ST. JEROME
COMMENTARY ON DANIEL

Ancient Christian Writers

THE WORKS OF THE FATHERS IN TRANSLATION

ADVISORY BOARD

Rev. Brian Dunkle, SJ
(Fordham University, Chair)

Rev. Boniface Ramsey, OFM

Dr. Thomas Cattoi
(Jesuit School of Theology of Santa Clara University)

Dr. Thomas Clemmons
(Catholic University of America)

Dr. Dawn LaValle Norman
(Australian Catholic University)

Dr. Erin Galgay Walsh
(University of Chicago)

No. 77

ST. JEROME
COMMENTARY ON DANIEL

TRANSLATED AND INTRODUCED BY
THOMAS P. SCHECK

THE NEWMAN PRESS
New York / Mahwah, NJ

Scripture quotations are from The Catholic Edition of the Revised Standard Version of the Bible, copyright © 1965, 1966 National Council of the Churches of Christ in the United States of America. Used by permission. All rights reserved worldwide.

Caseside design by Sharyn Banks
Book design by Lynn Else

COPYRIGHT © 2024 BY THOMAS P. SCHECK

All rights reserved. No part of this publication may be reproduced, stored in a retrieval system, or transmitted in any form or by any means, electronic, mechanical, photocopying, recording, scanning, or otherwise, without either the prior written permission of the Publisher, or authorization through payment of the appropriate per-copy fee to the Copyright Clearance Center, Inc., www.copyright.com. Requests to the Publisher for permission should be addressed to the Permissions Department, Paulist Press, permissions@paulistpress.com.

Library of Congress Cataloging-in-Publication Data
Names: Jerome, Saint, -419 or 420 author. | Scheck, Thomas P., 1964– translator, writer of introduction.
Title: Commentary on Daniel / St. Jerome ; translated and introduced by Thomas P. Scheck.
Other titles: Commentarii in Danielem. English (Scheck) 2024 | St. Jerome: commentary on Daniel
Description: New York: The Newman Press, [2024] | Series: Ancient Christian writers ; no. 77 | Translation of: Commentarii in Danielem. | Includes bibliographical references and index. | Summary: "This is an English translation, along with historical-literary commentary, of St. Jerome's Commentary on the Book of Daniel"—Provided by publisher.
Identifiers: LCCN 2023043019 (print) | LCCN 2023043020 (ebook) | ISBN 9780809106707 (hardcover) | ISBN 9780809187737 (e-book)
Subjects: LCSH: Bible. Daniel—Commentaries—Early works to 1800.
Classification: LCC BS1555 .J453 2024 (print) | LCC BS1555 (ebook) | DDC 224/.507—dc23/eng/20231122
LC record available at https://lccn.loc.gov/2023043019
LC ebook record available at https://lccn.loc.gov/2023043020

ISBN 978-0-8091-0670-7 (hardcover)
ISBN 978-0-8091-8773-7 (e-book)

Published by The Newman Press
an imprint of Paulist Press
997 Macarthur Boulevard
Mahwah, NJ 07430
www.paulistpress.com

PRINTED AND BOUND IN COLOMBIA

To my friend Mark Reasoner

CONTENTS

Introduction to St. Jerome 1

Translation of Jerome's Preface to the Vulgate
Version of Daniel 37

TRANSLATION OF JEROME'S COMMENTARY
ON DANIEL 41

Preface 43

Book One 47
    Vision 1 (1:1–21) 47
    Vision 2 (2:1–49) 51
    Vision 3 (3:1–100[4:1]) 60
    Vision 4 (4:1–34) 68

Book Two 76
    Vision 5 (5:1–31) 76
    Vision 6 (6:1–28) 82
    Vision 7 (7:1–28) 88
    Vision 8 (8:1–27) 97

Book Three 104
    Vision 9 (9:1–27) 104
    Vision 10 (10:1—12:13) 122

Origen's Notes on Susanna and Bel (Dan 13:1–64; 14:17) ... 157

CONTENTS

APPENDIX 163
    Julius Africanus's Letter to Origen on the Authenticity
    of Susanna (translated by Frederick Crombie) 164
    Origen's Response to Julius Africanus
    (translated by Frederick Crombie) 165

Notes 179

Bibliography 233

General Index 239

Scripture Index 245

INTRODUCTION TO ST. JEROME

St. Jerome (331/347–419/20)[1] is widely recognized as the most learned biblical scholar of the Western church. Pope Benedict XV's encyclical *Spiritus Paraclitus*, dated September 15, 1920, describes Jerome as the Catholic Church's "greatest doctor, divinely given her for the understanding of the Bible."[2] This specifies Jerome's most important ecclesiastical charism as his ability to translate and interpret Scripture. In his Wednesday Audiences in 2007, Pope Benedict XVI dedicated two catecheses to St. Jerome.[3] Among other things he noted that Jerome exhibited a lifelong devotion to the Word of God; Jerome affirmed the need to have recourse to the original texts of Scripture, Greek and Hebrew, and he made a fundamental criterion of the proper interpretation of Scripture harmony with the church's magisterium.

Then perhaps most importantly, on September 30, 2020, Pope Francis highlighted the life and figure of St. Jerome in an apostolic letter celebrating the 1,600th anniversary of the Doctor of the Church's death. Pope Francis says that the anniversary of Jerome's death

> can be seen as a summons to love what Jerome loved, to rediscover his writings and to let ourselves be touched by his robust spirituality, which can be described in essence as a restless and impassioned desire for a greater knowledge of the God who chose to reveal himself. How can we not heed, in our day, the advice that Jerome unceasingly gave to his contemporaries: "Read the divine Scriptures constantly; never let the sacred volume fall from your hand"?[4]

And then in a new liturgical initiative, inspired by Jerome's exemplary devotion to Holy Scripture, Pope Francis set aside the Third Sunday in Ordinary Time as Sunday of the Word of God.

These magisterial statements make clear that Jerome stands apart from other church fathers in his mastery of Scripture's original languages (Hebrew, Greek, and Aramaic). Jerome's linguistic expertise led him to complete a new translation of the Old and New Testaments called the Latin Vulgate, which at the popular level is probably his best-known achievement. Moreover, Jerome immersed himself in the antecedent Greek, Latin, and Hebrew exegetical traditions.[5] In multiple places in his writings, he indicates that he regarded the aim of his life to be to instruct and edify the Latin church by writing commentaries that had assimilated Hebrew learning and Greek Christian exegesis. Thus, he wanted to make his linguistic knowledge productive for the Western church and forge a unified exegetical theology that integrated the Greek East and the Latin West. Jerome did not separate the Bible from its tradition of Christian interpretation, and in a unique way he found great value in reporting and reflecting on Rabbinic (Hebrew) exegetical traditions.

Jerome equipped himself for the task of writing commentaries first by becoming a Latin translator of Greek works (mainly works of Origen but also some of Eusebius and Didymus the Blind). When he eventually launched his career as a scriptural commentator, he carefully consulted Greek and Hebrew sources and made them productive in his Latin exegesis. It is true that two of Jerome's predecessors, Hilary of Poitiers (315–68) and Ambrose of Milan (339–97), had relied on Greek interpreters to some extent, especially Origen, in their own exegetical works; but Jerome far surpassed them in his knowledge of the Greek tradition of exegesis, and his endeavor to incorporate Hebrew (Rabbinic) learning into Christian scholarship was a novelty in the Latin-speaking world.

In a sense official ecclesiastical recognition of Jerome in the West culminated in his being honored as one of the four great Doctors of the Latin Church, alongside Ambrose of Milan (d. 397), Augustine of Hippo (d. 430), and Gregory the Great (d. 604).[6] Pope Francis helpfully qualified this stature as an elevation that was presented to him by the "Christian iconographic tradition."[7] Erasmus of Rotterdam in 1516 also qualified this medieval reduction of church doctors to four with some sarcastic criticisms. He writes:

> It is worthwhile listening to the opinion of that learned crowd which reduces everything to a set number. It was an attractive idea to have four Doctors of the Church and

likewise four senses of Holy Scripture, to correspond of course with the four evangelists. To Gregory they assign tropology, to Ambrose allegory, to Augustine anagogy, and to Jerome, to assign him something, they leave the literal and grammatical sense. For this is how they divide these terms, though Jerome makes no distinction between the first three. First, from so many distinguished doctors, they wanted only four to be so designated. This they did from a kind of fairness rather than from their heart, to prevent the suspicion that they found none of the ancient Fathers acceptable; and yet they do not even read these writers at all except as examples of the apocryphal and long since obsolete. They generously accord some recognition to them, reserving the verities however for themselves. I would like very much to compare in a few words those who feel this way about Jerome with Jerome, but I will keep myself in check. I do not want honest theologians to think that my remarks about those wretched fellows will have been directed against themselves. But this one thing I cannot leave unsaid: Jerome has proved his worth by his many published works. If any one of those dolts could understand a single volume of Jerome on his own, if forty theologians of that party by common effort and concerted scholarship could hammer out one little book in any way worthy of comparison with Jerome's works, even with those Jerome dictated but did not write out, we will confess that Jerome is not a theologian.[8]

To my mind, when Erasmus's words are measured fairly by the times in which he lived, and by the quality of theological writing that was then being produced in the late fifteenth and early sixteenth centuries, one must conclude that he was justified in speaking up on Jerome's behalf like this and endeavoring to make room for Jerome at the table of the exegetes and theologians. The spirit Erasmus was combatting has still not been overcome.[9]

Jerome's Life and Career

Jerome was born in Stridon, a village near modern Ljubljana, Slovenia (Roman Emona) under northern Italian influence, not far distant from Aquileia, which was one of the great cities of the Roman

Empire. Scholars still differ about the year of his birth.[10] Some, such as his renowned English biographer J. N. D. Kelly as well as Erasmus, place it in 331, which would make him nearly ninety when he died in 419/420. But many contemporary scholars think he was born sixteen years later, in 347, which would make him around seventy-two at the time of his passing. When he was about twelve (presumably), his parents sent him to Rome to complete his literary studies. He received a thorough Latin education under Aelius Donatus, the famed Roman teacher of grammar and rhetoric.[11] He transcribed a great number of Latin authors, and perfected his prose ability to the point where his Latin letters are ranked, stylistically, alongside the epistolary collections of Cicero, Seneca, and Pliny the Younger. Jerome may have lost his virginity during this time in Rome, since he seems to deny that he possessed it.[12] At the age of eighteen or nineteen (or thirty-six, again depending on the date in which we place his birth), in Lent 367, Jerome requested baptism, possibly from Pope Liberius. Later that year he traveled to Gaul, where, in Trier, he decided to pursue monastic life. He copied out works by Hilary of Poitiers (d. 367), which introduced him to an irenic use of the great early Greek exegete, Origen of Alexandria (d. 254).[13] Jerome later remarked that he would gladly trade his knowledge of Scripture with Origen, who "knew the Scriptures by heart, and toiled day and night in the study of their meaning." Then he added pointedly, "Who can fail to admire Origen's enthusiasm for the Scriptures?" (*Ep* 84.8). Even when his admiration for Origen later turned to animosity during the Origenist controversies, Jerome's respect for Origen's exegetical and linguistic work, especially the Hexapla, remained.

In 374, Jerome began living as a hermit in the desert of Chalcis, where he made the acquaintance of a converted Jew named Baranina who introduced him to the Hebrew language. Jerome was the first Latin Christian scholar to attempt to make productive use of the OT's original Semitic languages in his scholarly works. He attained competence in Hebrew and Aramaic to go along with his fluency in Greek. He recounts the difficulties involved in this pursuit in his preface to his Vulgate version of Daniel, a translation of which is prefixed to the translation of his Commentary on Daniel in this volume. Jerome's literary debut took place at this time in the composition of his three monastic lives of Paulus, Hilarion, and Malchus.[14] In a famous incident at Chalcis, Jerome had a dream in which Christ scourged him for being a Ciceronian rather than a Christian. It moved him to vow never again to own or read books of pagan literature (*Ep* 22.30). He apparently kept the vow for several years but later relaxed his stance. Jerome went to Antioch in 379 and was ordained a presbyter by Paulinus of Antioch (not to be confused with St. Paulinus of Nola). He heard lectures there from the grammarian Apollinaris the Younger (d. 390), who eventually became bishop of Laodicea. Apollinaris was an opponent of Arianism, but also the author of christological teaching that was later deemed heretical, namely, the view that Christ's human soul was replaced by the indwelling Logos.

While living in Constantinople around the year 380 Jerome became a pupil of Gregory of Nazianzus (d. 389), who encouraged him to make Origen's scriptural exegesis his own. It is known that Basil of Caesarea and Gregory Nazianzus had produced an anthology from the works of Origen entitled *Philocalia*, so high was their esteem for the Alexandrian theologian. *Philocalia* means "love of the beautiful or choice thoughts." At this time, Jerome translated into Latin Eusebius of Caesarea's *Chronicle of World History* (381) and then Origen's *Homilies on Isaiah, Jeremiah,* and *Ezekiel*.[15] A few years later, he would render Origen's *Homilies on the Song of Songs* into Latin and dedicate the work to Pope Damasus.[16] In his preface to Origen's *Homilies on Ezekiel*, he said that he was considering translating a significant portion of Origen's entire corpus into Latin. Later, he gave up on the idea and turned to becoming a writer. Rufinus of Aquileia (345–411) would pick up where Jerome left off as a translator of Origen. It is Rufinus whose lifework would result in the saturation of the West in Latin translations of Origen's writings. In 388/9 Jerome composed a *Commentary on Ecclesiastes* that was heavily influenced by Origen's thoughts.[17]

Returning to Rome in the early 380s as a member of a delegation headed by Eastern bishops, Jerome entered the employ of Pope Damasus as secretary and theological adviser. At that time, he wrote a polemical defense of Mary's perpetual virginity (*Against Helvidius*), a work of lasting value for the position it defends but not necessarily for the polemical way the case is made.[18] Jerome had a stridently satirical style of writing against those he deemed heretics. This tendency is exemplified even more glaringly in another work *Against Jovinian*, to say nothing of his *Apology against Rufinus, Against Vigilantius,* and his *Diatribe against Bishop John of Jerusalem*. While living in Rome he also became embroiled in controversy when his extreme standards of asceticism were faulted in the death of Blesilla, the twenty-year-old daughter of his friend and correspondent Paula. The young girl had died from excessive fasting. After his patron Pope Damasus passed from the scene in December 384, Jerome was banished from the city by the priestly council of Rome, which he called "senate of the Pharisees." Jerome traveled to Palestine and visited the holy sites while also making a brief visit to Egypt, where he stayed with Didymus the Blind (d. 398). Soon he published a Latin translation of Didymus's *Treatise on the Holy Spirit*, a project undertaken with the unworthy motive of exposing to Latin readers that Ambrose of Milan had plagiarized his book on the Holy Spirit from the Greek work of Didymus. While in Egypt, Jerome persuaded Didymus to write commentaries on the prophets. The blind scholar complied, and his Greek *Commentary on Zechariah* was especially influential on Jerome's Latin *Commentary on Zechariah*.[19] I have discussed Jerome's involvement in the Origenist controversies elsewhere and refer the reader to the standard studies.[20]

JEROME'S COMMENTARY ON DANIEL

Jerome's commentaries on the prophets are widely regarded as his most important contribution to biblical studies. He wrote on all sixteen of them: the twelve Minor and the four Major Prophets. The last three decades of his life, from around 392 until his death in 419/420, were largely devoted to this enterprise. He would later refer to it as his *opus prophetale*,[21] a phrase that appears to indicate "a unified conception of the undertaking."[22] No other church father came even close to matching the scholarly depth found in Jerome's *opus* on the Hebrew prophets. Kamesar comments:

> He clearly had a sense of its tremendous scope, for, in the prefaces to the commentaries on Isaiah, Ezekiel and Jeremiah, he enumerates the number of books he has completed, as though tracking his own progress. He also knew that it was his last project and felt a great need to complete it before his death (*Comm. Isa.* 14, preface; *Comm. Ezech.* 14, preface). He fell just short.[23]

The last statement refers to the fact that Jerome died before completing his *Commentary on Jeremiah*. Where does his *Commentary on Daniel* fit into this epic achievement? It was composed in 407 CE, after the completion of his commentaries on the twelve Minor Prophets and inaugurating his work on the four Major Prophets: Daniel, Isaiah, Ezekiel, and Jeremiah.

INTRODUCTION TO ST. JEROME

Date	Title	Dedicatee(s)	Length (PG 17-11, PL 30-22)
379-82	Origen's 9 *Hom in Isaiah*	—	35
	Origen's 14 *Hom in Jer*	—	96
	Origen's 14 *Hom in Ezek*	Vincentius	96
383–84	Origen's 2 *Hom in Cant*	Damasus	21
386–87	*In Philemonem*	Paula and Eustochium	17
	In Galatas	" "	130
	In Ephesos	" "	115
	In Titum	" "	45
388–89	*In Ecclesiasten*	" "	107
392	Origen's 39 *Hom in Lk*	" "	99
392–93	*In Nahum*	" "	41
	In Michaeam	" "	79
	In Sophoniam	" "	50
	In Aggaeum	" "	29
	In Habacuc	Chromatius, bishop of Aquileia ...	63
396	*In Ionam*	" "	35
	In Abdiam	Pammachius	21
397	*In Visiones Isaiae*	Amabilis, bishop	53
398	*In Mattaeum*	Eusebius of Cremona, monk	201
406	*In Zachariam*	Exsuperius, bishop of Toulouse	124
	In Malachiam	Minervius and Alexander, bishops	37
	In Osee	Pammachius	131
	In Ioelem	" "	41
	In Amos	" "	107
407	*In Danielem*	Pammachius and Marcella	93
408–10	*In Isaiam*	Eustochium	661
410–14	*In Ezechielem*	" "	475
414–16	*In Hieremiam*	Eusebius of Cremona	223

Interestingly, in the prologue to the *Commentary on Daniel*, the seemingly weary Jerome announces an adjustment in his commentary method. In his previous commentaries on the Minor Prophets, he had left no stone unturned and discussed every single verse, usually based on a double-lemma, that of the LXX and that of the Hebrew.[24] For the present *Commentary on Daniel*, Jerome says that he will adopt a more concise method and will write more briefly and at intervals, explaining only those things that are obscure, lest his lengthy amount of writing become tedious to the reader. In the commentary that immediately succeeds Daniel, namely, the *Commentary on Isaiah*, Book 11 Preface, Jerome makes an interesting back-reference to the *Commentary on Daniel*.

> It is difficult, no, impossible, to please everyone, and the differences of opinion are not as great as the number of persons. To some I seemed to take longer in the explanation of the twelve prophets than I should have, and for this reason I tried to be brief in my little commentary on Daniel, except in the last and second-to-last visions, where I had to lengthen the discussion because of their great obscurity, and especially in the explanation of the seven, sixty-two, and one weeks [cf. Dan 9:25–27]. In discussing these, I have briefly summarized what Africanus, the chronologist, Origen, Eusebius of Caesarea, and also Clement, a priest of the Alexandrian church, Apollinarius the Laodicean, Hippolytus, the Hebrews, and Tertullian thought. I left it to the reader to choose what to select from the many views presented. And so, what we did out of modesty in forming judgments and out of consideration for those who would read the work, displeases some people perhaps, who long to know not the opinions of the ancients, but our judgment. It is easy to say to them in response that I did not want one man to be received in such a way that I seemed to be condemning the others. And, at any rate, if such great and learned men displease fastidious readers, what will they make of me who expose myself to the bites of the envious on account of the slenderness of my meager talent? But if, moreover, I have called the men mentioned above "teachers of the church," let them understand that I do not approve the faith of them all, who in any case contradict each other; but I spoke to the distinction between Josephus and Porphyry, who argued a great deal about this question.

INTRODUCTION TO ST. JEROME 9

But if I have translated discordant things in the explanation of the statue and of its feet and fingers, the iron and the clay as the Roman kingdom, because Scripture foretells that it was first strong, then weak, let it not be ascribed to me, but to the prophet [cf. Dan 2:31–45].[25]

Clearly, Jerome's new approach adopted for Daniel did not find favor with some readers, just as his older more exhaustive method had generated criticism for its verbosity. It is interesting to observe that he did not return to the Danielic method.[26] His final commentaries on Isaiah, Ezekiel, and Jeremiah are exhaustive in their treatment of the text.

Jerome understood that the purpose of a commentary is to elucidate what is unclear. This is the reason he gives for reporting the views of many exegetes and indicating how they have understood the text. The reader can then choose which interpretation is preferable. Jerome does not always feel compelled to weigh in on the truth or reliability of the interpretations provided. For him that is the task of the reader. Jerome shows considerable flexibility in allowing his readers to choose from the smorgasbord of interpretations he has provided, his only norm for selection being guidance from trusty Christian predecessors.

Sources of Jerome's Exegesis of Daniel

Origen's Hexapla

In 385 Jerome settled in Bethlehem, making use of the library in Caesarea, which possessed Origen's Hexapla. The title of this work means "Sixfold [Bible]." It displayed the entire text of the OT in six parallel columns. The first column contained the Hebrew version of the Old Testament, which was transliterated into Greek in the second column. Such a location demonstrates how Origen recognized the primacy of the Hebrew text in some sense, despite his simultaneous firm adherence to the divine inspiration and ecclesiastical authority of the Septuagint version (the fifth column). Indications are that Origen's Hebrew text agrees substantially with the Masoretic Text (MT), which is the medieval Hebrew text on which modern versions of the Hebrew Old Testament are based. Aquila's Greek version occupied the third column of Origen's Hexapla. Aquila was a Jewish scholar of the second century, a native of Sinope in Pontus (though some modern scholars conjecture that he was Palestinian). He lived at the time of Emperor

Hadrian (117–38) and published a slavishly literal Greek translation of the Hebrew Old Testament intended to replace the Septuagint, which was in use by the Christians and had become objectionable to the Jewish rabbis. Aquila's version is viewed to be of great value to modern textual critics who aim to determine the Hebrew wording that underlies it. Jerome admitted the fidelity of Aquila's translation to the Hebrew.[27] The fourth column of Origen's Hexapla was occupied by Symmachus's version, between Aquila's translation and the Septuagint. According to Epiphanius, Symmachus lived in the time of Emperor Severus (193–211) and was a Samaritan who became a Jewish proselyte. Eusebius, on the other hand, claims that he was an Ebionite, that is, a judaizing Christian.[28] Jerome follows Eusebius.[29] Symmachus's rendering was more literary than Aquila's. Jerome judged that he aimed to express the spirit of the Hebrew rather than the letter. The fifth column of the Hexapla contained a revision of the LXX. Finally, the sixth column was occupied by the Greek version of Theodotion, whose translation, according to Epiphanius, was completed during the reign of Commodus (180–92).[30] Jerome calls Theodotion an Ebionite,[31] whereas Irenaeus makes him a proselyte (a convert to Judaism) at Ephesus.[32] Theodotion's translation is a revision of the Septuagint, harmonized with the Hebrew text. It is of singular importance for the Book of Daniel, because Theodotion's version of Daniel had supplanted the LXX in the Christian churches of Jerome's day. Jerome discusses this in his preface to the Vulgate Daniel and in his *Commentary on Daniel* of 407. I will say more about Theodotion's version of Daniel below in the section that introduces Jerome's preface to his Vulgate version of Daniel. Some sections of Origen's Hexapla, particularly the Psalms, contained a fifth and sixth Greek version alongside the other four.

The Septuagint (LXX)

The Greek Septuagint is named from the Latin word *septuaginta*, which means "seventy." It is often identified simply by the Roman numerals LXX (70). It was the Alexandrian Greek translation of the Hebrew Bible that was begun in the third century BCE and became the Bible of the Jewish Diaspora in pre-Christian times. However, the Septuagint is more than a translation of the Hebrew Old Testament: it contains Greek additions to some books of the Hebrew Bible, such as Esther and Daniel, as well as independent works. Some of these books, such as Sirach, Tobit, and 1 Maccabees, are Greek translations of Hebrew or Aramaic texts, while others, such as Wisdom and 2 Maccabees, are original Greek compositions. Ancient (pre-Christian) Jews held the Septuagint in extremely high regard, some even claiming that it was a divinely inspired translation of the Hebrew Scriptures. The oldest Jewish historical tradition about this is recorded in the *Letter of Aristeas* (100 BCE), which reports that Ptolemy II Philadelphus (ruler of Egypt 283–246 BCE) wanted to provide a copy of the Hebrew Scriptures for the library at Alexandria. Seventy-two Jewish translators (six from each of the twelve tribes) were commissioned for the translation of the Pentateuch. Working together, they harmonized their translations by mutual comparison, that is, by collating the manuscripts, in a manner apparently similar to the way the text of Homer had been standardized. The first-century-CE Jewish scholar Philo introduced to this historical tradition the important element of divine inspiration. He says that the translators were secluded on the island of Pharos off the coast of Alexandria and then came under divine inspiration, "as though dictated to by an invisible prompter." The seventy-two translators allegedly produced a word-perfect identical translation of the Hebrew text of the Pentateuch. Philo does not mention Aristeas's letter. Rabbinic tradition later added a new embellishment: that the translators worked independently in isolated cells and God inspired them individually. However, in a reaction against Christianity in later centuries, rabbinic Judaism came to reject the Septuagint in its entirety as an untrustworthy translation. It commissioned new Greek translations to be made of the Hebrew Bible, for example, those by Symmachus and Aquila. The Jewish rabbis had been in conflict with the Christians, who preferred the Septuagint translation and based their apologetics upon it. It was the version used by the apostles and the earliest church fathers. Eventually, Jews adopted what is called the Palestinian Canon, which contains only the Hebrew books with none of the Greek additions.

Many of Jerome's Christian predecessors accepted Philo's version of the divine inspiration of the Septuagint. Jerome boldly dismissed both this legend and the later embellished tradition about the translators being sequestered into seventy separate cells. As evidence against this embellishment, he cites the silence of Aristeas and Josephus regarding the cells. Indeed, the latter scholars claim that the LXX translators were assembled in a single hall and consulted with each other. Jerome was perfectly justified in doubting the story about the seventy cells.

However, he takes his hesitations about the LXX one step further and calls into question the canonicity of some of the books added in the Septuagint. In the "Helmeted Preface" to his version from the Hebrew of the Books of Samuel and Kings, Jerome lists as books to be reckoned as apocryphal writings Wisdom, Sirach, Judith, Tobit, Additions to Daniel, and Maccabees. He recognized that the church reads the Books of Maccabees but claimed that it does not reckon them among the canonical writings.[33]

THE *HEBRAICA VERITAS* (HEBREW TRUTH)

In the fifth column of the Hexapla where he presents the LXX, Origen used critical signs adapted from the great Homeric critic Aristarchus. He marked with an asterisk or star (*) words or lines lacking in the Septuagint but present in the Hebrew (as attested by the other Greek versions displayed in the Hexapla). *Asterisk* comes from ἀστερίσκος, a small star used as a typographical mark placed before imperfect, deficient passages. Origen marked with an obelus (†) words or lines that were lacking in the Hebrew. *Obelus* comes from ὀβελός and refers to a critical mark shaped like a spit or small dagger placed opposite suspect passages. Obelus is also rendered "obelisk," a pointed square pillar. Origen's intention by this system was not to advocate for a new public text of Scripture in the Christian churches based on this reconstructed text. Rather, he desired merely to show Christians what readings were obtained among the Jews. Origen was wary of displacing the old Bible (the LXX) with a new version. Yet, his "corrected" text of the Septuagint was transmitted to posterity as the fifth column of the Hexapla. Eusebius of Caesarea believed that Origen's revised LXX was the original authentic text. He reproduced and published it, aided by St. Pamphilus, around 307, at first with the critical signs included, but eventually they were deleted. The result was to circulate a version that was not the original text of the LXX and that, in reality, consisted of a mixture of the LXX with Aquila and Theodotion. This is called the Hexaplaric recension of the LXX. Jerome, like Eusebius, viewed this text as reproducing the original Hebrew. It is noteworthy that in Jerome's view, passages marked by an asterisk were not deficient but authentic, since he believed they had been found in the original Hebrew *Vorlage* of the LXX.

Some scholars whose primary interest is focused on Hebrew textual criticism and the use of the LXX in the task of recovering and establishing the original Hebrew text have expressed concern over the net result of Origen's text-critical efforts. The British Old Testament scholar S. R. Driver, for instance, admired Origen and said his work on the Hexapla was projected with the best intentions and became the means of preserving to posterity much of priceless value that would otherwise have perished. But Driver added that Origen failed in restoring the genuine translation of the LXX, since he (wrongly) assumed that the original Septuagint was that which agreed most closely with the Hebrew text as he knew it. Origen was guided partly by this Hebrew text and partly by the other versions of Aquila, Theodotion, and Symmachus, which were based substantially upon it. Where the Septuagint text differed from the current Hebrew text, Origen systematically altered it to bring it into conformity with the Hebrew. Driver justly criticizes this from the perspective of a modern Hebrew textual critic and says that this was a step in the wrong direction:

> Where a passage appears in two renderings, the one free, the other agreeing with the existent Hebrew text, it is the former which has the presumption of being the more original: the latter has the presumption of having been altered subsequently, in order that it might express the Hebrew more closely. Origen, no doubt, freed the text of the LXX from many minor faults; but in the main his work tended to obliterate the most original and distinctive features of the Version. To discover the Hebrew text used by the translators we must recover, as far as possible, the text of the Version as it left the translators' hands; and Origen's labors, instead of facilitating, rather impeded this process.[34]

To me it appears that Driver has raised valid concerns. When Eusebius and Pamphilus published Origen's Hexaplaric recension, they may not have fully grasped the principles of textual transmission. Jerome seems to have inherited these mistakes and wrongly assumed that the Hebrew text that appeared in the first column of Origen's Hexapla represented the original text on which the Septuagint version of the fifth column must have been based.

Jerome's goal of restoring Christian Old Testament exegesis to the Hebrew truth was, of course, extremely commendable, and he was a bold and path-breaking scholar. What Jerome may not have fully appreciated was that the Septuagint translators were following different Hebrew textual traditions that were alternative to the Masoretic Text (Origen's first column). Their versions were at least a millennium older than the oldest Masoretic manuscripts available to modern scholars.[35] Thus, from the perspective of the modern science of Hebrew textual criticism, when Jerome accuses the Septuagint of "adding" something to the Hebrew, following the indications of Origen's critical apparatus, he seems to assume wrongly that his (Origen's) Hebrew *Vorlage* was identical to that used by the Septuagint translators. M. Hale Williams comments on this assumption:

> Although modern textual critics of the Hebrew Bible are far from according the Septuagint the inspired status it enjoyed among Jerome's Christian contemporaries, they hold it in much higher esteem than did Jerome. Jerome's privileging of the Hebrew text used by the Jews, together with its attendant traditions of interpretation, as the ultimate sources of biblical truth was by no means a simple recognition of scientific fact. Rather, it was an idiosyncratic insight, which allowed Jerome to construct for himself a unique position as an authority on the scriptures.[36]

By pointing out these deficiencies, I do not mean to disparage Jerome's path-breaking contribution to the study of the Hebrew Old Testament. Despite the limitations of Jerome's knowledge of some textual and linguistic issues, it is impossible to refrain from commending his unique Christian devotion to the original biblical languages on which his exegesis was based.

An additional point of clarification has been made by Kamesar, who observes that Jerome's Hexaplaric revision must be understood not in terms of a LXX versus Hebrew opposition, but rather in the context of the rivalry between the recensions of the LXX. There were three competing recensions of the LXX in the East, and the Hexaplaric recension had not attained universal recognition. Jerome's Hexaplaric recension was his attempt to extend in the West the influence of the recension of the LXX he believed to be correct. Kamesar writes:

> That this was his view is evident from Ep. 106.2, where he describes the Hexaplaric LXX as "incorrupta et inmaculata septuaginta interpretum translatio," ["incorrupt and faultless translation of the seventy translators"] and compares it

with the corrupt κοινη, which he identifies with the recension of Lucian....Jerome therefore took a firm position regarding the rivalry between the recensions, and maintained that position throughout his life.[37]

Recently I produced a new translation of Jerome's Epistle 106 in which I discuss these matters in sufficient detail.[38]

Rabbinic Exegesis

In addition to his use of the Hebrew and Aramaic originals as the basis of his new Latin translation of Daniel, aided by Theodotion's Greek version, Jerome also made use of rabbinic exegesis in his *Commentary on Daniel.* James A. Montgomery observed: "Any study of Jewish commentation upon the Scriptures should certainly include Jerome as almost the sole witness for an age otherwise dark, since the Jewish interest in Dan. as an object of learned or midrashic comment appears only in later literature."[39] Fortunately, there is now a fine study of Jerome's use of Hebrew exegetical traditions that focuses precisely on his *Commentary on Daniel.*[40] I have gratefully incorporated many of Braverman's analyses and assessments into the notes of this translation.

Origen's *Stromateis*

Not only did Jerome use Origen's Hexapla as well as Jewish exegetical traditions, but he also consulted Origen's exegetical writings, which appeared to him to be an indispensable source. If he writes a commentary on a book, such as the Gospel of Matthew, or merely on a verse of Scripture, such as in his exegetical epistles, Jerome searches out a corresponding homily by Origen on such a book or verse. If he lacks the good fortune of finding such a homily, for instance in commenting on a passage of Psalm 126, he apologizes to his correspondent and says that Pamphilus no longer possessed the homily.[41] But Jerome regrets the thought that Origen wrote something that did not survive. Similarly, in his massive *Commentary on Isaiah,* Jerome takes note that the twenty-sixth of Origen's thirty books on Isaiah cannot be found. Courcelle comments on Jerome's practice of compiling Origen with respect to the prophet Daniel:

If Jerome knows that Origen did not make any particular commentary on a book of Scripture, for instance the Book of Daniel, he looks for explanations in another of Origen's works, namely the *Stromateis*. But he feels particularly satisfied when he has at his disposal for a single subject (as in the case of the Psalms, Isaiah, and Hosea) a large amount of Origen's works to compile. It is therefore not surprising that Jerome's contemporaries were even then charging him with compiling Origen.[42]

The use of Origen's no-longer-extant *Stromateis* in the *Commentary on Daniel* is particularly noteworthy. It is explicitly named and compiled in 4:5a (8); 9:24, and for the exposition of Daniel 13—14. Origen's exegetical ideas are referred to passim. Origen's angelology and demonology particularly influenced Jerome's theological thought. As an heir to Origen's exegesis and a good steward of it, Jerome lets Origen's legacy bear fruit. Generally, in his commentaries on the prophets, Jerome explores the theme of Nebuchadnezzar as a figure of the devil even more widely than Origen had done.[43] However, Jerome does not blindly follow all of Origen's speculations. Specifically, Jerome rejects Origen's allegorical explanation of Daniel 4, which saw in Nebuchadnezzar's madness and restoration to sanity a figure of the devil's ultimate salvation.

The narrative in Daniel 4 reports that for being excessively proud, Nebuchadnezzar was afflicted by God with the outward resemblance and behavior of a wild beast for seven years, at the end of which he is finally restored to his throne. Origen was apparently unable to fathom a literal historical defense of this story. Therefore, this deposition of King Nebuchadnezzar was, for Origen, the image of the fall of the devil. He understood this whole chapter as an allegory of Lucifer's apostasy, and then of the hoped-for restoration of the devil to sanity at the end of time. This is called the "doctrine" (or better, "speculation") of *apocatastasis* (the "restoration"), according to which, at the end of time, Satan hopefully would do penance and be restored to his throne and to his original dignity. It was one of Origen's most controversial theological speculations—and that is precisely what it was: a query, not a dogmatic assertion—yet Jerome categorically rejects this opinion and considers it to be contrary to the Christian faith. For Jerome, Daniel 4 is a defensible historical narrative and contains no such allegorical meaning that would relate it to a speculative *apocatastasis*. Yet

Jerome still follows many of Origen's links between Nebuchadnezzar and the devil, whereby the prince of Babylon represents the prince of this world. Jerome knows how to set limits to Origen's use of allegories, when they no longer seem to conform to Christian doctrine. It is thus an essential principle of Jerome's exegesis that, far from being bowled over by Origen's allegories, he wants above all to be a faithful disciple of the faith of the Church. Jerome rejects Origen on points where the church has found him to be heretical or in error; but this does not prevent Jerome from receiving much valuable material from Origen's exegetical reservoir.

A passage from his *Commentary on Jonah* 3:6–9 resonates with his Daniel commentary and confirms Jerome rejection of Origen's *apocatastasis* speculation. Jerome writes:

> I know that very many[44] interpret the king of Nineveh as a symbol of the devil at the end of the world. As the last to hear the preaching, he would both come down from his throne and cast aside his original adornment. And clothed with sackcloth he would sit in ashes. And not content with his own conversion, he along with his leaders shall also preach repentance to others, saying: let men and beasts, both oxen and cattle be tormented by hunger. Let them be covered with sackcloth. And let them betake themselves without reservation from their former damnable vices to repentance. For [they say that] no rational creature that has been made by God should perish. When he comes down from his own pride, he shall repent and be restored to his original place. To prove this interpretation, they also cite the following passage from Daniel, when Nebuchadnezzar performed penance for seven years and is restored to his original kingdom [cf. Dan 4:28–37]. But since sacred Scripture does not say this, and since this interpretation completely undermines the fear of God—for men easily fall into vices when they think that even the devil, who is the author of evils and the fount of all sins, is able to be saved by repenting—let us cast this thought from our minds. And we should know that the sinners in the Gospel are cast into the eternal fire, which is prepared for the devil and his angels [cf. Matt 25:41]. And it is said of them: 'Their worm shall not die, and their fire shall not be

quenched'" [Isa 66:24; Mark 9:48]. To be sure, we know that God is mild, and we who are sinners do not delight in his cruelty, but we read: "The Lord is merciful and just, and our God shows mercy" [Ps 115:6]. The justice of God is surrounded by mercy; it proceeds toward the judgment by this kind of campaign: it spares so that it may judge, it judges so that it may show mercy. "Mercy and truth have met: justice and peace have kissed" [Ps 85:10]. Otherwise, if all rational creatures are equal, and of their own accord either are raised on high by their virtues or are plunged into the depths by their vices, and there shall be a restitution of all things and a single ranking for the soldiers, after a long cycle and infinite ages, what difference shall there be between virgin and prostitute? What distinction shall there be between the mother of the Lord and—what is criminal even to say—the sacrificial victims of the lusts of public prostitutes?[45] Shall Gabriel and the devil be the same? Shall the apostles and the demons be the same? Shall prophets and false prophets be the same? Shall martyrs and persecutors be the same? Imagine what you like, double the years and time, and heap up infinite ages for the torments. If the end for everyone is the same, the entire past counts for nothing, since we seek not what we were at one time but what we shall be forevermore. Nor am I unaware of what they ordinarily say in opposition to this, and to prepare hope for themselves and salvation with the devil. But now is not the time to write in more detail against perverse doctrine and the devil's σύνφρεγμα [defense] from those who teach this in private and then deny it in public. It suffices for us to have made known our perceptions of this passage and, as is appropriate for a commentary, to have briefly hinted at who is the king of Nineveh whom the word of God reaches last of all.[46]

This passage is consistent with Jerome's arguments against the *apocatastasis* speculation recorded in the *Commentary on Daniel*. It is of interest to note, however, that I. Ramelli openly questions the fairness of Jerome's arguments against Origen's *apocatastasis* speculation. She writes: "Jerome is misrepresenting Origen's thought. In the latter's view, there will be a big difference between saints and sinners in the next life, and this will disappear only after the complete purification of all sinners."[47] Furthermore, Ramelli insightfully observes that Jerome has arbitrarily equated Origen's eschatological views with those of Jovinian, who had been condemned by synods in Rome and Milan in 390. Jovinian had maintained that all Christians will have the same reward in the next world—in particular, ascetics and nonascetics alike—because baptism levels all differences in merits.[48] In *Against Jovinian*, Jerome had argued that it was impossible that a virgin and a prostitute would have the same reward in the next world.[49] Jerome's discussion in the *Commentary on Jonah* borrows from this and also agrees with what he says in *Apol* 2.12; *Ep* 84.7. In many of his polemical disputations with alleged "heretics," including Origen, Helvidius, Rufinus, and Pelagius, Jerome drew unwarranted inferences from the statements of his opponents. Yet none of this diminishes the fact that Jerome's intent is categorically to repudiate the speculations Origen had made on the possibility of the devil's future restoration, because these speculations are not stated in Scripture, and they clash with the general mind of the church.[50] Courtray summarizes Jerome's critical reception of Origen this way:

> Despite this restriction [of Jerome's rejection of the *apocatastasis* speculation], Jerome has followed Origen in his instruction of us on the traces of the devil through allegorical readings which make the prince of Babylon the Prince of this world. By bringing together remarks disseminated in his works, it is thus possible to reconstruct a coherent demonology, ranging from the fall of the devil on earth to his ruin at the end of time. The monk knows how to set limits to his use of allegories, when they no longer seem to conform to Christian doctrine. He thus affirms an essential principle of his exegesis: far from being fascinated by allegory, he wants above all to be a faithful disciple of the faith of the Church.[51]

Some scholars have claimed that Jerome adhered to the so-called Antiochene tradition of interpretation, with its preference for the historical, literal sense, as opposed to the allegorizing "Alexandrian" approach. The evidence cited in support of this claim is Jerome's rejection, in his exegesis of Daniel 4, of Origen's attempt to regard Nebuchadnezzar as a symbol of the devil.[52] I believe, on the contrary, that this stark dichotomy between Alexandrian and Antiochene method is untenable. Jerome merely rejected one specific allegorical interpretation of Origen, the one that surmised the final restoration of Lucifer to salvation, based on Nebuchadnezzar's restoration to sanity; but this does not entail a general repudiation of Origen's "Alexandrian" allegorical method. Moreover, Yarbro Collins displays little appreciation of Jerome's exegetical charism when she condescendingly claims that the main value of Jerome's *Commentary on Daniel* is in his preservation of Porphyry's insights and, to a lesser extent, in his citations of rabbinic exegesis. She gives no credit at all to Jerome's own exegetical insights.[53] On the other hand, in the commentary portion of this same volume, John J. Collins engages Jerome extensively and respectfully.

Porphyry and Modern Critical Interpretation of Daniel

Alongside Origen, an important interlocutor of Jerome in the *Commentary on Daniel* is the Neoplatonist philosopher and critic of Christianity, Porphyry (232–305). Porphyry was a disciple of Longinus and of Plotinus (204/5–270 CE), and he became the editor of Plotinus's writings. A brilliant philosopher in his own right, Porphyry authored a deeply inspiring philosophical treatise addressed to his wife, Marcella.[54] Unfortunately, he was also a critic of Christianity who authored a ferocious attack in fifteen books entitled *Against the Christians*, in which he pointed out the mistakes and faults in the Christian Scriptures.[55] It is hard to imagine that this work would not have added fuel to the fire of the Roman government's animus to the Christians and aggravated the persecutions that broke out at the end of Porphyry's life. Among these alleged contradictions, Porphyry claimed that the Book of Daniel was a forgery composed during the Maccabean period (167–164 BCE). In the preface to his *Commentary on Daniel*, Jerome tells us that Porphyry

> refuses to admit that it was composed by the person whose name it bears, but he says someone wrote it who was living in Judea at the time of the Antiochus who was called Epiphanes [165 BCE]. Porphyry says that it was not so much Daniel who spoke of things to come as that other person who narrated past events. In effect, he says that whatever the book says up to the time of Antiochus contains true history, but anything it conjectures beyond that

point is false, since the writer could not have known the future.

According to Porphyry, Daniel's "prophecies" (esp. chap. 11) were written *ex eventu* and describe events of the recent past that transpired in the Seleucid period of history, as well as actions of Antiochus IV Epiphanes (reigned 175–164 BCE). Although Porphyry's work has perished, several ecclesiastical writers responded to it, including Eusebius, Apollinaris, and Methodius, whom Jerome mentions in his preface.

A majority of twentieth- and twenty-first century students of the Book of Daniel hail Porphyry as the victor over Jerome and his Christian predecessors (Methodius, Eusebius, and Apollinaris) regarding his grasping the key to interpreting the Book of Daniel. Some have gone as far as to portray Porphyry as a persecuted victim of Christian obscurantism. P. M. Casey writes:

> The position of the neoplatonist philosopher Porphyry in this debate has been remarkable. Centuries before the advent of modern biblical criticism, Porphyry already knew that the book of Daniel was a Maccabean pseudepigraph. For this and other scholarly crimes against the regnant ideology of the later Roman empire, "impius Porphyrius" was vilified and his work destroyed, so that we are dependent for our knowledge of it on fragments preserved by hostile critics. Modern scholars have naturally been more sympathetic towards him for his "brilliant and definitive demolition of the traditional date of Daniel."[56]

It is certainly true that Jerome regarded Porphyry as "impious." Still, it seems to me somewhat inverted to depict Porphyry as an innocuous scholarly gentleman persecuted by Christians for crimes "against the regnant ideology of the later Roman empire," when in reality Porphyry was on the side of the Roman persecutors. At least one of his Christian disputants, Methodius, died as a martyr.[57] Another, Eusebius of Caesarea, lived through the period of Roman persecution against the Christians that preceded Constantine, losing his closest priest-friend, Pamphilus the Martyr, to imprisonment and beheading.

The assessment of Porphyry by Jerome's renowned English biographer J. N. D. Kelly resembles Casey's. "[Jerome's] failure to grasp the critical problem, in spite of Porphyry's having supplied the key, was understandable, perhaps inevitable. But it is ironical that the sharp-witted pagan critic of Christianity should have outmaneuvered him as a biblical scholar."[58] For many modern scholars, the debate over the pseudepigraphic nature and second-century-BCE Maccabean date of Daniel is outdated. Casey writes: "Daniel is now accepted as a pseudepigraph written, at least in its present form, in the Maccabean period, and few Christians lose sleep over its origin."[59]

On the other hand, a scholar who has lost some sleep over this question is E. J. Young. He admits that Porphyry sometimes showed himself to be a serious interpreter who approaches grammatical-historical exegesis, but he thinks that Porphyry cannot be regarded as a truly scientific interpreter of the Bible, mainly because of his philosophical precommitments.

> His [Porphyry's] work is founded upon the presupposition that predictive prophecy is impossible (*si quid autem ultra opinatus sit, quia futura nescient, esse mentitum*). It is upon the basis of this assumption that Porphyry came to his conclusion that the book of Daniel was a product of the second century B.C.[60]

I agree with Young's philosophical critique of Porphyry here. On the other hand, I would still concur with Casey and Kelly on the point that Porphyry's skills in historical criticism of Daniel were exceptional and worthy of respect. This obtains even if a careful reading of Jerome's commentary shows that Porphyry himself made many historical and linguistic mistakes, and indeed, as a philologist, he can hardly be compared with Jerome.

In my view, the main lines of Jerome's interpretation of Daniel as well as his critique of Porphyry are still plausible, and it was Jerome who showed himself to be a truly liberal scholar when, in his *Commentary on Daniel*, he preserved for posterity, without distortion, many of Porphyry's interpretations of the book. These would have been lost forever were it not for Jerome's effort to record them. Indeed, one of the great modern commentators on Daniel, James A. Montgomery, credited Jerome's method, especially in chapter 11, for providing his readers with the excellent historical insights of his fierce opponent Porphyry. This had beneficial results for the West:

Western scholarship has been delivered from the vagaries of apocalyptic exegesis through the mediation of Jerome. Porphyry, the heathen commentator of Daniel, in his argument against the Christian interpretation of Daniel as a Messianic prophecy, had given a detailed historical interpretation of c. 11, proving step by step that it is veiled history culminating with the Maccabean period, and hence logically the earlier cc. must be similarly interpreted. He has many characteristics of an ingenious modern scholar, as when he identifies Maozin with Modin the home of Maccabees, or Ephedano with a place between Euphrates and Tigris as the scene of Antiochus' actual death. Jerome honestly allowed himself to follow his reprobated opponent's excellent historical criticism, only parting company with him at v. 21, when for him the Antichrist appears. But he continues what is one of the greatest services contributed by any Patristic commentary in still presenting in parallel Porphyry's adverse views, so that Western scholarship has been in general committed to a sane exegesis of the chapter. Catholic theologians themselves have divided in part as between Jerome and Porphyry, some treating the whole of vv. 22ff. as referring to Antichrist, others introducing this figure only at v. 36, in this respect following Theodoret (see Knabenbauer, p. 320).[61] Chrysostom, however, found the Antichrist throughout the chap. (*Adv. Jud.*, v, 7 = PG 48, 894).[62]

It is noble of Montgomery to give Jerome due credit for his scholarly service in preserving Porphyry's adverse views.

In his prologue to the *Commentary on Daniel*, Jerome clarifies his opinion that Porphyry's assumption that Daniel could not have known the future prophetically through divine revelation threatens the standing of Daniel as a prophet. For such a stature had been affirmed by Jesus Christ himself (cf. Matt 24:15). Of great interest, however, is the observation that for Jerome, the rejection of Porphyry's unreasonable philosophical assumptions does not mean that Porphyry was wrong in providing a Maccabean interpretation of many of Daniel's oracles. Rather, Jerome admits that Porphyry is very often correct when he explains Daniel's words by referring to the deeds of Antiochus IV Epiphanes. Yet these historical explanations do not exhaust the meaning of the original passages, as they came from the mouth of the sixth-century-BCE Jewish prophet of Babylon and Persia. For Jerome, Daniel via divine revelation had accurately foreseen historical figures and events, which were shadows and types, which would be more fully fulfilled in the conflict between the Antichrist and the saints of the Lord. Under Daniel 11:21, Jerome cites the precedent of the messianic Psalm 72, which primarily describes King Solomon, but which contains language that necessarily points beyond Solomon to a fuller meaning that can only be apprehended in Jesus Christ. Jerome concludes that just as Solomon does not fulfill all the words of this psalm in a literal sense, so the Maccabean interpretation does not fulfill all the elements of Daniel 11:21ff in a literal sense. In Jerome's mind the eschatological interpretation, which sees the little horn as the Antichrist, is a much more complete interpretation, and it applies to events that are still to come.[63]

As mentioned above, modern biblical criticism of Daniel generally regards Porphyry (not Jerome) as its guiding light and polestar. Yet there remains a plurality of interpretive approaches to Daniel to the present day. To verify this, one has only to compare two major English commentaries on Daniel that appeared in the same year: Joyce G. Baldwin's *Daniel* (Tyndale, 1978) and Hartman and Di Lella's *The Book of Daniel* (Anchor Bible, 1978). Hartman and Di Lella's approach to the Book of Daniel is the purely higher-critical one. Its basic interpretive principle is formulated by J. Collins, who says:

> Conservatives have often argued that the critical position rests on a dogmatic, rationalistic denial of the possibility of predictive prophecy. For the critical scholar, however, the issue is one of probability. That Daniel's predictions have particular relevance to the time of Antiochus Epiphanes is not in dispute. This was recognized already by Josephus, and Jerome granted that events predicted the Antichrist in Daniel 11 were prefigured under Epiphanes. *There is no apparent reason, however, why a prophet of the sixth century should focus minute attention on the events of the second century.* Moreover, the references to Hellenistic history in chap. 11 are essentially accurate, whereas those to the Babylonian and Persian periods in the earlier chapters are notoriously confused. A further consideration, to which we will return in connection with the genre of Daniel, is the fact that

pseudonymity and *ex eventu* prophecy are well-known conventions of apocalyptic literature and are characteristic of other Jewish writings of the Hellenistic period.[64] In view of these considerations, the balance of probability is overwhelmingly in favor of a Maccabean date, at least for the revelations of chaps. 7–12, which clearly have their focus in that period.[65]

The answer Jerome would give to the italicized words is that divine revelation about the future would bring consolation to the captives who are serving God in their captivity.[66] The interpretation that results from the higher-critical approach is that, in agreement with Jerome's great opponent Porphyry, the Book of Daniel is viewed as a Maccabean pseudepigraph and fictional religious romance. It compiles religious folklore riddled with egregious historical blunders and *vaticinia ex eventu* (predictions composed after the historical events) as well as outright erroneous predictions (Dan 11:40–45). Many of these scholars believe the book can be precisely dated to 165 BCE and can be explained entirely based on the Maccabean events without any reference to Jesus and the future.[67] The majority of contemporary scholars of Daniel support this approach.

A more traditional approach to interpreting Daniel is exemplified by Joyce G. Baldwin, who published her commentary in the same year as Hartman and Di Lella's. She rejects Porphyry's idea that the Book of Daniel is a pseudepigraph from the Maccabean period and treats the prophet Daniel as a historical personage whose book (excluding the deuterocanonical additions) comprises substantially reliable historical narratives and miraculous revelations of divine knowledge and power. For this traditional Christian approach to the book, the key to interpreting Daniel correctly recognizes the interpretive authority of Jesus and the New Testament.[68] In the Gospels Jesus refers to Daniel's seventy weeks solely in terms of "the abomination of desolation" (Matt 24:15; Mark 13:14), which is to be the sign of the coming destruction of Jerusalem. This prediction was fulfilled in 70 CE. This implies that for Jesus the significance of the abomination was not exhausted by its applicability to the crimes and sacrileges of Antiochus Epiphanes. Moreover, the Book of Revelation takes up the symbolism of Daniel's "half of the week." In Revelation 11:2 this is expressed as forty-two months, during which the holy city is trampled upon. And in Revelation 13:5 the beast has authority for the same length of time. If Revelation was written, as most scholars claim it was, after the fall of Jerusalem, it makes a further application of Daniel's text to an end-time yet to be.[69] Thus there is strong support in the New Testament for the view that, while there are interim events that bear out the truth of Daniel's imagery, his book points forward to a culmination at the end of history.[70]

It is also worthwhile to report some new developments that have occurred in modern Gospel interpretation that may bear on the interpretation of Daniel. The "assured position" of Gospel scholarship long held that Jesus's apocalyptic discourse (Matt 24; Mark 13; Luke 21:5–36) must have been written after the destruction of Jerusalem in 70 CE, which that discourse predicts. According to this school, Jesus's discourse was similar to Daniel 11 in that it gave what purported to be a prophecy about the impending fall of Jerusalem, and together with that blended signs and warnings about the end of all things. But the foundation for this post-70 dating of the Gospel discourses was undermined by C. H. Dodd, who argued that Mark 13 fits better *before* the destruction of the temple it purports to prophesy. Dodd claimed that the language in Luke 21 deals with the regular commonplaces of ancient warfare: "So far as any historical event has colored the picture, it is not Titus's capture of Jerusalem in 70 CE, but Nebuchadrezzar's capture in 587 BCE. There is no single trait of the forecast which cannot be documented directly out of the Old Testament."[71] Similarly, at least some modern scholars would contend that in Daniel 11 likewise, "there is no feature which requires that the prophecy must have been written after the event."[72]

Interestingly, on the Catholic side of contemporary biblical criticism, J. Bergsma and B. Pitre have recently weighed in on the question of Daniel allegedly being a second-century BCE pseudepigraph.[73] One of the arguments that is used to question this view resembles that of C. H. Dodd cited above, namely, the observation that Antiochus IV Epiphanes did not destroy Jerusalem or the temple, as Daniel 9:26 states would happen. He only defiled them (cf. 1 Macc 1–2). If Daniel 9:26 is an *ex eventu* prophecy of Antiochus IV Epiphanes, why does it not comport with the actual events? Pitre and Bergsma comment:

> The difficulty all of this raises for the second-century dating of Daniel is that if these central oracles—Daniel 2, 7, and 9—are referring to a post-Hellenistic empire that would actually destroy the Jerusalem Temple, then—to be

consistent in the interpretation of the book as *ex eventu* prophecy—the date of the book of Daniel should not be placed in the Greek period (second century B.C.) but needs to be moved forward into the Roman period (ca. first century A.D.). But this is, of course, impossible, since the book of Daniel is already being quoted in books written before and during the first century A.D. (for example, 1 Mac 2:59–60; *Sib. Or.* 3:397; Mt 24:15; Josephus, *Ant.* 10.266–68; 3 Mac 6:6–7). So one ends up with a certain inconsistency and a selective use of prophecies to demonstrate the *ex eventu* dating of the book.[74]

The upshot of this recent reassessment of the prevailing scholarly "consensus" is that all theories about the composition of Daniel pose some interpretive difficulties, and the debate within the scholarly community continues. These questions should not be viewed as closed.

For my part, I would add the following pieces of evidence in support of the historical authenticity of the Book of Daniel. The most ancient external attestation to the historicity of the prophet Daniel is three apparent mentions of him in Ezekiel (14:13–14, 20; 28:3), where he is named alongside Job and Noah as a pattern of righteousness and wisdom. Ezekiel 14:13–14 states:

> Son of man, when a land sins against me by acting faithlessly, and I stretch out my hand against it and break its staff of bread and send famine upon it, and cut off from it man and beast, even if these three men, Noah, Daniel, and Job were in it, they would deliver but their own lives by their righteousness.

In 28:3 Ezekiel says sarcastically of the prince of Tyre: "You are indeed wiser than Daniel; no secret is hidden from you." Ezekiel ranks his contemporary Daniel with Noah and Job in his wisdom and uprightness. It is true that some modern scholars dispute the identification of the referent in Ezekiel. In the original texts in Ezekiel the name can be vocalized *Danel*, which coincides with the name of an ancient Phoenician sage known to us from the Ras Shamra (Ugaritic) literature of the twelfth century BCE. Some think Ezekiel is referring to him. The church fathers, as well as older conservative scholarship, identified Ezekiel's Daniel as the Jewish prophet Daniel. Saydon writes:

"It is generally believed that the Daniel, who is mentioned by Ezekiel...is the prophet and diplomat of the Babylonian court."[75] D. Block observes: "If the Daniel of the book by this name was indeed a historical figure, it is inconceivable that Ezekiel's audience would not have been familiar with him, and it might even be surprising if Ezekiel had never mentioned him."[76] Block argues that the biblical Daniel could have earned the right to stand alongside Noah and Job because of his upright character and miraculous deeds; moreover, Daniel's fame is attested elsewhere (in 1 Macc 2:60). Block also thinks that it is hard to imagine that Ezekiel's audience would have accepted the association of a pagan worshipper of foreign gods (the Ugaritic Danel) alongside the biblical Noah and Job.

In addition to the apparent references in Ezekiel, an indisputable mention of the person of Daniel is found in 1 Maccabees 2:59–60, a second-century-BCE text from a book universally regarded as historically reliable.[77] On his deathbed in 166 BCE, Mattathias, the father of Judas Maccabeus, refers to Daniel and his Judean companions, naming them at the end of a long list of Israel's great heroes that began with Abraham and ran through the prophet Elijah. Mattathias tells his sons: "Hananiah, Azariah, and Mishael believed and were saved from the flame. Daniel because of his innocence was delivered from the mouth of lions." Referring to events described in Daniel 1, 3 and 6, Mattathias shows himself to be quite familiar with the exploits of Daniel. The first-century-CE Jewish historian Josephus confirms the historicity of Daniel.[78] Moreover, as we have seen, Jesus and the authors of the NT did not look upon the Book of Daniel as a fictional romance but as real history and prophecy. Jesus's own self-understanding as the Son of Man was dependent on Daniel 7:13 (cf. Matt 26:64), and he refers to the "prophet Daniel" in Matthew 24:15. Jerome builds upon this stream of tradition, which was perpetuated in the rabbis and in his Christian predecessors.

JEROME'S PREFACE TO THE LATIN VULGATE VERSION OF DANIEL

In addition to the *Commentary on Daniel*, I have also provided a new translation of Jerome's Preface to his Latin Vulgate version of the Book of Daniel, so that readers may be equipped with the fullness of Jerome's scholarship on the Book of Daniel. My translation is based on the revised and corrected edition of this Latin preface edited by Aline Canellis in SC 592 450–464.[79] I consulted Fremantle's older English translation found in NPNF2 6.492–93, as well as Canellis's new French translation and notes. Jerome's new translation of the Book of Daniel was dedicated to Paula and Eustochium and published in 392 or 393. What is most noteworthy is Jerome's report that the Book of Daniel is read in the churches not according to the common version of the Septuagint but according to the edition of Theodotion. He says he does not know how this has come about and offers some speculations, but in any case, he strongly concurs with the decision that the LXX version of Daniel deserves to be rejected, since it differs so widely from the Hebrew truth.

Swete observes that the church's rejection of the LXX version of Daniel was so universal that only one Greek copy has survived, the Chigi MS of the ninth century CE.[80] Theodotion's Greek version was substituted in all other extant Greek MSS of Daniel.[81] Both Greek forms of Daniel (Theodotion and the sole surviving manuscript of the LXX) contain the additional stories that are not found in the Masoretic (Hebrew) text. In Theodotion's version, the story of Susanna precedes Daniel 1:1 (probably because the events took place in Daniel's youth). Yet the story had circulated independently and was sometimes associated with the name of Habakkuk. The LXX was composed before the Christian era and placed the story of Susanna in an appendix to Daniel (at the end of the book). The tale of Bel and the Dragon follows Daniel 12:13. After Daniel 3:23 a digression of sixty-seven verses (3:24–90) is found, consisting of the prayer of Azariah (24–45); details as to the heating of the furnace and the preservation of Azariah and his friends (46–51); the Song of the Three Children (52–90). Swete informs us that in the Greek MSS no break or separate title divides these Greek additions from the rest of the text, except that when Daniel is divided into "visions," the first is made to begin at 1:1. Thus, Susanna is excluded from the number of visions. The story of Bel is treated as the last of the visions.[82] Swete comments about these added stories within the Christian tradition:

> From the Fathers, however, it is clear that in the earliest Christian copies of the LXX, both Susanna and Bel formed a part of Daniel, to which they are ascribed by Irenaeus and Tertullian and implicitly by Hippolytus. The remarkable letter of Julius Africanus to Origen, which throws doubt on the genuineness of Susanna, calling attention to

indications of its Greek origin, forms a solitary exception to the general view; even Origen labors to maintain their canonicity.[83]

Interestingly, modern scholars (including Swete) believe that Susanna, Bel, and the addition to Daniel 3:23 once existed in Aramaic or Hebrew originals.[84] Thus Julius Africanus's arguments to the effect that Susanna was a Greek composition have been invalidated.

Jerome continues his preface by observing that Daniel is distinguished from the other books of Scripture in that it has been composed in three different languages: Hebrew, Aramaic, and Greek.[85] Although this observation does raise the question of the canonicity of the Greek portions, Jerome's primary intent is to criticize Porphyry for his inability to distinguish the textual traditions found in Daniel. Based on the Greek wordplays found in the Story of Susanna, the Neoplatonist scholar seems to have thought that the whole Book of Daniel was an original Greek composition and thus a forgery that does not belong to the Hebrew Scriptures.

Jerome mentions some Jewish opinions he has encountered that have been quite dismissive of the Greek portions of the book, especially the stories of Susanna, Bel and Dragon, the Prayer of the Three Children in the Fiery Furnace, and Daniel's encounter with Habakkuk. Jerome also points out that among contemporary Jews, Daniel is not found among the Prophets but among the Hagiographa. For the rabbis divide the Old Testament into three parts, the Law, the Prophets, and the Hagiographa.[86] Jerome does not pronounce himself for or against the canonicity of the Greek portions of Daniel. As a faithful servant of the tradition, he is content to report the text as it appears in the editions of the churches. He does not advance his own authority in this regard but leaves it to the reader to decide whether these parts should be received in the canon.[87]

Rufinus of Aquileia accused Jerome of judaizing by transmitting these facts and opinions and of thereby undermining the Christian canon. He quotes the legend of the divine inspiration of the LXX as proof that these portions of Daniel should not be removed from the place where they stood.[88] Jerome replies to this accusation in his *Apology against Rufinus* 2.33:

> In reference to Daniel, my answer will be that I did not say that he was not a prophet; on the contrary, I confessed in

the very beginning of the Preface that he was a prophet. But I wished to show what was the opinion upheld by the Jews; and what were the arguments on which they relied for its proof. I also told the reader that the version read in the Christian churches was not that of the Septuagint translators but that of Theodotion. It is true, I said that the Septuagint version was in this book very different from the original, and that it was condemned by the right judgment of the churches of Christ; but the fault was not mine who only stated the fact, but that of those who read the version. We have four versions to choose from: those of Aquila, Symmachus, the Seventy, and Theodotion. The churches choose to read Daniel in the version of Theodotion. What sin have I committed in following the judgment of the churches? But when I repeat what the Jews say against the Story of Susanna and the Hymn of the Three Children, and the fables of Bel and the Dragon, which are not contained in the Hebrew Bible, the man who makes this a charge against me proves himself to be a fool and a slanderer; for I explained not what I thought but what they commonly say against us. I did not reply to their opinion in the Preface, because I was studying brevity, and feared that I should seem to be writing not a Preface but a book.[89]

It is noteworthy that elsewhere in his corpus, Jerome not only admits Daniel to the number of the prophets, but he even asserts that none of the prophets spoke so clearly about Christ (preface to *Commentary on Daniel*). In *Ep* 53.8 to Paulinus of Nola, Jerome mentions Daniel as one of the four prophets, along with Isaiah, Jeremiah, and Ezekiel.

In an interesting autobiographical passage in this Preface to the Vulgate version of Daniel, Jerome points out the difficulties he himself had experienced in trying to learn Aramaic, after grappling with Hebrew for so many years. He says that he found Daniel to be so difficult to master that he almost despaired and gave up. Through the encouragement of a Hebrew acquaintance, he persevered and acquired the ability to read and understand Aramaic, but not to speak it very well. At the end of the preface, Jerome notes that the Book of Daniel had been criticized by the philosopher Porphyry, to whom Methodius of Olympus, Eusebius of Caesarea, and Apollinaris of Laodicea had responded at length. He requests the prayers of his dedicatees, Paula and Eustochium, in light of the changing judgments that his contemporaries have of his work. The fruit that was borne from Jerome's perseverance in learning the Semitic languages in addition to Greek was the ability to translate the original text of the Book of Daniel. He completed his Vulgate translation in 392, and this achievement formed the basis of his commentary on Daniel's text. R. Courtray summarizes Jerome's achievement as a translator of Daniel in these words:

> His endeavor marks a real advance over the Old Latin translations which circulated until then. In his concern to offer "Latin ears" a text reflecting the biblical *veritas* (truth), Jerome was able to make his translation benefit from the contributions of the ancient translations that he was able to achieve, in particular those of Theodotion and the Old Latin, but above all he retranslated the book from the original languages which he learned sometimes at the price of great effort. Certainly, we have noted the deviations of Jerome and his deviations from the principles followed, but his translation considerably renews the biblical text. However, despite his constant concern for literalness, we were able to note some interpretations of the text that reveal Jerome's faith; for he does not translate the Bible merely as an exegete, he also translates it as a Christian for Christians; the Bible is the word of God, it reveals mysteries, and the work of the translator is similar in this respect to the work of the prophet Daniel who was charged with explaining to kings the hidden secrets of their dreams.
> One could accuse Jerome of having "changed the Scriptures," one could reproach him for having given too discreet a place to the deuterocanonical parts to the point of making them disappear behind the *obeli*. But this would amount to ignoring the fundamental achievement of the monk, which will serve as a reference text throughout the Middle Ages and will be used until our time in the liturgy of the Catholic Church. Moreover, tradition is not mistaken about the value of his work; to realize this, it suffices to open the Latin translation of the Bible published about twenty years ago by the Vatican editions[90]: the translation

of the Book of Daniel which is given there is based on that of Jerome; of course, the progress of exegetical knowledge has considerably improved the monk's text, but the corrections remain ultimately few compared to the whole. Jerome, in his work as a translator, therefore offered Bible readers a "treasure for all times."[91]

I certainly concur with this summary of Jerome's charism in translation, which made him the patron saint of translators. Indeed, St. Jerome, pray for us!

Translator's Acknowledgements

My rendering of Jerome's Preface to the Vulgate version of Daniel is based on Aline Canellis, ed., *Jérôme: Préfaces aux Livres de la Bible*, Textes Latins des Éditions de R. Weber et R. Gryson et de L'Abbaya Saint-Jérôme (Rome), Revus et Corrigés, SC 592 (Paris: Cerf, 2017). The new translation of Jerome's *Commentary on Daniel* uses the new edition by Régis Courtray, ed. and trans, *Jérôme, Commentaire sur Daniel*, SC 602 (Paris: Cerf, 2019). I was fortunate to have learned about Courtray's new volume after I had completed a draft translation that had been based on the older critical edition by Franciscus Glorie, ed., *S. Hieronymi Presbyteri Commentariorum in Danielem Libri III <IV>*, CCSL 75A (Turnholt: Brepols, 1964). I was able to rework the entire translation according to Courtray's new edition.

In 1958, the American scholar Gleason L. Archer, Jr. produced, without an introduction, a very literal and accurate English translation of the Migne text of Jerome's Commentary.[92] He inserted linguistic annotations into the body of his work. I have benefitted from Archer's path-breaking work and esteem him as a rigorous Semitic scholar and a helpful scholarly interlocutor with Jerome. Archer's name appears frequently in the endnotes. Also, the reader will soon discover the debt I owe to the scholarship of Régis Courtray, which can hardly be measured. He has not only produced a beautiful new critical edition of Jerome's text but has also fortified it with helpful footnotes and a lengthy bibliography of studies of fundamental importance. Moreover, his French translation was flowing and precise.

Important Dates for the Book of Daniel[93]

BABYLON	612	Fall of Nineveh. Effective end of Assyria
	605	Battle of Carchemish. Nebuchadnezzar defeated Egypt and deported Daniel and his friends (Dan 1:1). Accession of Nebuchadnezzar II (605–562)
	597	Jerusalem taken by Nebuchadnezzar; many Jews exiled; city subjugated but not yet destroyed
	587	Fall of Jerusalem
	562–560	Amel-Marduk (Evil-Merodach 2 Kgs 25:27–30), King of Babylon
	560–556	Neriglissar, son-in-law of Nebuchadnezzar
	556	Labashi-Marduk
	556–539	Nabonidus (Belshazzar acting in Babylon)
	539	Fall of Babylon
PERSIA	539–530	Cyrus: the Achaemenid dynasty
	530–522	Cambyses
	522–486	Darius I
	486–465/4	Xerxes I (Ahasuerus)
	464–423	Artaxerxes
	423–404	Artaxerxes II
	359/58–338/37	Artaxerxes III
	338/37–336/35	Arses
	336/35–331	Darius III
GREECE	334–331	Conquests of Alexander of Macedon (331–323)
	323	Death of Alexander, empire divided into four areas, of which the Egyptian and the Syrian become prominent

EGYPT (Ptolemies)		**SYRIA** (Seleucids)	
323–285	Ptolemy I	312–281	Seleucus I
285–245	Ptolemy II	281–260	Antiochus I
247–221	Ptolemy III	260–246	Antiochus II

INTRODUCTION TO ST. JEROME 35

221–203	Ptolemy IV	245–223	Seleucus II and III
203–181	Ptolemy V	222–187	Antiochus III "The Great"
198	Syria took over Palestine from Egypt		
		187–175	Seleucus IV
		175–164	Antiochus IV "Epiphanes"
ROME	The rising power	168	Antiochus expelled from Egypt by Roman consul (Dan 11:30)
		167	(Dec. 25) erection of Greek altar in the Jerusalem temple

HERE BEGINS JEROME'S PREFACE ON THE PROPHET DANIEL[1]

1. The churches of our Lord and Savior[2] do not read the prophet Daniel according to the Septuagint translators, but they use Theodotion's edition,[3] and I do not know why this happened. For it is not known to me whether it is because the language is Chaldee [i.e., Aramaic] and differs from our speech in certain of its characteristics, and that the Seventy translators refused to keep those same lines in their translation; or because the book was published in the name of the Seventy by someone or other who did not know Chaldee adequately; or if there is some other reason. One thing I can affirm is that it differs widely from the original (*veritate*), and is rejected by a just judgment.[4] For one should know that Daniel especially and Ezra were written in Hebrew letters to be sure, but in the Chaldean language.[5] There is also one section of Jeremiah [cf. Jer 10:11], and Job, too, with a close affinity with the Arabic language.[6]

2. In fact, I too, when I was a young man, after reading Quintilian,[7] Tully [= Cicero],[8] and also the flowery rhetoricians, sequestered myself in the mill[9] of learning this language,[10] and with much sweat and a great deal of time, I barely began to pronounce the puffing and hissing words.[11] I seemed to be walking through some sort of underground passage (*cryptam*), seldom seeing any light from above, when at last I dashed my foot against the Book of Daniel.[12] I was so affected by the tedium of it that I suddenly became deeply depressed and wanted to forget about all my past efforts. But a Hebrew man showed up who encouraged me. He kept quoting in his own language the adage: "Unrelenting toil conquers everything."[13] So I who deemed myself to be a smatterer[14] among them once again became a student of Chaldean. To admit the truth, to the present day I can read and understand the Chaldean language better than I can speak it.

3. The reason I tell you these things is to point out the difficulty of [the Book of] Daniel. Among the Hebrews, it does not contain the story of Susanna [Dan 13], the hymn of the three children [Dan 3:24–90], or the stories (*fabulas*) of Bel and the Dragon [Dan 14]. We have appended them here, since they are spread throughout the world, but we have marked them with an obelus[15] set in front ready to slay these passages. We did this to avoid appearing to the uneducated to have cut off a significant portion of the book. I once heard a certain Jewish teacher making fun of the story of Susanna and saying that it was fabricated by some Greek or other. He raised the same objections that Africanus put to Origen, that these etymologies[16] of *scisai* from *scinov* and *prisai* from *prinov* derive from Greek [cf. Dan 13:54–59].[17] We can provide understanding of this matter to our Latin readers if we should say, for instance, that the speaker made a play on the word holm oak tree (*ilice*) by saying: "May you die on the spot" (*ilico pereas*)[18]; or a play on the word mastic tree (*lentisco*): "May the angel crush you into lentils" (*lentem*)[19]; or: "May you die but not slowly" (*non lente*); or: "May you be pliantly" (*lentus*), that is, flexibly, "led off to death"; or any other word-play that matches the name of the tree.[20] The Hebrew scholar also made fun of the three youths for having enough free time in the furnace of raging fire for the diversion of writing poetry and even of summoning all the elements in turn to praise God [cf. Dan 3:51–90]. He also asked: What divinely inspired and miraculous sign is there in the killing of a dragon with a lump of pitch [cf. Dan 14:26–27], or in uncovering the schemes of the priests of Bel [cf. Dan 14:1–21]? These things, he said, were done more by the intelligence of a shrewd man than by a prophetic spirit.[21] But when he came to the story of Habakkuk and read attentively that he was carried from Judea into Chaldea to bring a plate of food to Daniel [cf. Dan 14:32–38], he asked where in the entire Old Testament do we read of an instance of any saint with a heavy body flying through the air, and in an instant of time traversing such a great distance of land. When one of our own people who was a little too ready to speak adduced the instance of Ezekiel, and said that he was transferred from Chaldea into Judea [cf. Ezek 8:3], he scoffed at the man and proved from the book itself that Ezekiel saw himself transported in spirit.[22] Lastly, he said that even our own apostle, who was an educated person who had learned the law from the Hebrews [cf. Acts 26:4–5], did not dare to affirm that he had been caught up in the body, but said: "Whether in the body, or out of the body, I do not know; God knows" [2 Cor 12:2]. By these

and similar arguments he leveled accusations against the apocryphal stories in the church's book.[23] 4. I leave the decision about this matter to the judgment of the reader. I give warning that among the Hebrews Daniel is not found among the Prophets, but among those who wrote the Hagiographa. For they divide all Scripture into three parts, the Law, the Prophets, and the Hagiographa, which have respectively five, eight, and eleven books.[24] Now is not the time to discuss such matters.

5. On the other hand, Methodius,[25] Eusebius,[26] and Apollinaris[27] are witnesses of the things that Porphyry[28] objects to in this prophet, or rather, contrary to this book. For they replied to his madness in many thousands of lines. I do not know whether they have satisfied the curious reader. Therefore, I beg you, O Paula[29] and Eustochium,[30] to pour out your prayers to the Lord on my behalf, that as long as I am in this frail body [cf. 2 Pet 1:13], I may write something pleasing to you, useful to the church, worthy of posterity. For I am not much moved by the judgments of the present generation, for they slip off in both directions, whether out of love or hatred.

[JEROME'S COMMENTARY] ON THE PROPHET DANIEL[1]

PREFACE

Porphyry wrote his twelfth book against the prophet Daniel.[2] He refused to admit that it was composed by the person whose name it bears, but said someone wrote it who was living in Judea at the time of the Antiochus who was called Epiphanes.[3] Porphyry said that it was not so much Daniel who spoke of things to come as that other person who narrated past events. In effect, he said that whatever the book said up to the time of Antiochus contained true history, but anything it conjectured beyond that point was false, since the writer could not have known the future. In response to him and with very great skill, Eusebius, Bishop of Caesarea, wrote in three volumes, the eighteenth, nineteenth, and twentieth; so did Apollinaris in a single large book, namely, his twenty-sixth; prior to these men Methodius made a partial reply.[4]

But since our purpose is not to reply to the calumnies of an adversary, which would require a lengthy discourse, but to discuss for our people, that is, for Christians, what the prophet said, I will record the following prefatory remark, that among the prophets, no one has spoken so openly of Christ [cf. Matt 24:15]. For [Daniel] writes not merely that he will come—he has this in common with the others—but he shows at what time he will come, and he arranges the kings in order and counts the years, and announces in advance very clear signs.[5] Porphyry saw that all these things had been fulfilled and he could not deny that they had come to pass. Overcome by the truth of history, he rushed into this calumny, and contended that the things that were said concerning the antichrist, as things that will happen at the consummation of the world, were fulfilled under Antiochus Epiphanes, in view of the resemblance of events in certain respects.[6] But his attack is a witness to the truth.[7] For the reliability of the statements was so great, that it did not seem that a prophet spoke to unbelieving men about future events, but that he narrated things that were already past. However, when the occasion offers itself in the course

43

of explaining this same book, I shall attempt to respond briefly to his calumny and, by means of a simple explanation, to contradict the artifices of his philosophy, or rather, his worldly malice, by which he strives to undermine the truth and hide from our eyes the clear light by certain deceptions of his.

And so, I implore you, Pammachius,[8] foremost lover of learning,[9] and Marcella,[10] singular example of sanctity in Rome, since you are united by faith and blood, to help my efforts by your prayers, that our Lord and Savior might, for the sake of his own cause, reply with his thoughts by means of my mouth. For he says to the prophet: "Open your mouth and I will fill it" [Ps 81:10]. Indeed if he warns us not to think over what we ought to respond when we are arrested and taken before judges and tribunals [cf. Matt 10:19; Mark 13:11; Luke 12:11; 21:12–14], how much more is he able to fight his own wars against enemies who blaspheme and win the victory in his servants! And this is why a great number of psalms contain as something recorded in their titles that Hebrew expression *lamanasse*, which the Septuagint translated as "to the end," or better: "for the victory."[11] For Aquila[12] translated it as τῷ νικοποιῷ, that is, "To him who grants the victory." Symmachus[13] renders it as ἐπινίκιον, which properly signifies "the triumph and the palm."[14]

But we need to know that among his other arguments, Porphyry objects to the Book of Daniel, that it appears to be a forgery and is not held in regard by the Hebrews, but it is an invention of the Greek language. For in the story of Susanna, Daniel says to the elders, ἀπό τοῦ σχίνου σχίσει σε ὁ Θεός, καὶ ἀπὸ τοῦ πρίνου πρίσει σε [cf. Dan 13:54–55, 58–59 Theod.]. The wordplay[15] works better in Greek than in Hebrew. Both Eusebius and Apollinaris have replied to him in the same tone, that the stories of Susanna and of Bel and the Dragon are not contained in the Hebrew, but rather they constitute a part of the "Prophecy of Habakkuk, the son of Jesus of the tribe of Levi" [Dan 13:65 LXX], as is recorded in the title of that same story of Bel according to the Septuagint translators: "There was a certain priest named Daniel, the son of Abda, a companion of the king of Babylon" [Dan 14:1 LXX]. And yet Holy Scripture testifies that Daniel and the three youths were of the tribe of Judah [cf. Dan 1:6; 2:25b].[16] And this is why, when I translated Daniel many years ago,[17] I marked these visions with an obelus,[18] thereby signifying that they were not found in the Hebrew.[19] And I am surprised that certain fault-finders[20] are angry with me, as if I am the one who curtailed the book, when both Origen,

Eusebius, Apollinaris, and other churchmen and teachers of Greece acknowledge that, as I have said, these visions are not found among the Hebrews, and that they were not obligated to answer to Porphyry for these portions, which exhibit no authority as Holy Scripture.[21] I warn the reader again of the following, that the churches read Daniel not according to the Septuagint translators, but according to Theodotion, who assuredly was an unbeliever who lived after the coming of Christ, although some claim that he was an Ebionite, which is another kind of Jew.[22] But Origen too, starting from the work of Theodotion, placed asterisks[23] in the common version [of the Greek Old Testament], showing that the material added was missing [in the Septuagint], and conversely he marked some of the lines with obeli, thus designating everything that was superfluous.[24] And since all the churches of Christ, both those of the Greeks, Latins, Syrians and Egyptians, publicly read this version [i.e., Theodotion's] under the asterisks and obeli, let my envious detractors pardon my effort, in that I wanted our own people to have what the Greeks habitually read in the versions of Aquila, Theodotion, and Symmachus. For if the Greeks, for all their wealth of learning, do not despise the scholarly pursuits of Jewish men,[25] why should the impoverished Latin church look down upon a man who is a Christian, so as to take displeasure in his effort?[26] At least my good intentions should be welcomed.[27]

But now it is time for us to weave together the words of the prophet himself, not in our usual manner whereby we set forth everything and discuss everything, as we have done in our commentaries on the Twelve Prophets, but briefly and at intervals, explaining only those things which are obscure, lest the extent of our countless books wear down the reader.[28]

But to understand the final portions of Daniel,[29] a detailed investigation of Greek history is necessary, namely, of such authorities as Sutorius Callinicus,[30] Diodorus,[31] Hieronymus,[32] Polybius,[33] Posidonius,[34] Claudius Theon, and Andronicus surnamed Alypius.[35] These are writers whom Porphyry claims to have followed.[36] It is also important to know Josephus[37] and those whom he cites, and especially our own Livy, Pompeius Trogus, and Justin.[38] These men narrate the entire history of Daniel's final vision [cf. Dan 10—12], carrying it beyond the time of Alexander to the days of Caesar Augustus in their description of the Syrian and Egyptian wars, that is, those of Seleucus, Antiochus, and the Ptolemies. And if we are compelled at times to record some things from secular literature that we have long ago left to the side[39] and to speak of what is therein contained, this is not done willingly on my part, but, so to speak, by very serious necessity, in order to prove that what was foretold by the holy prophets many centuries before is contained in the literature of both the Greeks, the Latins, and other nations.[40]

BOOK ONE

Vision 1

1:1. *In the third year of the reign of Jehoiakim* (Joachim), *king of Judah, Nebuchadnezzar[1] king of Babylon came to Jerusalem and besieged it.* Jehoiakim was the son of the Josiah [cf. 2 Kgs 23:34, 36; 24:8; 2 Chr 36:5][2] in whose thirteenth year Jeremiah rose up to prophesy [cf. Jer 1:2–3], under whom also the woman Hulda (*Holda*) prophesied [cf. 2 Kgs 22:14]. He is the one who is called by another name, Eliakim [cf. 2 Kgs 23:34], and he reigned eleven years over the tribe of Judah and over Jerusalem [cf. 2 Kgs 23:36; 2 Chr 36:5]. His son Jehoiachin (*Joachin*), surnamed Jechoniah, succeeded him in the kingdom [cf. 2 Kgs 24:6; 2 Chr 36:8]. Jehoiachin was taken captive by Nebuchadnezzar's generals on the tenth day of the third month of his reign, and he was brought to Babylon [cf. 2 Kgs 24:6–17]. In his place his paternal uncle, Zedekiah, a son of Josiah, was appointed [cf. 2 Kgs 24:17], and in his eleventh year Jerusalem was captured and destroyed [cf. 2 Kgs 25:2–10; 2 Chr 36:17–20]. Let no one therefore think that the Jehoiakim (*Joachim*) in the beginning of Daniel is the same one who is recorded as Jehoiachin (*Joachin*) at the commencement to the Book of Ezekiel [cf. Ezek 1:2]. For the latter has "-chin" as its final syllable, whereas the former has "-kim." And it is for this reason that in the Gospel according to Matthew there seems to be a generation missing, because the second group of fourteen terminates in Jehoiakim, son of Josiah, and the third group begins with Jehoiachin, son of Jehoiakim [cf. Matt 1:11–12]. By his ignorance of this, Porphyry constructs a calumny against the church, displaying his own incompetence, as he tries to prove the evangelist Matthew guilty of error. It is also written that Jehoiachim was "handed over" [cf. Dan 1:2], which shows that the victory was not due to the valor of his adversaries but to the will of the Lord.

1:2b. *And a portion of the vessels of the house of God; and he carried them away into the land of Shinar (Sennaar) to the house of his god, and he brought the vessels into the treasure house of his god.*
The *land of Shinar* is a place in Babylon where the plain of Dura (*Duram*) was located [cf. Dan 3:1], and the tower that those who had migrated[3] from the east attempted to build all the way up to heaven [cf. Gen 11:1-8]. And this is why from the confusion of tongues the place received the name "Babylon," which translates into our language as "confusion" [cf. Gen 11:9].[4] And at the same time, one should notice in accordance with the anagogical interpretation,[5] that the king of Babylon was not able to transfer all of the *vessels* of God, and place them in the idol house which he had fabricated for himself, but only *a portion of the vessels* of the temple *of God*. These ought to be understood as the dogmas of truth. For if you go through all the books of the philosophers, you will inevitably discover that a *portion of the vessels of God* is in them. Thus, in Plato[6] you find that God is the fashioner of the world;[7] in Zeno the chief of the Stoics,[8] that there is an underworld, that souls are immortal, and that moral beauty (*honestatem*) is the one good.[9] But because they combine truth with falsehood and ruin the good of nature with many evils, for that reason they are said to have captured *a portion of the vessels of God*, and not all the vessels in their completeness and perfection.

1:3-4a. *And the king told Ashpenaz, the master of his eunuchs, to bring in some from the sons of Israel and from the royal seed and of the rulers,*[10] *youths in whom there was no blemish.*
Instead of *Ashpenaz* (*Asphanez*)[11] I found "Abiesdri" written in the common (*vulgata*) edition,[12] and for the word *phorthommin*, which is what Theodotion recorded, the Septuagint and Aquila translated "the chosen ones," whereas Symmachus rendered "Parthians," understanding it as the name of a nation instead of a common noun.[13] I have translated it as *rulers*, as one accurately[14] reads it in the Hebrew edition, especially since it is preceded by *from the royal seed*. This is why the Hebrews think that Daniel, Hananiah, Mishael, and Azariah were eunuchs,[15] thus fulfilling that prophecy which is spoken by Isaiah to Hezekiah: "And they shall take of your seed and make eunuchs of them in the house of the king" [Isa 39:7 LXX].[16] But if they were *from the royal seed*, there is no doubt that they were from the line of David,[17] unless the words that follow contradict this meaning:

1:4a,c. *Youths (or young men), in whom there has been no blemish, to have them learn the literature and language of the Chaldeans.*

Philo[18] thinks that the Chaldean language is the same as that of the Hebrews because Abraham came from the Chaldeans [cf. Gen 11:27–28, 31; 15:7; Acts 7:4]. But if we accept this, we must ask how the Hebrew *youths* could now be ordered to *learn a language* which they already knew; unless perhaps, we should say in accordance with the opinion of some, that Abraham knew two languages, both that of the Hebrews and that of the Chaldeans.

1:7. *And the master of the eunuchs gave them names, calling Daniel Belteshazzar (Balthasar), Hananiah Shadrach (Sidrac), Mishael Meshach (Misac), and Azariah Abednego (Abdenago).*

Not only does the *master* or teacher *of the eunuchs*, and as the others have translated it, the ἀρχιευνοῦχος (chief eunuch), change the names of saints, but so did Pharaoh who called Joseph in Egypt *Somtophaneg*[19] [cf. Gen 41:45]. They did not want them to have Jewish names in the land of captivity. And this is why the prophet says in the psalm: "How shall we sing the Lord's song in a foreign land?" [Ps 137:4]. The Lord in turn changes old names in a good sense, and according to circumstances *gives* the names of virtuous qualities. Thus, he named Abram Abraham, and Sarai Sarah [cf. Gen 17:5, 15]. In the Gospel too, the former Simon received the name of Peter [cf. Matt 10:2; 16:17–18; Mark 3:16; Luke 6:14; John 1:42], and the sons of Zebedee were called "sons of thunder" [cf. Mark 3:17]—which is not *boanerges*, as most people suppose, but is more correctly read *banereem*.[20]

1:8a. *Now Daniel purposed in his heart that he would not be defiled from the king's table, nor from the wine of his drink.*

One who does not want to eat *from the king's table* and *from the wine of his drink, that he would not be defiled*, assuredly would never have consented to learn what was not allowed, if he knew that the wisdom and teaching of the Babylonians was a sin [cf. Dan 1:4]. But they[21] do learn it, not in order to follow it, but to judge it and convict it of error; just as if someone inexperienced in learning (μαθήματος) exposes himself to ridicule by wanting to write against the astrologers (*mathematicos*);[22] or one who is ignorant of the teachings of philosophers conducts disputations against the philosophers. Therefore, they learn the teaching of the Chaldeans with the same mindset with which Moses had learned all the wisdom of the Egyptians [cf. Exod 2:9–10; Acts 7:22].

1:9. *God gave to Daniel grace and mercy in the sight of the prince of eunuchs.*

He who was led into captivity on account of the sins of his ancestors received an immediate recompense on account of the greatness of his own virtues. For he had "purposed in his heart not to be defiled from the king's table" [Dan 1:8], and he had preferred common food to royal banquets. Therefore, through the Lord's generosity *he received grace and mercy in the sight of the prince of the eunuchs.*[23] From this we understand that, if ever due to the necessity of circumstances saints are loved by unbelievers, this comes from the mercy of God, not from the goodness of perverse men.

1:12. *Put us to the test, I pray, your servants, for ten days, and let vegetables be given us to eat and water to drink.*

The extent of his faith is unbelievable, not only to promise himself a fleshy body[24] by the eating of poorer nourishment, but even to set a time for this. Therefore, their contempt for the royal banquets comes not from temerity but from faith.[25]

1:17. *But God gave these youths knowledge and learning in every book and wisdom, but to Daniel [he gave] the understanding of all visions and dreams.*

Note that *God gave* the holy *youths knowledge and learning* in secular literature, *in every book, and wisdom.* Symmachus translated this "skill in grammar," of the sort that resulted in their understanding everything they read, and by the Spirit of God, in their making judgments about the knowledge of the Chaldeans. But Daniel had this distinction over and above the three *youths*, that with his sagacious mind he could discern *visions and dreams* in which things to come are shown forth by means of certain symbols and αἰνίγματα (enigmatic sayings), so that what the others saw only as shadowy images, he could perceive clearly with the eyes of his heart.

1:18. *And so, when the days were completed after which the king had said they should be brought in, the master of the eunuchs brought them before the presence of Nebuchadnezzar.*

By *the days were completed,* understand the three-year period that the king had established, "that being nourished for three years, afterward they might stand before the king" [Dan 1:5].

1:20. *And in every word* (verbum)[26] *of wisdom and understanding that the king inquired of them, he found them ten times better than all the soothsayers and magi who were in all his kingdom.*

For *soothsayers* and *magi* the common version [of the Septuagint] translated "sophists"[27] and "philosophers"—not in the sense of the philosophy and sophistic instruction that a Greek education promises, but the instruction of a barbarian nation that the Chaldeans pursue as philosophy up to the present day.[28]

1:21. *And Daniel lived until the first year of king Cyrus.* In what follows we shall tell how Daniel, who is here described as having *lived until the first year of king Cyrus*, later on is said to have lived to the third year of the same king Cyrus and to the first [year] of Darius [cf. Dan 9:1; 10:1].²⁹

VISION 2

2:1a. *In the second year of the reign of Nebuchadnezzar, Nebuchadnezzar saw a dream etc.* If the youths entered into his presence after three years [cf. Dan 1:18], as he himself had commanded [cf. Dan 1:5], how is it that he is now said to have *seen the dream in the second year of his reign*? Here is how the Hebrews solve [the difficulty]: the *second year* refers here to his rule over all the barbarian nations, not merely over Judea and the Chaldeans, but also over the Assyrians, Egyptians, Moabites, and the rest of the nations that he had conquered with the Lord's consent. And this is why Josephus writes in the tenth book of the *Antiquities*: "After the second year of the devastation of Egypt, king Nebuchadnezzar saw a wonderful dream."³⁰

2:1b. *And his spirit was terrified and his dream fled from him.* The impious king saw a dream about the future, in order that God would be glorified, when the saint interprets what he had seen, and there would be great consolation for the captives who were serving God in their captivity. We read this same thing in the case of Pharaoh [cf. Gen 41:1–13], not that Pharaoh and Nebuchadnezzar deserved to see [visions], but because Joseph and Daniel stood out as worthy, as those who would be preferred over all others, because of their interpretation.³¹

2:2a. *Therefore the king ordered the soothsayers, the magi, the evil charmers, and the Chaldeans to be summoned.* Those whom we have translated as *soothsayers* (*harioli*), others have rendered ἐπαοιδούς, that is, "enchanters."³² Well then, it seems to me that *enchanters* are people who carry out an action using words; *magi* are those who philosophize about everything; *evil charmers* are those who use blood and animal sacrifices and often touch the bodies of the dead. On the other hand, I believe that among the Chaldeans the term γενεθλιαλόγους³³ signifies what the common people call astrologers.³⁴ But common speech and usage understand the term *magi* as *evil charmers*. Yet among their own nation they are regarded differently, since they are the philosophers of the Chaldeans, and even the kings and princes of that nation do everything in conformity with the knowledge of this art. And that is why, at the birth of our Lord and Savior, they were the first to understand his birth, and they came to holy Bethlehem to worship the child, with the star above them showing the way [cf. Matt 2:1–11].

2:3. *And the king said to them: I saw a dream, and being confused in my mind, I do not know what I saw.*

There remained in the king's heart a kind of shadow, so to speak,[35] and a glimpse and trace of the dream. Thus, when others relate it, he would be able to recall what he had seen, and lying fabricators would have been unable to deceive him.

2:4a. *The Chaldeans replied to the king in Syriac.*

Up to this point, what has been read is reported in the Hebrew language. From this passage until the vision of the third year of King Balthasar [*Belshazzar*], which Daniel saw in Susa [cf. Dan 8:1–2], the account is written in Hebrew characters, to be sure, but in the Chaldaic language, which they here call Syriac.[36]

2:5b. *Unless you tell me the dream and its interpretation* (conjecturam), *you yourselves shall perish and your houses shall be confiscated, etc.*

He has threatened a punishment and he sets forth rewards [cf. Dan 2:6], so that if they should be able to tell the dream, he consequently would also give credence to those things which are uncertain, namely, what the dream means. But if they are unable to tell the things about which the king was able to recall for the most part confusedly, they would also forfeit credibility in respect to their forthcoming interpretation. After all, it follows:

2:9b, 11. *Tell me the dream, that I may know that you are speaking a true interpretation* (interpretationem) *of it as well.... The word* (sermo) *that you seek, O king, is difficult. Nor can anyone be found who will make it known in the presence of the king, except for the gods whose commerce is not with men.*

The magi confess, the soothsayers confess, and all the knowledge of secular literature confesses, that foreknowledge of the future does not belong to humans but to God. This proves that the prophets who sang about the future spoke by the Spirit of God.[37]

2:12–13. *When he heard this, the king flew into a rage and in his great anger gave orders that all the wise men of Babylon should perish. And when the sentence went forth, the wise men were being killed, and Daniel was sought for and his companions, that they should perish.*

The Hebrews ask why Daniel and the three youths did not enter before the king along with the other wise men, and why, once the sentence was published, they are ordered to perish along with the rest. They explain it this way. At the time when the king was promising rewards and gifts and very great honor [cf. Dan 2:6], they refused to go, lest they should seem to be shamelessly seeking after the riches and dignity of the Chaldeans. Or else, the Chaldeans themselves, being jealous of their glory and knowledge, entered alone, as if they alone would obtain the rewards. But later, when they came into danger, they wanted to have as their companions those whom they had rejected in their hope of glory.[38]

2:15a. *And he asked the one who had received authority from the king as to why so cruel a sentence had gone forth from the presence of the king.*

The Chaldeans knew that Daniel and the three youths were wise and had understanding ten times beyond that of all the soothsayers and magi who were in the whole of Chaldea [cf. Dan 1:20]. Therefore, they concealed the king's inquiry from them, lest they should be preferred to themselves in the interpretation of the dream. And that is the reason Daniel *asks* about the *cruelty* of the *sentence*. He did not know why he was in danger.

2:16. *Daniel went in and asked the king to grant him time to make known the solution to the king.*

He requests *time*, not in order to search out secrets by investigation and wisdom of mind, but in order to pray to the Lord of secrets. And therefore he associates Hananiah, Mishael, and Azariah in his prayers [cf. Dan 2:17–18], lest he should seem to presume this solely based on his own merit. Thus, those who shared a common danger share prayer also in common.[39]

2:19a. *Then was the mystery revealed to Daniel by a vision in the night.*

He learns the king's dream by his own dream; or rather, by God's revelation he comes to know both the dream and its interpretation. What the demons were ignorant of, the wisdom of the world could not know [cf. 1 Cor 1:21]. Whence also the apostles, by the Lord's revelation, come to know the mystery that had been unknown to all previous generations [cf. Eph 3:5; Col 1:26].

2:19b. *And Daniel blessed the God of heaven.*

In order to distinguish him from those who dwell on earth and delude earthly places with demonic arts and deceptions, *Daniel blesses the God of heaven.* For "the gods who did not make heaven and earth will perish" [Jer 10:11].

2:21a. *He changes times and ages, he transfers kingdoms and establishes them.*

Let us then not be amazed if from time to time we see kings succeed kings and kingdoms succeed kingdoms, which are governed, *changed*, and ended by God's decision. And the reasons for each of these things, he knows who is the creator of all things, and often he allows evil kings to arise, so that evil men may punish the evil men. And at the same time, he gives a glimpse[40] and by a general discussion prepares the listener to hear that the dream he saw was about the changing and succession of *kingdoms*.

2:21b. *He gives wisdom to the wise and knowledge to those who understand instruction.*

This agrees with what is written: "The wise man will hear and increase his wisdom" [Prov 1:5]. "For he who has, to him it shall be given" [Matt 13:12; Mark 4:25; Luke 8:18; cf. Matt 25:29]. And the Spirit of God is freely poured into the soul which burns with a love of wisdom, but "wisdom will not enter into a perverse soul" [Wis 1:4].

2:22. *He reveals deep and hidden things and knows what is set in darkness, and light is with him.*

The one to whom God *reveals deep things* and who can say: "O the *depth* of the riches of the wisdom and of the knowledge of God!" [Rom 11:33], is one who, by the Spirit that dwells within him, "searches even into the *deep things* of God" [1 Cor 2:10]. And he digs the deepest wells in the *depth* of his soul and carries off all the earth which used to cover the *deep* waters [cf. Gen 26:18], and he observes the commandment that says: "Drink the waters from your own vessels and from the spring of your wells" [Prov 5:15 LXX]. As for what follows, *He knows what is set in darkness, and light is with him*: *darkness* signifies ignorance, *light* [signifies] knowledge and doctrine. And so, just as what is perverse does not escape God, so what is right surrounds him and envelops him. Or one should interpret it thus, that the dark things signify all that is mysterious and *deep* in the sense of what we read in Proverbs: "He will understand also a parable and dark speech" [Prov 1:6 LXX]. It means the same thing as what we read in the Psalms: "Dark water in the clouds of the air" [Ps 18:11]. For one who climbs to the heights and abandons earthly things like the birds aspires for the thinnest air and everything ethereal [cf. Phil 3:13]. He is made into a cloud that the truth of God reaches and that is accustomed to shower down rain upon the saints [cf. Ps 57:10; 108:4]. And when he is filled with an abundance of knowledge, he contains in his heart much dark water [cf. Ps 18:11] and is wrapped in the deep darkness which Moses alone enters [Exod 20:21] and speaks with God face to face [cf. Exod 33:11], of whom it is written: "He made darkness his hiding place" [Ps 18:11].

2:23a. *To you, O God of my fathers, I confess, and I praise you.*

Lest it should seem that what [Daniel] has procured is due to his own merit, he refers it to the justice *of his fathers* and to the truth of *God,* who takes pity upon their seed even in captivity.

2:23c. *And now you have shown me what we asked of you.*

What the four *ask* for is *shown* to one of them, that he might both flee from arrogance, seeming to have procured the request on his own, and give thanks, since he alone heard the mystery of the dream.

2:24b. *Do not destroy the wise men of Babylon.*

He imitates the clemency of the Lord, who prays for his persecutors and does not want them to perish by whose fault he himself was going to perish [cf. Luke 23:34].

2:25b. *I have found a man of the sons of the transmigration of Judah who will make known the solution to the king.*

He[41] refers [what came from] God's grace to his own diligence, and he claims to have *found* him himself, though Daniel is the one who had offered himself of his own accord to be brought before the king [cf. Dan 2:24]. In this is shown the ἦθος (customary manner) of the messengers: When they have good news to declare, they want it to appear to be their own doing. But the one who promises the *solution* to the dream is certainly going to relate the dream beforehand. And note that Daniel is said to belong to the *sons of Judah*; he is not a priest, as the story of Bel at the end has it [cf. Dan 14:27].[42]

2:26b. *Do you really think that you can make known to me the dream that I saw, and its interpretation?*

He maintains order in the question, so that he asks first about the *dream*, which the magi had replied that they did not know it [cf. Dan 2:10–11], and then about the *interpretation* of the dream. Thus when he has heard the dream and recognizes the things he had seen, then he would trust also in the interpretation, which is susceptible to various explanations.

2:27b. *The mystery that the king asks about, neither the wise men, the magi, the soothsayers nor the diviners are able to make known to the king.*

For *diviners* (*haruspices*), as we have translated it, the Hebrew[43] has *gazarenos*,[44] which only Symmachus has rendered as θύτας (sacrificers), and which the Greeks usually call ἡπατοσκόπους (inspectors of livers),[45] because they inspect entrails and make predictions about the future based on them. Now by calling the succession of a revealed dream a *mystery*, Daniel shows that whatever is hidden and unknown by men can be named a *mystery*. Moreover, he removes the king's perverse idea that thinks that what is reserved to the knowledge of God alone can be discovered by human ingenuity.

2:28a. *But there is a God in heaven who reveals mysteries.*

Therefore, it is in vain that you seek from people on earth what God alone in heaven knows. Also, by secretly drawing Nebuchadnezzar away from the worship of many gods, he directs him to the knowledge of the one God.

2:28b. *Who has made known to you, King Nebuchadnezzar, the things that are going to take place in the last times.*

Avoiding the vice of adulation by his union with the truth, he speaks flattery as to a king, and says that God has *revealed* to him *mysteries* that *will take place in the last times*. Now either these *last* days are to be reckoned from the time when the dream was revealed to Daniel until the consummation of the world, or else the entire interpretation of the dream should be understood as applying to that end, when the image and statue that is seen is to be smashed to pieces [cf. Dan 2:34–35, 40, 44–45].

2:28c. *Your dream and the visions of your head upon your bed are of this sort.*

He did not say, *the visions* "of your eyes," lest we should think it was something bodily,[46] but *of the head*. For "the eyes of a wise man are in his head" [Eccl 2:14], that is, in the principal part (*principali*) of the heart, in accordance with what we read in the Gospel: "Blessed are the pure in heart, for they shall see God" [Matt 5:8]; and: "What are you thinking in your hearts?" [Luke 5:22; cf. Matt 9:4; Mark 2:8]. In fact, on the pretext of this chapter, others surmise that τὸ ἡγεμονικὸν (the ruling part) lies not in the heart but, as Plato says, in the brain.[47]

2:29a. *You, O king, began to think on your bed about what should come to pass after these things.*

Instead of *after these things*, the Septuagint alone translated: "in the last days." But if it is read that way, we must inquire quite carefully where "last days" have been written; and we should refute those who think the world will not perish.[48] For they would not be called the "last days" if the world were eternal. And as for what is said: *You, O king, began to think*, this shows the causes of the dream; for God revealed to him the mysteries of the future, because the king himself wanted to know what would come to be. Also, in order that Nebuchadnezzar might marvel at the gracious gift of divine inspiration, he sets forth not only what he saw in the dream, but what he was thinking about in silence before the dream.

2:29c. *And he who reveals mysteries has shown you what shall come to pass.*

That which we read in the Gospel: "Who makes his sun to rise upon the good and the evil" [Matt 5:45], we understand to have been fulfilled in the case of Nebuchadnezzar also. For the mercy of almighty God is so great that he even *revealed* to Nebuchadnezzar the *mysteries* of his providential governance by which he rules the world. Let us ask those who assert that there are different kinds of natures,[49] what kind do they understand Nebuchadnezzar to have had: good or evil? If good, why is he called impious?[50] If evil, as is certain,[51] why did God show his mysteries (*sacramenta*) to one who was evil and of the earth (*terreno*), that is to say, from clay (*choico*) [cf. Gen 2:7; 1 Cor 15:47–48]?

2:30a. *To me also this mystery* (sacramentum) *has been revealed not by any wisdom which is in me more than in all the living, but that the interpretation might be made manifest to the king.*

The king had thought that a knowledge of the future could be grasped by the ingenuity of the human mind, and that is why he had ordered the wise men of Babylon to be killed [cf. Dan 2:12]. Daniel therefore excuses even those who were unable to speak, and he himself avoids their ill will, lest anyone should think that he had said what he was about to say by his own *wisdom*. But the cause of the prophetic revelation is the desire of the king, who wanted to know what was coming. Therefore, he honors the king, when he says that it was for the sake of the king's knowledge that the mysteries have been revealed by God. And one should take this into consideration, that dreams in which certain coming events are indicated and in which truth is pointed out, as it were, through a cloud, are not accessible to the interpreters and to the judgment of the human mind, but to the knowledge of God alone.

2:31–35. *You, O king, looked, and behold [there was] as it were a huge statue. This statue was great and tall of stature and it stood before you, and the sight of it was terrible. The head of this statue was of finest gold, but the chest and the arms of silver; moreover, the belly and the thighs were of bronze, but the legs were of iron. The feet were partly of iron and partly of clay. Thus you saw it, until a stone was cut without hands, and it struck the statue upon its feet that were of iron and of clay, and broke them in pieces. Then were the iron, the clay, the bronze, the silver, and the gold broken to pieces together, and became like the chaff of a summer's threshing floor, and they were carried away by the wind; and there was no place found for them. But the stone that had struck the statue became a great mountain, and it filled the whole earth.*

Instead of *statue*, that is, ἀνδριάντι,[52] which is the translation of Symmachus alone, others have translated it as "image," intending by this term to show the likeness to future events. Let us follow the prophet's interpretation, and as we go through[53] Daniel's words, let us explain more extensively the things which he has said with brevity.[54] He says, "Now you, O king, are the head of gold" [Dan 2:38]. By this, it is shown that the first kingdom is that of Babylon. It is compared to very precious *gold*. "And after you there shall arise another kingdom inferior to you" [Dan 2:39], namely, that of the Medes and Persians, which bears a resemblance to *silver*. It is *inferior* to the former, and not greater than the one that follows. "And a third kingdom, another, of bronze, which shall hold command over all the earth" [Dan 2:39]. This signifies Alexander and the kingdom of the Macedonians, and of Alexander's successors. Now it is rightly said to be *of bronze*, for among all the metals *bronze* has greater resonance and it rings out more clearly, and its sound spreads far and wide.[55] Thus he showed not only the fame and power of that kingdom, but also the eloquence of the Greek language. "And a fourth kingdom," which clearly applies to the Romans, "is of iron," which "crushes and subdues all else" [Dan 2:40]. But its "feet and toes are partly of iron and partly of potter's clay" [Dan 2:41]. This is a reality that is most clearly demonstrated at the present time. For just as in the beginning there was nothing stronger or tougher than the Roman Empire, so at the end of affairs there is nothing weaker, since we require the assistance of barbarians of other tribes, both in our civil wars and against different nations.[56] But at the end of all these kingdoms of gold, silver, bronze and iron, "a stone"— the Lord and Savior—"was cut off without hands" [Dan 2:45], that is, from a virgin's womb, without sexual intercourse and the involvement of human seed.[57] And when all these kingdoms have been crushed, "it became a great mountain and filled the whole earth" [Dan 2:35]. The Jews and the impious Porphyry wrongly apply this to the people of Israel, whom they want to believe will be the strongest at the end of the ages, and will crush all kingdoms and will reign forever.[58]

2:45b. *The great God has shown to the king what will come to pass hereafter.*

Again he says that the revelation of the dream is not due to his own merit,[59] but has been granted to make the interpretation clear to the king and to show the king that God alone ought to be worshipped.

2:46. *Then King Nebuchadnezzar fell on his face and worshipped Daniel, and ordered them to sacrifice victims and incense to him.*

Porphyry raises a calumny over this passage when he says that this most proud king would never have *worshipped* a captive. As if the Lycaonians too did not want to offer animal sacrifices to Paul and Barnabas on account of the greatness of the signs [cf. Acts 14:10–12]! Therefore, one should not impute to the Scripture an error of pagans, who think that all that is beyond themselves are gods. Scripture is simply relating all that took place. But we can say this too, that the king himself explains the reasons for his *worship* and for his *offering of victims and incense* and sacrifice, when he says to Daniel:

2:47b. *Truly your God is the God of gods and the Lord of kings, and a revealer of mysteries* (mysteria*); since you were able to discover this mystery* (sacramentum*).*

Therefore, he does not so much worship Daniel as the God who, in Daniel, had revealed the *mysteries*.[60] We read that Alexander, king of the Macedonians, did this too in respect to the high priest Joiada (*Yaddua*).[61] But if this explanation is displeasing, one should say this, that Nebuchadnezzar was confused by the greatness of the signs and by his own sense of wonderment. He did not know what he was doing, so that when he came to understand the true God and Lord of kings, he worshipped his servant and burned incense to him.

2:48. *Then the king raised Daniel to a high position, and gave him many great gifts, and he made him prince over all the provinces of Babylon and prefect of the magistrates over all the wise men of Babylon.*

In this matter also the malicious accuser of the church [Porphyry] tries to criticize the prophet for not refusing the *gifts* and for freely receiving the Babylonian office. He fails to consider the fact that the reason the king saw the dream, and the mysteries of its interpretation were revealed through the youth, was for Daniel to increase and, in the place of captivity, to become *prince* over all the Chaldeans and to make known the omnipotence of God. Indeed, we read that this happened both to Joseph in the home of Pharaoh in Egypt [cf. Gen 41:37–46],[62] and also to Mordecai at the court of Ahasuerus [cf. Esth 8:1–2]. Thus in every nation, the captives and sojourners from the Jews had consolation, when they saw that a man of their own people was a *prince* of the Egyptians or of the Chaldeans.

2:49a. *But Daniel requested of the king, and he appointed Shadrach, Meshach, and Abednego over the works of the province of Babylon.*

He does not forget those with whom he had prayed to the Lord, and who had been in danger with him.[63] And so he makes them judges of provinces; but he himself does not leave the king's side [cf. Dan 2:49b].

VISION 3[64]

3:1a. *King Nebuchadnezzar made a golden statue sixty cubits in height and six cubits in breadth.*

How quickly he forgets the truth![65] The man who a short time ago had been worshipping a servant of God [cf. Dan 2:46] as if he were God now commands a *statue* to be made for himself, in order that he himself might be worshipped in the statue! Now the fact that it is *of gold* and is of measureless weight is in order to produce a sense of wonder in the onlookers and so that a vain thing may be worshipped as God, while everyone hallows his own greed [cf. Isa 56:11; Jer 6:13; 8:10].[66] Also an opportunity of salvation is granted to the barbarian nations on the occasion of the captives, so that those who had first come to know the power of the one God by Daniel's revelation might learn from the courage of the three youths to despise death and not worship idols.[67]

3:1b. *And he set it up in the plain of Dura (*Duram*) of the province of Babylon.*

For *Dura*, Theodotion has "Deira," Symmachus "Doraum," and the Septuagint translated it περίβολον,[68] which we can express as "live game park" or "an enclosed place."

3:2a. *He sent to assemble the satraps, magistrates, judges, captains, rulers, prefects, and all the princes of the regions.*

The heights stand closer to danger, and the lofty more quickly fall.[69] The *princes* are *assembled* to worship the statue, in order that through their princes the nations also might be led astray. For those who are rich and powerful are tripped up more easily because they fear being without their riches and power. But once the *magistrates* are led astray, the submissive people perish by following the example of their elders.

3:4–6. *And a herald cried out forcefully: To you it is said, O peoples, tribes, and languages: in the hour that you shall hear the sound of the trumpet and of the flute and of the harp, of the sambuca,[70] and of the lute, and of the bagpipe, and of every other kind of musical instrument, you shall fall down and worship the golden statue which king Nebuchadnezzar has set up. But if anyone shall not fall down and worship, he shall the same hour be cast into a furnace of burning fire.*

It is not that all the *peoples* of all the nations could be assembled on the plain of Dura (*Duram*) to *worship the golden statue,* but that in the princes of all the nations, the whole nation and people are believed to have worshipped. Now as I mentally run through all of Sacred Scripture, unless my memory deceives me, I nowhere find a passage stating that any saint *worshipped* God by *falling down.*[71] But whoever worships idols, demons, and forbidden things is said *to worship by falling down,* as is said in this present passage, not once but repeatedly. And in the Gospel the devil says to the Lord: "All these things will I give you, if you will fall down and worship me" [Matt 4:9]. But it should also be said that all heretics who compose false doctrine with the brilliance of secular eloquence make a golden statue, and to the extent that they are able, they compel people, by their persuasiveness, to *fall down and worship* the idol of falsehood.

3:7a. *As soon as all the people heard the sound of the trumpet, the flute, and the harp.*

One should take this in the same sense as above, that we understand *all the peoples* in the princes.[72] For it would have been impossible for all the nations to be present at one time.

3:8. *And immediately at that time some Chaldeans approached who accused the Jews.*

They were jealous of those who had been put in charge of the king's work projects in Babylon, and they took offense at their foreign form of worship and their aversion to idols. Lighting upon this pretext, they bring criminal charges to the king, precisely as follows:

3:12a. *There are certain Jews whom you appointed over the works of the country of Babylon, Shadrach, Meshach, and Abednego, who have shown contempt for your decree.*

In a certain manner, they are saying this: "Those captives and slaves whom you preferred to us and made to be princes, they have become elated with pride and are showing contempt for your commands."

3:12b. *They do not worship your gods, and do not adore the golden statue that you set up.*

What we said at the beginning of this vision[73] is very clearly proven here: Nebuchadnezzar's gods are one thing; the golden statue, which he had ordered to be erected for the worship of himself, is something else. For in what comes next the king himself says:

3:14b. *Do you not worship my gods, and do you not adore the golden statue that I have set up?*

Some say that this is the custom of Holy Scripture, to speak of a single idol in the plural. For example, in Exodus, it says the following about the calf: "These are your gods, O Israel, who have brought you out of the land of Egypt" [Exod 32:4 LXX; cf. 1 Kgs 12:28]. Also in the Book of Kings, Jeroboam is said to have made idols, when he set up a golden calf in Bethel [1 Kgs 12:32–33]. On the other hand, multiple demons are designated in the singular number in Isaiah: "He bowed himself down and adores it and makes his vow and says: You[74] are my God!" [Isa 44:17 LXX; cf. Mark 5:9].

3:15b. *Prostrate yourselves and adore the statue that I have made; but if you do not adore, you shall be cast the same hour into the furnace of fire that is burning.*

Although it was while he was in a rage that he had ordered the youths to be brought, yet he gives them time to show regret, so that their previous guilt might be pardoned, if they should fall down and *adore*. But if they disdain adoring it, the punishment of the *burning furnace* will be immediate.

3:15c. *And who is the God who shall rescue you from my hand?*

Clearly he is the one whose servant you worshipped a short time ago [cf. Dan 2:46], who you said was truly "God of gods and Lord of kings" [Dan 2:47].

3:16b. *King Nebuchadnezzar, we do not have to answer you concerning this matter.*

The Hebrew text[75] does not have *King*, lest they should seem to flatter an impious man or to call him a *king* who was compelling wicked actions. But if some contentious person reads, *O king*, we would say that they were not recklessly provoking the king to shed their blood, but rendering to the king the honor that is owed him, without harm to the worship of God. But as for the words: *We do not have to answer you concerning this matter*, the sense is: "You do not have to listen to the words of those whose courage and constancy you will soon test by their very deeds."

3:17. *For behold our God whom we worship is able to rescue us from the furnace of burning fire and to deliver us from your hands, O king!*

The means by which he thought he was frightening the youths, he perceives has become in them the stuff of courage. Nor do they postpone the help to the distant future, but they promise that it is immediately present to themselves, saying: *For behold, our God whom*

we worship, he himself *is able to deliver us,* both from that fire that you threaten and *from your hands.*
3:18a. *But if he does not will it.*
It is nice[76] that in response to what he had said: "He is able to deliver us" [Dan 3:17], he did not add the opposite: "If he is not able," but: *if he does not will it.* Thus, if they perish, this will not be due to God's incapacity, but to his will.
3:18b. *Be it known to you, O king, that we do not worship your gods, and we do not adore the golden statue which you set up.*
Whether we wish to read *statue,* as Symmachus does, or "golden image," as the others have translated it, worshippers of God should not *adore* it. Therefore, let judges and princes of the world, who adore the statues and images of emperors, understand that they are doing precisely what these three youths pleased God by refusing to do. Moreover, the precision of terms deserves to be noted: They say that gods are worshipped, an image is adored, neither of which is befitting for God's servants to do.
3:19a. *Then Nebuchadnezzar was filled with fury and the aspect of his face was changed.*
In certain psalms, the titles are prefixed: "For those who will be changed"[77] [cf. Ps 45:1; 69:1; 80:1].[78] Therefore, talk of a *change* is ambiguous. It can refer both to change from good to evil and from evil to good. For a *change* of Nebuchadnezzar's face cannot be adjusted into a good sense, although some refer even the psalm titles to a change from good to evil.[79] They say that those who should have understood God by nature [cf. Rom 1:20–23] have been changed through the disturbance of mind and *fury* to oppose Christ and his saints.
3:19c. *And he ordered the furnace to be set ablaze seven times more than it was accustomed to being heated.*
As if a plain ordinary fire could not have consumed the bodies of the three youths! But fury and wrath, which border on insanity, are incapable of showing moderation. Also, he wants to terrify them by the threat of a far greater punishment, since he saw that they were ready to die.
3:21. *And immediately these men were bound, and they were cast into the midst of the furnace of burning fire, with their trousers, caps, shoes, and garments.*
Instead of *trousers,* which Symmachus translated as ἀναξυρίδας ("trousers worn by eastern nations"),[80] Aquila and Theodotion said *saraballa* (rather than the corrupt reading *sarabara*). Now human legs

and shinbones are called *saraballa* in the language of the Chaldeans,[81] and it is homonymous[82] with *trousers* which cover the legs (*crura*) and shinbones (*tibiae*), as if they were being called "leggings (*crurales*)" and "shinnies (*tibiales*)." Now *cap* (*tiara*) is a Greek word[83] that has, by usage, been turned into a Latin word also. Even Virgil uses it: "...both scepter and sacred tiara."[84] Now it is a kind of skullcap used by the Persian and Chaldean nations.[85]

3:22b. *Moreover the flame of the fire killed those men who had cast in Shadrach, Meshach, and Abednego.*

He is referring to those *men* of whom he had said above: "And he commanded the strongest men in his army to bind the feet of Shadrach, Meshach and Abednego and cast them into the furnace of fire that was burning" [Dan 3:20]. Thus, Nebuchadnezzar destroyed not just some chance servants of his, but men from all his army who were strong and most ready for war, so that he would not only become thoroughly frightened before the miracle, but would also feel the damage to his own army.

3:23. *But these men, that is, the three: Shadrach, Meshach, and Abednego, fell bound into the midst of the furnace of burning fire.*

It was a great miracle: *bound* men are cast into a *furnace* and *fall* headlong *into the midst of the fire*.[86] The chains with which they are *bound* burn up; and the flame, fearing the bodies of those in chains, does not touch them.

The Hebrews read it only up to this point. The intervening verses which follow as far as the end of the *Song of the Three Children* are not found in the Hebrew.[87] Lest we seem to have bypassed them altogether,[88] let us say a few things.

3:26–28a (vv. 3–4).[89] *Blessed are you, O Lord, the God of our fathers, and your name is worthy of praise and glorious forever. For you are just in all that you have done to us, and all your works are true, and your ways right, and all your judgments true. For you have executed true judgments in all the things that you have brought upon us.*

When we are pressed by different kinds of difficulties, let us say these words with the full feeling of our heart, and let us confess that, whatever happens to us, we are enduring it justly. That way the following scripture may be fulfilled in us: "The daughters of Judah have exulted and rejoiced in all your judgments, O Lord" [Ps 97:8].[90]

3:29 (v. 6). *For we have sinned and acted unjustly in departing from you, and we have trespassed in all things.*

Now surely the three youths did not *sin*, nor were they even of an age to be punished for their own faults, when they were brought to Babylon.[91] Therefore, they are saying this under the persona of[92] the people, just as one should read the following words of the apostle: "For I do not do what I wish; but what I do not want, that I carry into effect" [Rom 7:19], and the other things that are written in that same passage.[93]

3:37–39 (vv. 14–16). *For we, O Lord, are diminished more than all nations, and we are brought low in all the earth this day on account of our sins. Neither is there at this time prince, or prophet, or leader, or holocaust, or sacrifice, or oblation, or incense, or place of first fruits before you, that we may be able to find mercy.*

One should use these short verses, whenever the churches, on account of the sins of the people, suffer a poverty of holy men and teachers, who are most learned in the law of God; and whenever in times of persecution *sacrifice and oblation* is not being offered up.

Some apply this passage to the heavenly Jerusalem [cf. Heb 12:22] as well. They say that souls have fallen to the earthly regions and are put in a place of tears [cf. Ps 84:6; Heb 12:17] and confession.[94] They bewail the ancient transgressions and the other things that the prophetic discourse covers. But the church of God does not accept these things.[95]

3:39 (v. 16). *But let us be welcomed with a contrite soul and a spirit of humility.*

Based on the present passage, on the one that follows: "Bless the Lord, ye spirits and souls of the just" [Dan 3:86 (v. 64)], and on one in the Psalms: "The sacrifice for God is an afflicted spirit, a contrite and humbled heart God does not despise" [Ps 51:17], there are those who would have it mean that the human *spirit* is one thing, apart from the Holy Spirit, and the *soul* is something else;[96] but they will have their hands full explaining how there can be said to be two substances and two inner men in one man [cf. Col 3:9–10], separate from the flesh and from the grace of the Holy Spirit.[97]

3:46 (v. 23). *And the king's servants who had cast them in did not cease to kindle the furnace with naphtha, flax, pitch, and dry sticks.*

Sallust writes in his *Histories* that *naphtha* is a kind of tinder in use among the Persians that very greatly feeds fires.[98] Others think that *naphtha* is the name applied to olive pits, which are thrown away with the dried oil residue. This is why it is expressed in Greek as πυρίνη (fiery, enflamed), from the fact that it nourishes πῦρ, that is, fire.[99]

3:49–50 (vv. 26–27). *But the angel of the Lord came down into the furnace with Azariah and his companions, and he drove the flame of the fire out of the furnace and made the midst of the furnace like the blowing of a wind bringing dew. And the fire did not touch them at all, nor did it trouble them, nor do them any harm.*

When the soul is overwhelmed with troubles and occupied with various *causes of harm*, when it has despaired of help from men, and turns with its whole mind to the Lord, *an angel of the Lord*, that is to say, the divine word, *comes down* to it, it *drives out* the fierce heat of the *flame*, so that the flaming arrows of the enemy [cf. Eph 6:16] do not penetrate the secret places of our heart [cf. Ps 11:2], and we are not shut up within his *furnace*.

3:87 (v. 65). *O ye holy and humble of heart, bless the Lord.*[100]

The present brief verse teaches us to have humility of heart, as does what is said in the Gospel: "Learn from me, for I am meek and *humble of heart*, and you shall find rest for your souls" [Matt 11:29]. Now this humility of heart is that which is elsewhere called "poverty of spirit" [cf. Matt 5:3]. So let us not be lifted up in pride, let us not seek after glory by a feigned humility, but let us abase ourselves with our whole heart.

3:57a (v. 35). *All ye works of the Lord, bless the Lord.*

He speaks first in general terms of praise, that all creation ought to praise God. Then in what follows he exhorts the different classes of individual things to do this: the angels and the heavens [cf. Dan 3:58–59 (vv. 36–37)], the waters and the powers [cf. Dan 3:60–61 (vv. 38–39)], the sun and the moon [cf. Dan 3:62 (v. 40)], the rain and the dew [cf. Dan 3:64 (v. 42)], wind, fire, and heat [cf. Dan 3:66–67 (vv. 43–44)], the cold and the heat [cf. Dan 3:67 (v. 45)], and the other things, which would take too long to recount, so that he rouses to the praise of the Lord the springs also and the seas [cf. Dan 3:77–78 (vv. 55–56)], the sea monsters, the birds, the beasts and the cattle [cf. Dan 3:79–81 (vv. 57–59)]. He summons also the children of men [cf. Dan 3:82 (v. 60)], and after the entire human race, Israel [cf. Dan 3:83 (v. 61)], and within Israel itself the priests and servants of the Lord [cf. Dan 3:84–85 (vv. 62–63)], the spirits and souls of the just [cf. Dan 3:86 (v. 64)], and those who are holy and of humble heart [cf. Dan 3:87 (v. 65)]. And lastly he addresses Hananiah, Azariah, and Mishael, who are summoned to praise the Lord for his present kindness [cf. Dan 3:88 (v. 66)]. But all creation praises God not in words but in *works*. For it is by what is created that we subsequently understand the Creator [cf. Wis 13:5], and it is by each of his *works* and effects that the greatness of God is shown [cf. Sir 39:19–20].

3:91a (24). *Then Nebuchadnezzar the king was astonished and rose up in haste and said to his nobles.*

Up to this point, we have touched upon a few things from Theodotion's translation that are not found in the Hebrew, concerning the confession and praises of the three youths. But from this point on let us follow the Hebrew truth. *And he rose up in haste and said to his nobles.* After the princes were punished, the king is corrected, in order that he may glorify God while still alive. But he questions *his nobles*, upon whose accusation and counsel he had cast the three youths into the fiery furnace. That way, when they reply that they had cast three youths into the furnace, he might announce to them and point out:

3:92b (25). *Behold, I see four men loose and walking about in the midst of the fire, and there is no corruption in them, and the appearance of the fourth is the likeness of a son of God.*

I will say it again:[101] O how wise is the fire, how unspeakable the power of God! Their bodies were bound with chains; the chains are burnt up, but the bodies do not burn. As for *the appearance of the fourth*, which he says is *like a son of God*, either we should take it to be an angel, as the Septuagint has translated it, or else, as the majority think,[102] it is the Lord and Savior.[103] But I do not know how an ungodly king could have merited seeing the *Son of God*.[104] Therefore, angels are to be understood here, in accordance with Symmachus, who translated it: "But the appearance of the fourth is the likeness of the sons," not of God, but "of the gods." Angels are very frequently called gods and sons of the gods, or of God [cf. Gen 6:1–4; Ps 29:1; 89:6; Job 1:6; 2:1; 38:7]. I have said these things according to the history. But as for the type, this angel or *son of God* prefigures our Lord Jesus Christ, who descended into the furnace of hell, in which the souls of both sinners and of the just were being held and shut in, in order that he might deliver those who were held imprisoned by chains of death, without being burned or suffering harm to himself [cf. 1 Pet 3:19].[105]

3:93a (26). *Then Nebuchadnezzar came to the opening of the furnace of burning fire and said.*

Seized by terror and fear, he does not inquire of the youths through any messengers, but himself calls them by name, addressing them as *servants of the Most High God* [Dan 3:93b], and asking those whom he had cast into the furnace in chains to come out to him.

3:95a (28). *Blessed be the God of Shadrach, Meshach, and Abednego, who sent his angel and rescued his servants.*

The one whom above he calls a son of God [cf. Dan 3:92(25)] he here calls *an angel*, although higher up he was called the *likeness* of a son of God, not the "truth." Once again, therefore, Nebuchadnezzar accepts a confession of God [cf. Dan 2:46–47], and while condemning the idols, he praises the three youths who refused to serve and worship any god but their own God. And he is astonished that the fire was unable to touch the saints of God. And he says:

3:96 (29). *By me this decree is proposed: that any people, tribe, or language that speaks blasphemy against the God of Shadrach, Meshach, and Abednego shall be destroyed and his house shall be laid waste. For there is no other God who can save in this way.*

Some [commentators] very wrongly apply this to the devil.[106] They say that at the consummation and end of the world, even the devil himself will accept the knowledge of God and will exhort all to repent. They think that this is what the king of Nineveh signifies, who at the very end came down from his proud throne and obtained the rewards of humility [cf. Jon 3:6, 10].[107]

3:97 (30). *Then the king promoted Shadrach, Meshach, and Abednego in the province of Babylon.*

Those who say that higher up [cf. Dan 2:49] the three youths were not judges of provinces[108] but overseers of individual work projects in Babylon think this means that they were likewise appointed as judges over the provinces.[109]

3:98 (4:1).[110] *King Nebuchadnezzar, to all the nations and languages that dwell upon the whole earth: May peace be multiplied to you!*

The epistle of Nebuchadnezzar is recorded in the prophet's volume, in order that the book might not be thought to have been made up later by some other author, as the sycophant[111] [Porphyry] falsely claims, but is by Daniel himself.[112]

VISION 4

4:1a/4:4 (3:98). *I Nebuchadnezzar was at rest in my house.*

The history is indeed clear and does not need much interpretation.[113] For offending God, Nebuchadnezzar went insane. For seven years, he lived among the brute beasts and fed upon the roots of plants [cf. Dan 4:22, 29–30, 34; 5:20–21]. Afterward by the mercy of God "he was restored to his kingdom" [Dan 4:33], and "praised and glorified the King of heaven" [Dan 4:34]: "For all his works are true, and his ways judgments, and he is able to humble those who walk in pride" [Dan 4:34].

But there are those who want to understand Nebuchadnezzar as the opposing power of which the Lord speaks in the Gospel: "I saw Satan falling from heaven like lightning" [Luke 10:18]; and John in the Book of Revelation, that the dragon fell to the earth and dragged a third of the stars with him [cf. Rev 12:3–4]; and Isaiah: "How has Lucifer fallen, who used to rise in the morning?" [Isa 14:12 LXX].[114] They claim that it was in no way possible for a man raised in luxury to have fed on hay for seven years, and to have lived among wild beasts for seven years, without having his body torn to pieces. And how could the empire be preserved for a madman, and the most powerful kingdom exist without a king for such a long time? Or, if someone had succeeded him in the kingdom, one would have to reckon with that man's senselessness, in handing over the imperial authority, which he had possessed for such a long time, especially since the histories of the Chaldeans contain no such thing, nor is it possible that those who recorded matters of lesser significance should have been silent about matters of greater importance. Now they inquire about all these things and reflect that, since the history does not hold up, the devil is being signified by Nebuchadnezzar.[115]

We do not accept any of this. Otherwise, everything we read would appear to be shadows and fables.[116] For who has not seen crazy people living like brute animals in fields and forested places? And to pass over everything else, Greek and Roman history reveals that things that are even harder to believe have actually taken place, and fables tell us about Scylla[117] and the Chimaera,[118] the Hydra,[119] and the Centaurs,[120] birds, beasts, flowers and trees, stars and stones, made out of human beings.[121] What is so astonishing, if this was accomplished by the judgment of God, in order to show God's power and to humble the pride of kings?[122]

4:1b (4). *I was at rest in my house and flourishing in my palace* (or as Theodotion translated it, "upon my throne.")

Now those who follow the interpretation that we oppose understand by the devil's *house* that world of which both [the devil] himself speaks in the Gospel to the Savior: "All these things have been given over to me" [Matt 4:9]; and of which the apostle says: "The world is placed in wickedness" [1 John 5:19].

4:2a (5). *I saw a dream which terrified me.*

Let them respond what kind of *dream* the opposing power would have *seen*, unless perhaps everything he seems to have in this world is a shadow and a *dream*.

4:2c (5). *And the visions of my head greatly troubled me.* Note that even Nebuchadnezzar knew that his *visions* were not of the eyes and heart, but *of his head.* For the mysteries of the events to come are revealed to him for the sake of the glory of God's servants.

4:5a (8). *Until [their] colleague Daniel entered into my presence.* Apart from the Septuagint translators, who for some reason or other skipped over all these things,[123] the other three translators [Aquila, Symmachus, and Theodotion] rendered it *colleague.*[124] Whence it is that by the judgment of the teachers of the church, the Septuagint edition has been rejected in the case of this book, and it is the translation of Theodotion which is commonly read, since it corresponds with the Hebrew as well as with the other translators.[125] It is also for this reason that Origen asserts in the ninth book of his *Stromata* that, from this point on in the prophet Daniel, he is discussing the things that follow not in accordance with the Septuagint translators, who are at great variance from the Hebrew truth, but in accordance with Theodotion's version.[126]

4:5c (8). *Who has in himself the spirit of the holy gods.*

What is expressed here as *of the holy gods,* we read in the Chaldean language in which Daniel was written *helain cadisin,* which means *holy gods* and not "holy God," as Theodotion translated it. Nor is it surprising if Nebuchadnezzar errs and judges that anything he perceives to be beyond himself are gods, not God. Consequently, he says also in what follows:

4:6a (9). *Belteshazzar (Balthasar), prince of the diviners, whom I know that you have within you the spirit of the holy gods.* (*Belteshazzar, prince of the diviners,* or *enchanters,* as the others translated it.)

It is not surprising that he was appointed *prince of* all *the diviners,* since at the king's command he had learned the wisdom of the Chaldeans [cf. Dan 1:4] and had been found ten times wiser than all the rest [cf. Dan 1:20]. Let us ask those who do not accept the history in respect to this vision, who is this Nebuchadnezzar who saw the dream?[127] And who is the Daniel who explained his dream and predicts things to come? And how is it that this same Daniel—who assuredly according to them ought to be understood as a holy power—is appointed by Nebuchadnezzar *prince of the diviners,* and is called a *colleague* [cf. Dan 4:5]?

4:7-8 (10-11). *I was looking and beheld a tree in the midst of the earth, and the height thereof was exceeding great. The tree was great and strong, and its height touched heaven; the sight of it was even to the ends of all the earth.*

The prophet says not only of Nebuchadnezzar, the Chaldean king, but of all the impious: "I saw the impious highly exalted and lifted up like the cedars of Lebanon" [Ps 37:35 LXX]. They are *lifted up*, not by the greatness of their virtues, but by their own pride, and that is why they are cut down and fall [cf. Ezek 31:10-14]. This is why it is good to follow what the Lord teaches in the Gospel: "Learn from me, for I am meek and humble in heart" [Matt 11:29]. But as for what it says according to Theodotion, τὸ κύτος, that is, *the height thereof*—or ἡ κυρία, as he himself later translated it [cf. Dan 4:19], that is, "his dominion" which we rendered *the sight of it*—those who disdain the history of this passage[128] again speak with calumny and say that Nebuchadnezzar's *dominion* never possessed the whole world. For his rule did not reach the Greeks, the barbarians, and any of the nations in the north and west. He merely held sway over the provinces of the east, that is, over Asia, not over Europe and Libya. Because of this, they want it to be understood that all these things must be referred to the devil. Surely we ought to take all these things as having been spoken hyperbolically, on account of the pride of the impious king, who in Isaiah makes such a great boast that he vaunts to hold sway over heaven, as well as the inhabited world, as if it were a nest full of birds' eggs [cf. Isa 14:13-14; 10:14].

4:10b (13). *And behold a watcher and a holy one came down from heaven.*

Instead of *watcher*, Theodotion recorded the Chaldean word *hir*,[129] which is written with the three letters: *ain, iod, res*. It signifies the "angels," because they always watch and are ready for God's command. Whence also we imitate the services of angels by means of frequent vigils that last through the night. Also it is said of the Lord: "He who guards Israel has not slumbered nor will he fall sleep" [Ps 121:4]. Indeed, we read also in what follows:

4:14a (17). *The decree lies in the sentence of the watchers (that is, of the angels), and the word and request of the holy ones.*

Now it is the custom of both Greek and Latin speech to call the rainbow ἶριν, which is said to descend to earth in a multicolored arch.[130]

4:16a (19). *Then Daniel, whose name is Belteshazzar (Balthasar), began silently to think within himself for about one hour; and his thoughts* *troubled him. And the king answered and said: Belteshazzar, do not let the dream and its interpretation trouble you.*

Daniel understood *silently* that the *dream* was against the king, and he signaled the fear in his heart by the pallor of his face, and he was pained on behalf of the man who had granted him a lot of honor [cf. Dan 2:48]. And lest he should seem to insult the king and take joy over against him as an enemy, in the end he detests what he had come to understand and says to him:

4:16c (19). *My lord, may this dream be to them that hate you, and its interpretation be to your enemies.*

So then, when Nebuchadnezzar sees that Daniel is afraid of giving the appearance of saying anything unfavorable and contrary to the king, he exhorts him to speak out plainly and truly what he understands, without any fear.

4:17a, 19 (20, 22). *The tree which you saw high and strong, it is you, O king, who have grown great and have become mighty; and your greatness has increased, and has reached to heaven, and your power unto the ends of the whole earth.*

He explains the truth without doing injury to the king, so that he does not seem to be accusing the king of arrogance, but of having *power.*

4:20b (23). *And let him be chained with iron and bronze among the grass outside, and let him be sprinkled with the dew of heaven, and let his feeding be with the wild beasts, until seven times are changed over him.*

Above as well it is written in similar fashion [cf. Dan 4:12]. Those then who speak against the history ask us how Nebuchadnezzar would have been bound with chains of *iron* and *bronze,* or who would have *chained* him or bound him with fetters. Yet it is very clear that all raving lunatics are tied with chains to keep them from hurling themselves at other people and attacking them with iron weapons.

4:21 (24). *This is the interpretation of the sentence of the Most High that has come upon my lord the king.*

[Daniel] tempers the severity of the *sentence* by flattering words, and after he has first set forth the harsh aspects, he relieves the terrified king's spirit by gentler assurances. After all he adds:

4:23b (26). *Your kingdom shall remain to you, after you acknowledge that power comes from heaven.*

Whence those who speak against the history and want it to mean that the devil's original dignity will be restored to him have smooth sailing on this passage and say that after Nebuchadnezzar's torments and transformation into a wild beast,[131] after his feeding upon grass and hay, after his endurance of the cycles of the seven years, he would make a confession of the Lord and would be what he had been before.[132] But they need to answer the question of how it would be fitting for the angels who never fell away to have him [over them] again as their prince who has returned by means of repentance.

4:24 (27). *Wherefore, O king, let my counsel be pleasing to you, and redeem your sins with alms, and your iniquities with works of mercy to the poor. Perhaps he will forgive your transgressions.*

If he predicted God's verdict, which cannot be changed, how could he exhort the king to *almsgiving* and *mercy to the poor*, in order that God's verdict might be changed? This has an easy solution in the example of King Hezekiah, who Isaiah had said was going to die [cf. Isa 38:1]. Consider also the example of the Ninevites: "Yet three days, and Nineveh shall be destroyed" [Jonah 3:4]. And yet, God's verdict was changed in response to the prayers of Hezekiah and of Nineveh [cf. Isa 38:5; Jonah 3:10]. This was due not to the vainness of his judgment, but to the conversion of those who had come to merit pardon.[133] Besides, God also says in Jeremiah that he threatens evil against a nation, but if that nation does what is good, he will change his threats into clemency. On the other hand, he claims to make promises to one who does good; but if that person does evil, he says that he changes his own verdict. This is not due to the men themselves, but to their works which have changed [cf. Jer 18:7-9]. For God is not angry with men but with their vices; and when a man has no vices, God by no means punishes what has been changed. Let us express this even in another way: Nebuchadnezzar did indeed do *acts of mercy toward the poor*, in accordance with Daniel's advice, and for that reason the sentence against him was postponed until the twelfth month; but afterward, he walked about the courts of Babylon boasting and saying: "Is this not Babylon the great, which I myself have built as a home for the kingdom by the might of my power and for the glory of my name?" [Dan 4:27]. On that account, he forfeited the good of mercy by the evil of his pride.

4:24b (27). *Perhaps he will pardon your transgressions.*[134]

Seeing that the blessed Daniel, who had foreknowledge of the future, has doubts concerning God's judgment, those who audaciously promise pardon to sinners act rashly. And yet one should know that if pardon is promised to Nebuchadnezzar, provided that he does good works, it is much more promised to others who have committed lighter sins. We read in Jeremiah also of God's precept to the Jewish people, to pray for the Babylonians, since the peace of the captives lies in their peace [cf. Jer 29:7].

4:28 (31). *And while the words were still in the king's mouth, a voice fell from heaven: To you, O king Nebuchadnezzar, it is said: The kingdom has passed from you.*

The Lord punishes his arrogant boasting immediately. Therefore, the judgment is not postponed, lest mercy toward the poor seem not to have been of any benefit at all. But as soon as he spoke with arrogance, he forfeited the *kingdom* which had been preserved on account of almsgiving.

4:29a (32). *Until you know that the Most High holds dominion over the kingdom of men.*

Great is the consolation in misery, when one who is exposed to torments knows that prosperous times will follow; however, Nebuchadnezzar was a man of such great fury and madness that during the time of evils, he did not recall the good things that God had promised him.

4:31b (34). *I, Nebuchadnezzar, lifted up my eyes to heaven, and my intelligence was restored to me.*

Had he not *lifted up his eyes to heaven*, he would not have received back his former *intelligence*. But when he says that his *intelligence was restored to him*, he shows that he had not lost his [outward] form, but only his mind.[135]

4:31d (34). *And his kingdom is unto generation and generation.*

If we understand what is said in the Scriptures, *unto generation and generation*,[136] literally for what it is, "for all times to come," then no problem arises. But if—as we have said repeatedly—*generation and generation* signifies two generations, that of the Law and that of the Gospel,[137] then the question must be asked how Nebuchadnezzar could have known the mysteries (*sacramenta*) of God; unless perhaps we should say that after he *lifted up his eyes to heaven* and *received back* his former status, and exulted and blessed the God who lives forever [cf. Dan 4:34], he would not have been ignorant even of these things.

4:32 (35). *For he does according to his will, both in heaven and on earth, and there is no one who resists his hand and says: Why have you done this?*

He says this too as a man of the world. For God does not *do* that which he wills; but that which is good, this is what God wills. But Nebuchadnezzar spoke in such a way that, while he proclaims God's power, he seems to be accusing his justice, in that he was made to endure these punishments undeservedly.

4:33b (36). *And my nobles and my magistrates sought for me, and I was restored to my kingdom, and greater magnificence was added unto me.* Well then, according to those who speak against the history, all the angelic powers will *search for* the devil, and he will grow so much in power that the very one who was once so proud over against God will be greater than he was before his sin.[138]

4:34b (37). *For all his works are true and his ways are judgments, and those who walk in pride he is able to humble.*

Nebuchadnezzar has come to understand why he had endured a punishment lasting seven years [cf. Dan 4:23], and that he was humbled because he had become proud over against God.

BOOK TWO

VISION 5

5:1. *Belshazzar (Balthasar)[1] the king[2] made a great feast for a thousand of his nobles, and everyone drank according to his age.* One should know that this man was not the son of Nebuchadnezzar, as readers commonly think, but according to Berosus,[3] who is the author of a *History of Chaldea*, and Josephus, who follows Berosus, after Nebuchadnezzar, who reigned for forty-three years, a son named Evil-merodach succeeded in his kingdom.[4] Jeremiah also writes about the latter, that in the first year of his reign he lifted up the head of Jehoiachin (*Ioachim*), king of Judah, and led him forth from his home in prison [cf. Jer 52:31]. Josephus likewise reports that after the death of Evil-merodach, his son[5] Neglisar succeeded to his father's kingdom. After him in turn came his son Labor-sordech.[6] Upon the latter's death, his son, *Belshazzar (Balthasar)*,[7] obtained the kingdom, whom the Scripture now mentions. When he was killed by Darius, king of the Medes,[8] who was the maternal uncle of Cyrus, king of the Persians, the empire of the Chaldeans was destroyed by Cyrus the Persian. It was these two kingdoms [the Median and the Persian] which Isaiah calls a rider of a two-horse car, of a camel and a donkey [cf. Isa 21:9, 7]. Indeed Xenophon[9] also writes about this in *The Childhood of Cyrus the Great*; also Pompeius Trogus[10] and many others who have written histories of the barbarians. Some authorities think that this Darius was the Astyages[11] mentioned in the Greek books, while others think it was Astyages' son, and that among them he was known by another name. Now *every one* of the princes who had been invited *drank according to his age*. Or, as the other translators have rendered it: "The king himself drank wine in the presence of all the princes whom he had invited."[12]

5:2. *So then, being now drunk he commanded that they should bring the vessels of gold and silver which Nebuchadnezzar his father had brought away out of the temple that was in Jerusalem, so that the king and his nobles, his wives, and his concubines might drink from them.* The Hebrews hand down a story of this sort. Until the seventieth year, in which Jeremiah had said that the captivity of the Jewish people would be released [cf. Jer 25:11–12; 29:10; Dan 9:2], of which Zechariah also speaks in the beginning of his book [cf. Zec 1:12–17], Belshazzar (*Balthasar*) thought God's promise was futile and his assurance false. He turned this into an occasion of joy and "made a great feast" [Dan 5:1], mocking, as it were, the hope of the Jews and the vessels of the temple of God.[13] But vengeance followed immediately. Now for those who are familiar with the usage of Holy Scripture, the fact that the author calls Nebuchadnezzar the *father* of Belshazzar is not an error. In Scripture, all ancestors and elders are called "fathers." And one should also take the following into consideration, that the man is not sober when he does these things, but *drunk* and forgetful of the punishment that had come upon his ancestor, Nebuchadnezzar.

5:4. *They drank wine and praised their gods of gold, and of silver, of bronze, of iron, and of wood, and of stone.*

What madness! As they *drank* from the vessels of *gold, they praised gods of wood and of stone!* As long as the vessels were in the idol temple of Babylon, the Lord was not angry, for, granted it was in accordance with their own twisted beliefs, they nevertheless seemed to have consecrated the property of God to divine worship. But once they defile the divine things by letting human beings use them, there is punishment at once after the sacrilege. What is more, they *praise their own gods* and mock the God of the Jews, thinking that they were drinking from his vessels following the victory that their own gods had given them.

According to tropology, the following should be said, that all heretics and all doctrine that is contrary to the truth—which takes the words of the prophets and misuses the testimonies of Divine Scripture according to their own sense and allows those whom it deceives and with whom it has fornicated to *drink*—such doctrine carries off the vessels of God's temple and becomes drunk by them. Such a person does not *praise* the God whose vessels they are, but *the gods of gold and silver, of bronze, of iron, and of wood and stone.* To me it seems that the *gods of gold* are those that are composed of secular reasoning. Those *of silver* have charming eloquence and are composed with rhetorical skill. But those who introduce the fables of the poets and employ ancient traditions that are very different from each other, in terms either of elegance or of foolishness, these are called *bronze and iron.* And those who set forth completely ridiculous things are called *of wood or stone.* Deuteronomy divides these all into two categories when it records: "Cursed is the man who makes a graven or molten image, the work of the hands of a craftsman, and who will place it in a hidden place" [Deut 32:15 (LXX 27:15)]. For all heretics hide and cover over their lying doctrines, in order to "shoot their arrows from concealment against those who are upright in heart" [Ps 11:2].

5:5. *At the same hour there appeared fingers, as it were of the hand of a man, writing over against the candlestick upon the surface of the wall of the royal palace; and the king beheld the joints of the hand that wrote.*

It is nicely said: *At the same hour,* just as we read higher up concerning Nebuchadnezzar: "While the words were still in the king's mouth, a voice fell from heaven" [Dan 4:28]. That way he would know that the punishment inflicted upon him was for no other reason than on account of blasphemy. Now the *fingers* are seen writing on the *wall over against the candlestick,* lest the hand and what was written appear too far away from the light [to be clearly visible]. And they write upon the *wall of the royal palace,* in order that the king may understand that what is written pertains to him.

5:6a. *Then the king's face was changed.*

Here too one should note, in view of those psalms which are entitled: "For those who will be changed" [cf. Ps 45:1; 60:1; 69:1; 80:1], that the change pertains not only to the saint but also to the sinner.[14] For we read in what follows: "King Belshazzar (*Balthasar*) was much troubled and his countenance was changed" [Dan 5:9].

5:7a. *And so the king cried out loudly to bring in the magi, the Chaldeans, and the soothsayers.*

Forgetting about what had happened to Nebuchadnezzar, he follows the ancient and ingrained error of his nation. Thus instead of calling upon a prophet of God, he summons the *magi, the Chaldeans, and soothsayers.*

5:7c. *He shall be clothed in purple and he shall have a golden chain* (torquem auream)[15] *about his neck.*

It is, of course, ridiculous of me to dispute like a grammarian about the gender of words in a commentary on the prophets; but a certain person who knows nothing while promising everything has faulted me for translating *necklace* (*torquem*) in the feminine gender.[16] Therefore, I will briefly note that Cicero and Varro use *necklace* in the feminine gender while Titus Livy expresses it in the masculine.[17]

5:7d. *And he shall be the third man in my kingdom.*
Either *third* after me, or one of the three princes whom elsewhere we read of as the *tristatai* [cf. Exod 15:4 LXX; Ezek 23:23 LXX].[18]

5:10a. *Then the queen, on occasion of what had happened to the king and his nobles, came into the banquet hall and she spoke out and said.*
Josephus records that she was Belshazzar's grandmother;[19] Origen says that she was his mother.[20] She therefore knew about matters of the past of which the king was ignorant. Therefore let Porphyry wake up, who dreamed up the idea that she was Belshazzar's wife, and he mocks the way she knows more than her husband does.

5:11a. *There is a man in your kingdom who has the spirit of the holy gods in him.*
Apart from Symmachus, who followed the Chaldean truth, the rest translated it: "the spirit of God."

5:11b. *And in the days of your father, knowledge and wisdom were found in him.*
The queen calls Belshazzar's ancestor Nebuchadnezzar *father*, according to the custom of the Scriptures, as we said above.[21] But even among barbarians the manner of life of a holy man is deemed worthy of imitation, for the king's grandmother, or mother, extols him with such great praises in view of the greatness of his virtues.

5:17. *To which Daniel made answer before the king and said: Let your rewards be your own, and give the gifts of your house to someone else; but as for the writing, O king, I will read it to you and show you the interpretation.*
We should emulate Daniel, who despised the honor and *rewards* of the king and makes known the truth free of charge. Already at that time, he was following the gospel precept: "Freely you have received, freely give" [Matt 10:8]. In any case, it would have been improper for one who was announcing grievous news to accept *gifts* willingly.

5:19b. *Those whom he wanted, he killed, and those whom he wanted, he struck down, those whom he wanted, he lifted up, and those whom he wanted, he humbled.*
Daniel records the example of Belshazzar's ancestor Nebuchadnezzar, in order to teach the justice of God and corroborate that his descendant, too, is enduring similar chastisements due to his pride. Now if Nebuchadnezzar *killed those whom he wanted and struck down those whom he wanted, lifted up those whom he wanted and humbled those whom he wanted*, then it is not a question of God's providence or command in honors and strikes of this sort, in acts of lifting up and humiliation, but

it pertains to the will of those who strike down and lift up those whom they want.[22] If this is so, one should ask in what sense is the following written: "The heart of a king is in the hand of God: He will incline it wherever he wills" [Prov 21:1 LXX]; unless perhaps we should say that every holy person is a king, for whom "sin does not reign in his mortal body" [Rom 6:12], and whose heart is kept safe because it is in God's hand. But whatever is in the hand of God the Father, no one can snatch away from it [cf. John 10:28–29]; and it is understood that whoever is taken away was not in the Lord's hand.

5:22. *You also, his son Belshazzar (Balthasar), have not humbled your heart, though you knew all these things.*

Your ancestor, because "his heart was lifted up and his spirit was hardened in pride, was deposed from his royal throne and his glory was taken away" [Dan 5:20], etc. Therefore in your case too, since you knew these things about your relative and were aware that "God resists the proud but gives grace to the humble" [Jas 4:6; 1 Pet 5:5], you should not have lifted up your heart against the ruler of heaven and outraged his majesty and done the things that you have done. Some refer this passage to the antichrist and say that he has raised himself up against God by imitating the pride of his father, the devil.[23] But one should ask them who this Daniel is who translates God's writing for him, and who are these Medes and Persians who kill him and succeed him in his kingdom. Surely no one doubts that the saints will reign after the antichrist.

5:25–28. *But here is the writing that has been displayed: "mane, thecel, phares." And here is the interpretation of the words. "Mane": God has made an accounting of your kingdom and has brought it to an end; "Thecel": You have been weighed in the balance and found wanting; "Phares": Your kingdom is divided and is given to the Medes and Persians.*

He had indicated only three words written on the wall: *mene, thecel, phares.*[24] The first of these means "account," the second "weighing," the third "division."[25] And so, it was necessary not only to read it but also to interpret what he had read, in order to understand what these words were predicting, which was, namely, that *God* had *made an accounting of* that man's kingdom and had *brought it to an end*; and he had *weighed him in the balance* of his judgment, and a sword would slay him before nature would dissolve him; and his empire would be *divided* among the *Medes and Persians.* For as we have already said,[26] Cyrus the king of the Persians overthrew the empire of the Chaldeans in alliance with Darius, his maternal uncle.

5:29. *Then, by the king's command, Daniel was clothed with purple, and a chain of gold was placed around his neck, and it was proclaimed of him that he would have power as the third man in the kingdom* (or: *over a third of the kingdom*).²⁷

Now he received the royal insignia, a *chain* and *purple*, so that he would be better known to Darius, who was to be the successor in the kingdom, and thanks to that recognition, more esteemed. It is no wonder that Belshazzar, upon learning the grievous news, should have paid the promised price. For either he thought that what he had said would come to pass after a very long time, or he is hoping that, so long as he honors the prophet of God, he will obtain pardon; but if he did not procure it, one should believe that the sacrilege against God outweighed the honor he had rendered toward man.

5:30–31. *That same night Belshazzar (Balthasar) the Chaldean king was slain, and Darius the Mede succeeded to the kingdom at the age of sixty-two years.*

Josephus writes in the tenth book of his *Jewish Antiquities* that when Babylon was besieged by the Medes and Persians, that is, by Darius and Cyrus, Belshazzar, king of Babylon, came to forget himself to the point that he hosted that very famous banquet, and drank from the vessels of the temple, and, even while under a siege, made leisure for banquets.²⁸ Thus the history can stand firm, that he was captured and slain *that same night*, while everyone was either terrified and panicked by the vision and its interpretation, or occupied with the festivity and drunkenness of the banquet. As for the fact that Cyrus king of the Persians and Darius king of the Medes were the victors, but *Darius* alone is recorded to have *succeeded in the kingdom*, this is due to the order of age, parentage, and kingdom [cf. Dan 5:28; 6:1].²⁹ For Darius was *sixty-two years old*, and we read that the kingdom of the Medes was greater than that of the Persians, and being Cyrus's maternal uncle, by natural right he took precedence and ought to have been reckoned as successor in the kingdom. And this is why, in the vision against Babylon that one reads in Isaiah, after many things too lengthy to record, these matters pertaining to the future are recounted: "Behold I will raise up against them the Medes, who do not seek after silver nor desire gold; but who slay little children with their arrows and have no mercy upon women who suckle their young" [Isa 13:17–18]. And Jeremiah says: "Sanctify against her the nations, the kings of Media, its governors and all its magistrates, and all the land under its power" [Jer 51:28]; and in the things that follow: "The daughter of Babylon is like a threshing-floor, [during] the time of its threshing; yet a little while, and the time of its harvesting will come" [Jer 51:33]. Now Isaiah writes quite openly that Babylon, whom he exhorts to battle, was captured during a banquet: "Babylon, my beloved, has become a miraculous wonder to me.[30] Set the table, behold in the watchtower those who eat and drink; arise, O princes, take up the shield!" [Isa 21:4–5].

Vision 6

6:1–2a. *It pleased Darius to appoint over his kingdom one hundred and twenty satraps, that they might be throughout his whole kingdom; and over them there were three princes; Daniel was one of them.*

Josephus, of whom we have spoken above,[31] writes of the history of this passage and says the following:

> Now Darius, who destroyed the empire of the Babylonians, with his relative Cyrus helping him and fighting alongside of him, was sixty-two years of age at the time he captured Babylon; and he was the son of Astyages,[32] who is known to the Greeks by another name. And he took the prophet Daniel with him and brought him into Media, and made him one of the three princes who were in charge of his whole kingdom.[33]

From this we understand that when Babylon was overthrown, Darius returned to his own kingdom in Media and he brought Daniel with him, holding the same office to which Belshazzar had promoted him. There is no doubt that Darius had heard about the sign and portent that had happened to Belshazzar, and also about the interpretation that Daniel had expounded, and how he had predicted the kingdom of the Medes and the Persians. Let no one therefore be troubled by the fact that Daniel is sometimes said to have lived in Darius's kingdom [cf. Dan 6:1–2], and sometimes in the kingdom of Cyrus [cf. Dan 10:1]—instead of *Darius* the Septuagint translated "Artaxerxes" [cf. Dan 6:1 LXX]. It seems to me that the reason for the inversion of the order, that the history under Darius is told before that under Belshazzar [cf. Dan 6:1–2; 7:1; 8:1], who, we will read later, was put to death by Darius, is that the author has immediately linked history to history. For at the end of the earlier vision he had said: "And Darius the Mede succeeded to the kingdom at the age of sixty-two" [Dan 5:31]. It was under this Darius, then,

BOOK TWO   83

who had Belshazzar killed, that the events took place of which we are about to speak.

6:4a. *Moreover the king was thinking of appointing him over the whole kingdom; whence the princes and the satraps sought to find occasion [to destroy] Daniel from the side of the king.* Instead of *princes*, which is how Symmachus translated it, Theodotion interpreted it as τακτικοὺς (tacticians), Aquila as συνεκτικους (officers).[34] And while I was trying to determine who these *princes* were, tacticians or officers, I read it more clearly in the Septuagint version, which said: "and the two men whom he appointed with him, and the one hundred twenty satraps" [Dan 6:4 LXX]. And so, the occasion of their ill-will and plot arose from the fact that the king *was thinking of* making him the first, who had been the third among the other two princes. *They sought to find occasion [to destroy] Daniel from the side of the king.* On this passage the Hebrews surmise something like this:

> The side of the king refers to the queen, or his concubines and other wives who slept *at his side*. Therefore, *they sought an occasion* in things of this sort, [to see] if they could accuse Daniel for his speaking, touching, signaling, or his communication as a go-between. But, they say, "they could find no grounds for suspicion" [Dan 6:4b], since he was a eunuch, and they were unable to accuse him in the matter of violating what is honorable.[35]

This interpretation comes from those who are accustomed to composing long tales on the pretext of a single word [cf. 1 Tim 1:6–7; 6:20; 2 Tim 4:3–4; Titus 1:14; 3:9; 2 Pet 1:16]. I myself would simply interpret this to mean that they found no occasion against him in which he was guilty before the king.

6:4c. *For he was a faithful man and no suspicion of blame was found in him.* Instead of *suspicion*, Theodotion and Aquila translated it ἀμβλάκημα (error, fault, offense), which is said in Chaldean as *essaitha* (criminal infraction). And when I asked a Hebrew man for the meaning of this word, he replied that the basic force of it was δέλεαρ (snare), which we can express as "allurement," or σφάλμα, that is, a "mistake." Moreover, Euripides in the *Medeia* calls ἀμπλακίας—with a π not a β—ἁμαρτίας, that is to say, "sins."[36]

6:5. *Therefore those men said: We will not find any occasion [to destroy] Daniel, except perhaps in the law of his God.*

Happy is the life in which enemies find no *occasion*, except in the legal prescriptions of God!

6:6a. *Then the princes and satraps slipped away to the king and spoke as follows.*

He has nicely said *slipped away*, for they did not tell what they were planning to do, but were plotting an ambush against their enemy under the cover of honoring the king.

6:8a. *Now therefore, O king, confirm the sentence and write the decree, so that what is established by the Medes and Persians may not be changed.*

What we said above becomes clear here, that under Darius and Cyrus there was one kingdom of the Medes and Persians.[37]

6:10a. *Now when Daniel learned of it, that is, of the law that had been enacted, he entered his house, and with the windows in his upper room (*coenaculo*) opened up toward Jerusalem, he knelt down three times a day.*

From all of Holy Scripture we must swiftly gather from our memory the places where we read δώματα, which means in Latin either "walled enclosures" (*maeniana*), "houses" (*tecta*), or "sun-terraces" (*solaria*);[38] and also where we read ἀνάγαια, that is, *upper rooms*. Indeed even our Lord celebrates the Passover in an *upper room* [cf. Mark 14:15–17; Luke 22:12–14], and in the Acts of the Apostles the Holy Spirit comes down upon the one hundred and twenty souls of believers in an *upper room* [Acts 1:13–15; 2:1–5]. And now Daniel, showing contempt for the king's orders and placing his trust in God, prays not in a low place, but in a high place, and he *opens* the *windows toward Jerusalem*, where there was a vision of peace [cf. Ezek 13:16].[39] He prays according to God's command [cf. Deut 12:5, 11], and also according to what Solomon had said when he recorded that one should pray toward the temple [cf. 1 Kgs 8:29–30; 2 Chr 7:15–16]. Now there are *three times* when we should *kneel down* before God. The tradition of the church understands this to be the third, the sixth, and the ninth hours.[40] After all, it was at the third hour that the Holy Spirit descended upon the apostles [cf. Acts 2:4, 15]; the sixth, when Peter wanted to eat and went up to the *upper room* to pray [cf. Acts 10:9–10]; the ninth, when Peter and John went to the temple [cf. Acts 3:1].

6:11. *Therefore, those men watched him more carefully and found Daniel praying and making supplication to his God.*

From this passage, we learn that we should not rashly offer ourselves to dangerous situations, but as far as it lies within our power, we should avoid ambushes. Hence, Daniel too did not act against the king's command in the forum or on the streets, but in a hidden place in his home, so as not to neglect the commands of the true and almighty God.

6:12b. *O king, did you not establish that every man who should make a request to any of the gods, or men, for thirty days, but to yourself, O king, should be cast into the den (*lacum*) of the lions?*

They are silent about Daniel's name, so that once the king has replied that he has given this general order, he would be held to his own word, and not deal with Daniel otherwise than he has spoken.[41]

6:12d. *The word is true according to the decree of the Medes and Persians, which it is not permitted to violate.*

We have noted repeatedly[42] that when there has been talk of the kingdom *of the Medes and Persians*, we have solved that very difficult problem of why Daniel sometimes is said to have lived under Darius, and at other times under Cyrus [cf. Dan 6:1–2, 28].

6:13b. *Daniel, who is of the sons of the captivity of Judah.*

To make the despiser's act of dishonor greater, they say that the one who showed this contempt for the king's commands is a captive.

6:14a. *When the king heard this word, he was very grieved and on Daniel's behalf he set his heart to deliver him.*

He understood that he had been duped by his own reply [cf. Dan 6:12], and that their plot had been motivated by envy. And so, lest he seem to be acting against his own law, he wants to deliver Daniel from danger by means of reasoning and counsel, not by royal authority. And he labors and strives so hard for this that the most powerful king does not take any food until sunset [cf. Dan 6:14, 18]. And their obstinate adherence to evil is so great that they are unaffected by the king's will or by the injustice.

6:15. *But those men who understood the king said to him: Know, O king, that the law of the Medes and Persians is that no decree which the king has made is allowed to be altered.*

Just as the king understood that the princes were raising their accusation on account of envy, so they also understood the king's mind, that he wanted to rescue Daniel from imminent death. This is why they say that according to the *law of the Medes and Persians*, the king's orders cannot be annulled.

6:16b. *And the king said to Daniel: Your God, whom you always worship, he will deliver you.*

He yields to the multitude and does not dare to refuse a friend's death to adversaries who are in agreement; and he entrusts to the power of God what he himself was unable to procure. Nor does he speak in an uncertain manner, so as to say: 'If he be able to deliver you,' but he says boldly and confidently: *The God whom you always worship, he will deliver you.* For he had heard that three youths, who were lower than Daniel in rank, had vanquished the Babylonian flames [cf. Dan 3:25(94)], and that numerous mysteries had been revealed to Daniel [cf. Dan 2:47]. And this is why he singled him out for the highest office, a man whom he regarded as a captive.

6:17a. *And a stone was brought, and placed over the entrance of the den (*laci*).* *The king sealed it with his own ring and with the ring of his nobles.*

He *seals with his ring* the *stone* with which the *entrance of the den* was closed, to keep Daniel's enemies from trying to harm him. For he entrusts him to the power of God, and he is very anxious that the one who is safe from lions may not be safe from men. He also *seals* it *with the ring of his nobles*, lest he should seem to be at all suspicious of them.

6:18. *And the king went away to his house and slept without taking supper, and food was not set before him, moreover his very sleep departed from him.*

The king's goodwill was so great that he did not take in *food* night or day, he did not allow his eyes to *sleep*, but as long as the prophet was in danger, he was hanging in suspense out of strong feeling for him! But if a king who does not know God acts like this on behalf of another whom he wants to be delivered from danger, how much more, in view of our own sins, ought we incline God to mercy by going without food and by means of prayer vigils!

6:19. *Then the king arose at first light and went in haste to the lions' den (*lacum*).*

Den (*lacus*) is the name he gives to a deep pit, or a dry cistern, in which the lions were fed. Now at first light he goes in haste to the den, for he believed that Daniel was alive. In Latin, a body of fresh water is called a *lacus*, such as Lake (*lacus*) Benacus,[43] Lake Larius,[44] and others. The Greeks call this a λίμνην, that is, "a body of standing water" (*stagnum*).[45]

6:20a. *And coming near to the den, he called out to Daniel with a tearful (*lacrimabili*) voice.*

By his tears (*lacrimis*) he shows the deep feeling of his heart. Forgetting his royal dignity, the conqueror runs to the captive, the master to the slave.

6:20c. *Daniel, servant of the living God.*

He calls him *living* to distinguish him from the gods of the Gentiles, who are images of dead human beings.[46]

6:20d. *Do you think that your God, whom you serve always, was able to deliver you from the lions?*

He is not casting doubt on the power of God, of whom he had said above: "Your God, whom you worship always, he will deliver you" [Dan 6:16], but he tempers the ambiguous sentence in order that when the uninjured Daniel should appear, the king's indignation at the princes might seem more just, in proportion to the way the factual reality surpasses belief.

6:21b. *O king, live forever!*

He honors the one who honors [him], and prays for his eternal life.

6:22. *My God sent his angel, and shut the mouths of the lions, and they did not harm me, for before him, justice was found in me; and before you, O king, I have committed no transgression.*

It was not the ferocity of the lions that was altered but their angry gaping mouth that was *shut* by the *angel*, and it was closed because the prophet's good works had preceded. Thus, it was not so much grace of deliverance as repayment for justice.[47] And let every saint profess these words who has been rescued from the *mouths of* invisible *lions* [cf. 1 Pet 5:8] and from hell's den, because he has come to believe in his God.

6:25a. *Then king Darius wrote to all the peoples, tribes, and languages, dwelling in all the earth.*

A certain person interpreted Nebuchadnezzar, writing to the languages and nations, as referring to the hostile powers [cf. Dan 3:95–100].[48] He interprets Darius in the same way, that Darius is summoning everyone to repentance. And this person asks whether[49] this will take place in this world, or in another, or even after other worlds. We regard these things as delusional ravings and empty fables. We say only this: that signs among barbarian nations are done by God's servants, so that the worship and religion of the one God may be proclaimed.

6:28. *Moreover Daniel continued until the reign of Darius and the reign of Cyrus the Persian.*

So then, what we read above at the end of the first vision: "And Daniel lived until the first year of king Cyrus" [Dan 1:21], is not to be understood of the duration of his life; for indeed we read in the last vision: "In the third year of Cyrus, king of the Persians, a word was revealed to Daniel, whose surname was Belteshazzar (*Balthasar*)"

[Dan 10:1]. But this means that up to the first year of king Cyrus, who destroyed the empire of the Chaldeans, Daniel was in power in Chaldea, but afterward he was transferred to the Medes by Darius.

VISION 7

7:1a. *In the first year of Belshazzar (Balthasar), king of Babylon, Daniel saw a dream.*

According to history, this section (*pericope*) that we are now trying to explain, and the following one, of which we will speak, are anterior to the two previous sections.[50] For this section [chap. 7] and the one that follows [chap. 8] are recorded to have taken place in the *first* and third *year of king Belshazzar* [cf. Dan 7:1; 8:1]; but the section that was read before the one higher up [i.e., chap. 5], is recorded to have taken place in the last year, or rather on the last day, of Belshazzar's reign [cf. Dan 5:30]. And we read of this sort of thing not only in Daniel but also in Jeremiah [cf. Jer 21:1–2] and Ezekiel [cf. Ezek 29:17–21],[51] as we shall be able to show in those passages, if life remains our companion.[52] But in the things above [i.e., Dan 1–6], historical order is followed, namely, the miraculous signs that occurred under Nebuchadnezzar, Belshazzar, and Darius or Cyrus.[53] But in the passages now before us [i.e., Dan 7–12] an account is given of dreams that were seen at particular times[54]—of which the prophet alone was aware—and they have no great significance as a sign or revelation among the barbarian nations, but are recorded only in order that a remembrance of the things that were seen might remain among later generations.[55]

7:2–3. *In the night, I saw in my vision, and behold the four winds of heaven fought upon the great sea, and four great beasts were coming up out of the sea, differing from one another.*

The four winds of heaven are the angelic powers to which the principal kingdoms have been entrusted. This agrees with what we read in Deuteronomy: "When the Most High divided the nations, when he separated the sons of Adam, he established the boundaries of peoples according to the number of the sons of Israel. But the Lord's portion is his people; Jacob is the line of his inheritance" [Deut 32:8–9]. Now the *sea* signifies this world and age. It overflows with salty and bitter waves, just as the Lord interprets it in the parable of the dragnet cast into the *sea* [cf. Matt 13:47–50]. And this is why the dragon is called "king of all things that are in the waters" [Job 41:25 LXX]. And according to David his heads are crushed in the *sea* [cf. Ps 74:14]. And in Amos we read: "If he descends into the depth of the *sea*, there

I will command the dragon, and he will bite him" [Amos 9:3 LXX]. But as for the *four beasts* who *came up out of the sea* and *differed from one another*, we may know them from the angel's explanation, who says: "These four great beasts [are] four kingdoms [that] shall arise out of the earth" [Dan 7:17]. And as for the *four winds which fought upon the great sea*, they are called *winds of heaven* because each angel does for his realm that which is entrusted to him. It should also be noted that the ferocity and cruelty of the kingdoms is shown by the name of the *beasts*.

7:4. *The first [beast] was like a lioness and had the wings of an eagle. I beheld until her wings were plucked off; and she was lifted up from the earth and stood on her feet like a man, and his heart was given to her.*

The kingdom of Babylon is not called a lion but a *lioness*,[56] on account of its savageness and cruelty, or because of its luxurious life that is enslaved to lust.[57] In fact, those who have written on the characteristics of beasts say that lionesses are the fiercer, especially if they are nursing their cubs, and they are always eager to have sex.[58] And as for the fact that she *had the wings of an eagle*, this signifies the pride of the most powerful kingdom, whose prince says through Isaiah: "I will set my throne above the stars of heaven" [Isa 14:13 LXX] and "I shall be like the Most High" [Isa 14:14 LXX]. This is why he is told: "If you are borne on high like an eagle, I will drag you down from there" [Obad 4 LXX]. Moreover, just as the lion is the king of the beasts, so also is the *eagle* of the birds. But one should also say this, that the *eagle* lives for a long time, and the kingdom of the Assyrians held lordship for many generations. And as for the fact that the *wings* of the *lioness* or *eagle were plucked off*, this signifies the other kingdoms over which it formerly held power and flew in the world. It says: *And she was lifted up* (sublata) *from the earth*, namely, when the empire of the Chaldeans was overthrown.

And as for what follows: *And she stood on her feet like a man, and his heart was given to her*, if we understand this of Nebuchadnezzar, it is clear that after he lost his kingdom and his power had been taken away (*ablata*), he was once more restored to his original state and learned that he was not a *lioness* but a man, and he received back the heart that he had lost [cf. Dan 4:28–37]. But if, on the other hand, this is to be understood as applying in a general way to the kingdom of the Chaldeans, then it signifies that after Belshazzar (*Balthasar*) was killed and the Medes and Persians succeeded to imperial power [cf. Dan 5:30–31], then the Babylonians came to understand that they were human beings of humble and fragile natures. Note the order: the one who was called the golden head in the image [cf. Dan 2:32] is called a *lioness* here.[59]

7:5. *And behold another beast like a bear stood up on one side, and there were three rows in its mouth and in its teeth, and so they said to it: Arise, devour much flesh.*

The second *beast, like a bear,* is the same as that one of which we read in the vision of the statue: "His chest and arms were of silver" [Dan 2:32]. It is compared to a *bear* because of its hardness and fierceness. For the kingdom of the Persians was characterized by a rigorous and more frugal manner of life, like the Spartans, to the point that they used salt and nasturtium cress[60] as food. Read: *The Childhood of Cyrus the Great.*[61] As for the words: *he stood up on* one *side,* the Hebrews interpret this as follows: The Persians never treated Israel cruelly;[62] and this is why they are called "white horses" in the prophet Zechariah [Zech 1:8; 6:3, 6].

But as for the three *rows* or lines that *were in its mouth and in its teeth,* a certain man interpreted it to mean that the kingdom of the Persians was divided up among three princes, just as we read in the περικοπῇ (section) about Belshazzar (*Balthasar*) and Darius, that there were three princes who were in charge of the one hundred and twenty satraps [cf. Dan 6:1–2]. But other commentators affirm that these were three kings of the Persians after Cyrus, and yet they are silent about their names.[63]

In fact, we know that after Cyrus's reign of thirty years,[64] Cambyses,[65] his son, and his brothers, the magi, ruled among the Persians,[66] and then Darius, in whose second year the building of the temple began in Jerusalem [cf. Ezra 4:24].[67] The fifth [king] was Xerxes, the son of Darius;[68] the sixth was Artabanus;[69] the seventh, Artaxerxes, who was surnamed Μακρόχειρ (Long-hand);[70] the eighth was Xerxes; the ninth, Sogdianus;[71] the tenth, Darius, surnamed Νόθον (Bastard);[72] the eleventh, the Artaxerxes who is called Μνήμων (Rememberer);[73] the twelfth, the other Artaxerxes, who himself received the surname of Ochus;[74] the thirteenth, Arses, the son of Ochus;[75] and the fourteenth, Darius the son of Arsamus,[76] who was conquered by Alexander, the king of the Macedonians. How then can we say that these were three kings of the Persians, unless perhaps we select some who were especially cruel, whom we cannot discover in the historical accounts? Therefore, *the three rows in the mouth* of the kingdom of the Persians *and in its teeth* we must take to be the three kingdoms of the Babylonians, the Medes, and the Persians, which have been reduced

BOOK TWO 91

to a single kingdom. And as for what he adds: *And so they said to it: Arise, devour much flesh*, this refers to the time when in the reign of the Ahasuerus, whom the Septuagint calls Artaxerxes, the order was given, at the suggestion of Haman the Agagite, that all the Jews be slaughtered on a single day [cf. Esth 3:13]. And it is nice that it does not say: "He devoured them," but: *And so they said to it.* This shows that it was merely an attempt, but was not followed by any result.

7:6. *After this I looked and, behold, another like a leopard, and it had upon it four wings of a bird, and the beast had four heads, and power was given to it.*

The third kingdom is that of the Macedonians, of which we read in respect to the statue: "The belly and thighs were of bronze" [Dan 2:32]. It is compared to a *leopard*, a very swift beast and ὁρμητικᾷ (eager to attack). It lunges after blood headfirst, and with a leap rushes at death. *And it had four wings*. For there has never been a victory swifter than Alexander's, who passed all the way from Illyricum and the Adriatic Sea to the Indian Ocean and the Ganges River, not so much staging battles as victories. Within six years, he subjugated a portion of Europe and all of Asia to himself. Now the *four heads* refers to his generals, who subsequently rose up as successors of his kingdom: Ptolemy, Seleucus,[77] Philip,[78] and Antigonus.[79] The added words: *And power was given to it* show that this result came not from Alexander's bravery but from the Lord's will.

7:7a. *After this, I was looking at the vision of the night, and behold, a fourth beast, terrifying and astonishing and exceedingly strong. It had great iron teeth, eating and breaking in pieces, and treading down the rest with its feet.*

The *fourth* is the empire of the Romans, which now holds sway over the world.[80] It is said of it in respect to the statue: "Its lower legs were of iron, and part of its feet were of iron, and part of clay" [Dan 2:33]. And yet, Daniel now partly calls to mind the same iron, attesting that its *teeth* were *iron* and *great*. I find it quite astonishing that although above he recorded a lioness, a bear, and a leopard in respect to the three kingdoms [cf. Dan 7:4–6], he did not compare the Roman kingdom to any beast, unless perhaps he kept silent about its designation in order to make the beast terrifying. Thus, whatever we might think of as more ferocious among the beasts, this is how we should understand the Romans. The Hebrews think that what is here kept in silence is stated in the Psalms: "A boar from the forest has laid it waste, and a uniquely savage animal devoured it" [Ps 80:13][81] (for which the

Hebrew has: "All the beasts have torn it to pieces").[82] For we realize that all the kingdoms together that had previously been separated are included in the one empire of the Romans. And as for what follows: *eating and breaking in pieces, and treading down the rest with its feet*, this signifies that all nations have either been killed by the Romans or else have been subjugated to pay tribute and be enslaved.

7:7b. *It says: And it was different from the other beasts which I had seen earlier.* For in the former ones, there was only one characteristic trait; this one had them all. *And it had ten horns* [Dan 7:7c]. Porphyry places the last two beasts, that of the Macedonians and that of the Romans, in the single kingdom of the Macedonians, and he distinguishes them. He wants the leopard to be understood of Alexander himself, and the beast that is *different from the others* to represent Alexander's four successors. Then he lists ten kings all the way to Antiochus, surnamed Epiphanes, who were extremely cruel. He does not place the kings themselves in one kingdom, for example in Macedonia, Syria, Asia, and Egypt, but makes one series of kings from the different kingdoms, namely, in order that one should believe that the things that are written: "A mouth speaking great things" [Dan 7:8] have been said about Antiochus, not about the antichrist.

7:7c–8. *And it had ten horns. I considered the horns, and behold another little horn sprung out of the midst of them, and three of the first horns were torn off its face; and behold eyes like the eyes of a man were on this horn, and a mouth speaking great things.*

Porphyry vainly supposes that the *little horn* that *sprang out* after the ten horns is Antiochus Epiphanes and that the *three horns torn off* from the ten are: Ptolemy VI, surnamed Philometor, Ptolemy VII Εὐεργέτην, and Artaxias, king of Armenia. The first two of these kings died well before Antiochus was born. We know in fact that Antiochus indeed waged war against Artaxias, but the latter remained in his ancient realm.

We should therefore say what all the church writers have handed down, that at the end of the world, when the Roman Empire is to be destroyed, there shall be ten kings who will divide the Roman world among themselves. Then a *little* eleventh king will arise. He will overcome *three* of the ten kings, that is, the kings of the Egyptians, Africa, and Ethiopia, as we learn more clearly in what follows. Then, after they have been killed, the seven other kings also will submit their necks to the victor.[83] It says: *And behold eyes like the eyes of a man were on this horn.*

Let these words keep us from thinking, in accordance with the opinion of some commentators, that it refers either to the devil or a demon. Instead, he means one man among men whose body Satan will entirely inhabit.[84] *And a mouth speaking great things.* For he is "the man of sin, the son of perdition" [2 Thess 2:3], "so that he dares to sit in the temple of God, making himself out to be like God" [2 Thess 2:4].[85]

7:9a. *I was looking until thrones were set in place, and the Ancient* (antiquus) *of days sat down, and the rest.*

We read something similar in John's Revelation:

> After these things I was immediately in the Spirit. And behold, a throne was set in place in heaven, and there was one sitting upon the throne. And he who sat had the likeness of jasper stone and sardius. And there was a rainbow round about the throne like the appearance of emerald. And around the throne there were twenty-four other thrones, and upon the twenty-four thrones there sat twenty-four elders, clothed in shining garments and upon their heads were golden crowns. And lightning flashes came forth from the throne, and voices and thunderclaps. And in front of the throne there were seven lamps of burning fire, which are the seven spirits of God. And in front of the throne there was as it were a glassy sea like unto crystal. [Rev 4:1–6]

So then, the numerous *thrones* that Daniel saw seem to me to be those John calls the *twenty-four thrones.* And the Ancient (*Vetustus*) *of days* is he who according to John sits alone upon the throne. The Son of man, too, who comes to the Ancient of Days, is the same as he who, according to John, is called the "lion of the tribe of Judah, the root of David" [Rev 5:5], and other things similar to these [cf. Rev 1:13–14]. I think these thrones are the ones of which the apostle Paul also speaks: "Whether thrones or dominions" [Col 1:16]; and we read in the Gospel: "But you yourselves shall sit upon twelve thrones, judging the twelve tribes of Israel" [Matt 19:28; Luke 22:30]. And God is the one who *sits down* and is called the Ancient *of Days,* so that his character as eternal judge is shown.

7:9b. *His garment was white as snow, and the hair of his head pure as wool.*

The Savior too, when he was transfigured on the mountain and assumed the glory of his divine majesty, appears in *white* garments [cf. Matt 17:2; Mark 9:2–3; Luke 9:29]. And as for his *hair* being compared to very *pure wool,* this shows the purity and sincerity of his judgment, that he shows no partiality in exercising judgment. He is also described as elderly, in order to prove the maturity of his sentence.

7:9c. *His throne, a flame of fire.*

So that sinners may dread the extent of the torments and the just may be saved, "but only as through fire" [1 Cor 3:15].

7:9d. *Its wheels, a burning fire (or its chariot).*

In Ezekiel, too, God is presented seated in a four-horse chariot, and everything pertaining to God is in flames [Ezek 1:14–15, 26–27]. In another place, too, there is talk of this: "God is a consuming *fire*" [Deut 4:24], that we might know that wood, hay, and stubble are going to burn up on the day of judgment [cf. 1 Cor 3:12–15; John 15:6].[86] And in the Psalms we read: "*Fire* will go out before him, and will set aflame all his enemies round about him" [Ps 97:3].

7:10a. *A swift stream of fire issued forth from his face.*

This is to drag sinners into Gehenna.

7:10b. *Thousands of thousands ministered to him, and ten thousand hundreds of thousands stood before him.*[87]

It is not that this is the definitive number of ministers of God, but that human speech cannot express such a great multitude. These are the *thousands* and tens of thousands of which we also read in the Psalms: "The chariot of God has more than ten thousand; thousands who rejoice. The Lord is among them" [Ps 68:17]. And in another passage: "Who makes his angels spirits, and his ministers a burning fire" [Ps 104:4]. Now the duty of angels is twofold: Some distribute rewards to the just; others preside over each person's punishments.

7:10c. *The judgment sat down and the books were opened.*

The consciences and the works of each one are revealed to all, in both respects, whether good or evil works.[88] There is that good *book* of which we often read, the book of the living [cf. Ps 69:28; Dan 12:1; Phil 4:3; Rev 3:5; 13:8; 17:8; 20:12, 15; 21:27]; the evil book is held in the hand of the accuser, who is the enemy and avenger, of whom we also read in Revelation: "The accuser of our brethren" [Rev 12:10]. There is also the earthly book of which the prophet also speaks: "Let them be written in the earth" [Jer 17:13; cf. John 8:6].

7:11a. *I was looking on account of the voice of the great words which that horn spoke.*

The *judgment* of God comes to humble pride. Therefore, the Roman kingdom will be destroyed because *that horn speaks great words.*

7:11b–12. *And I saw that the beast was slain, and its body perished, and was given to the fire to be burnt. And that the power of the other beasts was taken away, and that times of life were appointed them for a time, and a time.*

In the one Roman Empire, all the kingdoms at once were destroyed because of the blaspheming antichrist. And there will be no earthly empire at all, but simply the association of the saints and the advent of the triumphant Son of God of whom it is said:

7:13b. *Behold one like a son of man was coming with the clouds of heaven.*

The one of whom it is written, in the dream of Nebuchadnezzar, as a stone cut without hands, which also grew into a large mountain and crushed the clay, the iron, the bronze, the silver, and the gold [cf. Dan 2:34–35], is now introduced under the persona of *a son of man,* so that in the Son of God the assumption of human flesh is signified [cf. Matt 26:64]. This agrees with what we read in the Acts of the Apostles: "Ye men of Galilee, why do you stand gazing into heaven? This Jesus, who has been taken up from you into heaven, shall come just as you have seen him going into heaven" [Acts 1:11; cf. Matt 26:64].

7:13c. *And he came up to the Ancient of Days.*

All that is said, that he was brought before Almighty God and received authority and honor and kingdom [cf. Dan 7:13–14], should be understood in accordance with the apostle's words:

> Who, since he was in the form of God, thought it not robbery to be equal with God; but he emptied himself, taking the form of a servant, he was made in the likeness of men, and was found in his condition as a man. He humbled himself, becoming obedient unto death, even death of the cross. [Phil 2:6–8]

7:14b. *And all the peoples, tribes and languages shall serve him. His power is an eternal power that shall not be taken away, and his kingdom shall not be corrupted.*

To what human being can this correspond? Let Porphyry answer.[89] Or who is so powerful as to break and crush the little horn, whom he interprets to be Antiochus? If he answers that Judas Maccabaeus defeated the generals of Antiochus [cf. 1 Macc 3:1–4, 35; 5:1–7, 47; 2 Macc 8–15], then he ought to show how Judas *like a son of man comes with the clouds of heaven,* and is brought to the Ancient of Days, and is given *authority and kingdom,* and *all peoples and tribes serve* him, and his *power is eternal* and not limited by any end.

7:17–18a. *These four great beasts: four kingdoms shall arise from the earth; but the saints of God most high shall receive the kingdom.*

The *four kingdoms* of which we have spoken above[90] were earthly: "For everything which is *from the earth* shall return to the earth" [Eccl 3:20]. But *the saints* shall never have an earthly kingdom, but a heavenly one. Therefore, let the fable of the thousand years cease [cf. Rev 20:1–6].[91]

7:18b. *And they shall possess the kingdom unto the age, and the age of ages.*

If this is understood of the Maccabees, let the one who claims this show how their kingdom is perpetual.[92]

7:25a. *And he speaks words against the High One.* Or, as Symmachus translated it: "He speaks words as if he were God."

Thus the one who assumes the power of God arrogates to himself the words of the divine majesty.

7:25b. *And he shall crush the saints of the Most High, and he shall think that he can change times and laws.*

Indeed, the antichrist will wage war against the saints and will overcome them, and he will be lifted up by such great pride that he will try to *change* God's *laws* and ceremonies. And he will be lifted up "against all that is called God" [2 Thess 2:4] and religion, subjecting everything to his own power.[93]

7:25c. *And they shall be delivered into his hand for a time, and times, and half a time.*

Time means "year." *Times,* according to the unique character of the Hebrew language, which also has the dual number, prefigures (*praefigurant*)[94] "two years."[95] But *half a time* stands for the "six months" during which the saints are to be given over to the power of the antichrist, in order that the Jews might be condemned who did not believe the truth but welcomed a lie [cf. 2 Thess 2:10–11]. The Savior also speaks of this time in the Gospel: "Unless those days had been cut short, absolutely no flesh would have been saved" [Matt 24:22]. In [our exposition of] the final vision,[96] we will speak about how this chronology does not fit Antiochus.[97]

7:26. *And the judgment will sit that [his] power may be taken away and be broken in pieces and perish even to the end.*

This refers to the Antichrist, that is, to the little horn that spoke the great words [cf. Dan 7:8], for his kingdom is to be destroyed forever.

7:27a. *But the kingdom, the power and the greatness of the kingdom which is over all heaven.*
This concerns Christ's empire, which is everlasting.

7:28a. *Thus far is the end of the word.*
Of this *word* and speech which the Lord revealed to me in this present vision.

7:28b. *I, Daniel, was much troubled with my thoughts, and my face was changed in me; but I kept the word in my heart.*
Up to this point, the Book of Daniel is written in Chaldean and Syriac speech. The rest that follows up to the end of the volume we read in Hebrew.

Vision 8

8:1a. *In the third year of the reign of King Belshazzar (Balthasar), a vision appeared to me.*
This *vision* came two years after the previous revelation. For the previous one was seen in the first year of Belshazzar [cf. Dan 7:1], this one in the *third*. This is why he adds: *After that which I had seen in the beginning* [Dan 8:1c].

8:2a. *I saw in my vision while I was in the fortress of Susa, which is in the country of Elam* (or, as Symmachus translated it, "city"—from which the *country* also took its name, just as the Βαβυλώνιοι were named from "Babylon," and the Elamites from *Elam*; which the Septuagint translated as: "the country of Elymais"[98]).

Now *Susa* is the metropolis of the *country of the Elamites*. According to Josephus's history, in it Daniel

> built a lofty tower and it was constructed of square blocks of marble, and was of such great size and beauty that it seems to be new even today. There also the remains of the kings of the Persians and Medes lie buried, and the guardian (or attendant) and priest of that place is a Jew.[99]

While I was in the fortress at Susa. Not that the city itself was a *fortress*—as we have said, it was a very powerful metropolis—but it was built with such great strength that it gave the appearance of being a *fortress.*

8:2b. *And I saw in the vision that I was over the gate of Ulai* (which Aquila translated as: "over *ubal* of Ulai," Theodotion: "over ubal," Symmachus: "over the swamp of Ulai," the Septuagint: "near the gate of Ulai").[100]

But one should know that *Ulai* is the name of a place, or of a gate, just as there was in Troy a gate called the *Skaia*,[101] and among the Romans the *Carmentalis*.[102] In each case, the names originated for their own particular reasons.

8:3a. *And I lifted up my eyes and I saw.*

Although the things that appear in dreams are *seen* in shadow and image, yet without *lifting up our eyes* we cannot *see* even these things.

8:3b. *And behold, a ram stood before a swamp* (or *before a gate*, which is expressed in Hebrew as *ubal*), *having lofty horns and one that was higher than the other and growing larger.*[103]

He calls Darius, Cyrus's uncle, *a ram*. He reigned over the Medes after his father, Astyages.[104] And the *one horn which was higher than the other, and growing larger,* points to Cyrus himself, who succeeded his maternal grandfather, Astyages. He held command over the Medes and Persians along with his uncle, Darius, whom the Greeks called Cyaxares.[105]

8:3c–4a. *Afterward I saw the ram brandishing its horns against the east, and against the north, and against the south.*

He does not mean the *ram* itself, that is, Cyrus or Darius, but a *ram* of the same kingdom as theirs, that is, the other Darius, who was the last king of the Persian Empire,[106] who was defeated by Alexander, the son of Philip, the king of the Macedonians. Now both Greek, Latin, and barbarian historical accounts record that this Darius was a very powerful and wealthy king.[107]

8:5a. *And I,* he says, *understood.*

For from the earlier visions, in which the second kingdom had been signified by the silver and the bear [cf. Dan 2:32, 39; 7:5], he now *understands* that he is perceiving the empire of the Medes and Persians.

8:5b–9a. *And behold a he-goat came from the west across the face of the whole earth, and he did not touch the ground; and the he-goat had a notable horn between his eyes. And he went up to the ram that had the horns, which I had seen standing before the gate, and he ran toward him in the force of his strength. And when he had come near the ram, he grew wild against him, and struck the ram and broke his two horns, and the ram could not withstand him; and when he had cast him down on the ground, he stamped upon him, and no one could deliver the ram out of his hand. And the he-goat became exceedingly great; and when he was grown, the great horn was broken, and there came up four horns under it toward the four winds of heaven. And out of one of them came forth a little horn, and it became great.* Lest anyone think that I am recording my own interpretation, let us learn the words of Gabriel as he explains the prophet's vision. He says, "The ram whom you saw that had the two horns is the king of the Medes and Persians" [Dan 8:20]. This refers, of course, to Darius the son of Arsamus, in whom the kingdom of the Medes and Persians was destroyed. There was, in addition, *a he-goat who came from the west*, and because of his incredible speed, he seemed *not to touch the ground*. This refers to Alexander, the "king of the Greeks" [Dan 8:21], who overthrew Thebes and then took up arms against the Persians. Initiating a battle at the Granicus River, he defeated Darius's generals and ultimately *struck the ram* himself and *broke his two horns*, the Medes and the Persians. And he *cast him* under his feet and subjugated both horns to his own empire. Now the *great horn* refers to the first king, Alexander himself [cf. Dan 8:21]. When he died in Babylon in the thirty-second year of his life, his four generals rose up in his place [cf. Dan 8:22] and divided his empire among themselves. For Ptolemy, the son of Lagos, held control over Egypt;[108] the Philip who was also called Aridaeus, the brother of Alexander, took over Macedonia;[109] Seleucus Nicanor[110] took over Syria, Babylonia, and all the kingdoms of the east; and Antigonus[111] reigned over Asia. "But not with his strength" [Dan 8:22], it says, since no one was able to equal the greatness of Alexander. "And after a long time there shall arise a king of Syria who shall be of shameless countenance and shall understand counsels" [Dan 8:22–23]. This refers to Antiochus Epiphanes, the son of the Seleucus who was also called Philopator.

Since Antiochus had been a hostage in Rome [cf. 1 Macc 1:1–42; 2 Macc 5:1–6:7], and without the Roman Senate knowing about it, he obtained rule deceitfully, he fought a war with Ptolemy Philometor, that is, *against the south* and against the Egyptians; and then again *against the east*, in opposition to those who were fomenting revolution in Persia [cf. 1 Macc 1:19–20]. Finally, he fought against the Jews, and after capturing Judea, he entered Jerusalem and set up in the temple of God the image of Jupiter Olympius[112] [cf. 1 Macc 1:21–28, 43–57; 2 Macc 5:11–26; 6:1–7]. "And even unto the strength of heaven" [Dan 8:10], that is, unto the sons of Israel, who were protected by the help of angels. "He roused his own greatness" [Dan 8:10] to the point that he subjected most of the saints to idolatry and, as it were, "trampled upon the stars of heaven beneath his feet" [Dan 8:10; cf. 1 Macc 1:30–42, 58–67; 2 Macc 5:24–27; 6:8–7:42]. And so it came to pass that he held the *south* and the *east*, that is, Egypt and Persia, under his imperial command. And as for the words: "And it was magnified even unto the prince of the strength" [Dan 8:11], this means that he was raised up against God and persecuted his saints. "He even took away the ἐνδελεχισμον,[113] that is, the continual sacrifice" [Dan 8:11], which was offered in the morning and the evening [cf. Exod 30:8; 29:38], and he defiled it and "cast down the place of his sanctuary" [Dan 8:11]. And he did not do this by his own power, but "because of the sins" of the people. And so it came to pass that "truth was cast down upon the earth" [Dan 8:12], and, as the cult of idols flourished, the religion of God went dormant.

8:13a. *And I heard one of the saints speaking, and one saint said to another, I do not know to whom, that was speaking.*

Instead of *to another whom I do not know*, which Symmachus translated as τινί ποτε, which we have followed, Aquila, Theodotion, and the Septuagint recorded the Hebrew word itself *phelmoni*. While keeping silent about the angel's name, he indicated in a general way that it was one of the angels, it does not matter which.

8:13b. *How long until the vision, the continual sacrifice, the sin of the desolation that is made, and the sanctuary and the strength be trodden under foot?*

One angel asks another angel for *how long* a time will the temple be desolated by the judgment of God, under the rule of Antiochus, king of Syria, and will the image of Jupiter stand in God's temple.

8:14. *And he said to him, Until the evening and the morning, two thousand three hundred days; and the sanctuary shall be cleansed.*

Let us read the Books of Maccabees and the history of Josephus. There we shall find it written that in the one hundred and forty-third year after the Seleucus, who was the first to reign in Syria after Alexander, Antiochus entered Jerusalem, devastated everything, and returned in the third year and set up the statue of Jupiter in the temple [cf. 1 Macc 1:11—4:58; 2 Macc 4:7—10:8].[114] And up until the time of Judas Maccabaeus, that is, up until the one hundred and forty-eighth year, during the six years of the devastation of Jerusalem and the three of the defiling of the Temple,[115] *two thousand three hundred days* and three months were fulfilled, at the end of which the Temple was purified. Some read "two thousand two hundred" instead of *two thousand three hundred*, apparently in order to avoid going beyond the six years and three months.[116] Most of our people refer this passage to the antichrist and say that what happened under Antiochus as a type must be fulfilled in truth under antichrist.

But as for what is added: *The sanctuary shall be cleansed*, this signifies the times of Judas Maccabaeus, who came from the village of Modein (*Modin*) [cf. 1 Macc 2:1]. Supported by the efforts of his brothers, relatives, and many of the Jewish people, he defeated the generals of Antiochus near Emmaus, which is now called Nicopolis [cf. 1 Macc 4:3–25; 2 Macc 8:1–36].[117] When Antiochus heard about this—the one who had risen up against the prince of princes [cf. Dan 8:25], that is, against the Lord of lords and king of kings [cf. Rev 17:14; 19:16]—he desired to despoil the temple of Diana in Elymais, which is in a region of the Persians, because it contained precious votive offerings [cf. 1 Macc 6:1–3; 2 Macc 9:1–2].[118] And it was there too that he lost his army and was destroyed "without hands" [Dan 8:25; cf. 2:34], that is to say, he perished out of grief and disease [cf. 1 Macc 6:9–16; 2 Macc 9:5–10, 28]. Now as for *evening and morning*, this refers to the succession of day and night.

8:15a. *And it came to pass that when I, Daniel, saw the vision and sought the understanding....*

He *saw the vision* by way of a picture and image, and he did not know the *understanding* of it. Therefore, not everyone who sees understands; it is as if we read the Holy Scripture with our eyes but do not understand it in our heart [cf. Matt 13:13–14, 19; Mark 4:12; Luke 8:10; John 12:40; Acts 28:26].

8:15b. *Behold, there stood before me as it were the appearance of a man.*

Surely angels are not men, but they are seen as *men* in *appearance*. For example, three men were seen by Abraham at the oak of Mamre [Gen 18:1–3] who certainly were not men. One of them is worshipped as the Lord; and this is why the Savior says in the Gospel: "Abraham saw my day and rejoiced" [John 8:56].

8:16. *And I heard the voice of a man between Ulai, and he cried out and said: Gabriel, make him understand the vision.*

The Jews claim that this man who ordered Gabriel to *make* Daniel *understand the vision* was Michael.[119] And it is logical that Gabriel is assigned this duty, for he is in charge of battles, and the vision had to do with battles and conflicts between kings, or rather, with the succession of kingdoms. Indeed, Gabriel translates into our language as "the force of" or "the mighty one of God."[120] Whence also, when the Lord was about to be born, to declare war on the demons, and to triumph over the world, Gabriel came to Zachariah and to Mary [Luke 1:11–19, 26–27].[121] And further on, we read in the Psalms concerning the Lord's triumph: "Who is this king of glory? The Lord strong and powerful, the Lord strong in battle; he is the king of glory" [Ps 24:8].[122] Now whenever medicine and healing are needed, Raphael is sent [cf. Tob 5:4], whose name means "the healing" or "medicine of God."[123] But this is only if one votes to accept the Book of Tobit.[124] And then, when promises of prosperity are made to the people, and ἱλασμὸς, which we can express as "propitiation" or "expiation," becomes necessary, Michael is directed to go, whose name means, "Who is like God?" The name [Raphael] of course when interpreted signifies that the true medicine is in God.[125]

8:17b. *And he said to me: Understand, O son of man.*

Ezekiel, Daniel, and Zechariah often perceive that they are in the company of angels [cf. Ezek 2:1–47; 6; Dan 7:16–27; 8:15–26; 9:21–27; 10:5—12:13; Zech 1:9–14; 2:2, 7; 4:4–5; 6:4–5]. In order to keep them from being lifted up in pride and imagining themselves to be of an angelic nature or dignity, they are reminded of their frailty, and they are addressed as *sons of men* in order that they would know that they are human beings.

8:18b. *And he touched me and set me on my feet.*

The prophet had fallen down out of fear and was lying on the ground on all fours. At the angel's touch, he is raised up in order to be able without fear to hear and understand what is being spoken.

8:26b. *You therefore seal up the vision because it shall come to pass after many days.*

The angel Gabriel explained the vision, which we have discussed above to the best of our ability. At the end he records: *You therefore seal up the vision, because it shall come to pass after many days.* By the word *seal* he shows that the things that were spoken are obscure and inaccessible to the hearing of many, nor can they be understood before they are fulfilled in events and works.

8:27a. *And I, Daniel, languished and was sick for some days.*

This is what we read in Genesis about Abraham, that after he had heard God speaking to him, he said that he was earth and ashes [cf. Gen 18:27]. So then, Daniel says that he *languished* before the horror of the vision, and *was sick*, and that when he got up, he did the works that had been commanded to him by the king [cf. Dan 8:27]. He renders all things to all people [cf. 1 Cor 9:22; Rom 13:7], since he knows the following saying from the Gospel: "Render unto Caesar the things that are Caesar's, and to God the things that are God's" [Matt 22:21; Mark 12:17; Luke 20:25].

8:27c. *And I was stunned by the vision, and there was no one to interpret it.* If *there was no one to interpret it,* how did the angel interpret it higher up? What he means is this: He had heard mention of kings but did not know their names. He had learned of things to come, but he wavered in doubt about when they would happen. And so, he did the only thing he could do: he *was stunned by the vision,* and left everything to the knowledge of God.

BOOK THREE

Vision 9

9:1. *In the first year of Darius the son of Ahasuerus of the seed of the Medes, who held command over the kingdom of the Chaldeans.*

This is the Darius who, with Cyrus, conquered the Chaldeans and Babylonians.[1] Let us not think that this is that Darius in whose second year the temple was built [cf. Ezra 4:24], as Porphyry supposes in order to prolong Daniel's years. Nor are we to think of the Darius who was defeated by Alexander, the king of the Macedonians. He therefore adds the name of his father and refers to his victory, saying that he was the first *of the seed of the Medes* to overthrow *the kingdom of the Chaldeans.* This removes the possibility of an error on the reader's part, owing to the similarity of the name.

9:2b–3. *I Daniel understood in the books the number of the years concerning which the word of the Lord came to Jeremiah the prophet, that seventy years would be accomplished for the desolation of Jerusalem; and I set my face to the Lord God, to pray and make supplication with fasting, sackcloth and ashes.*

Jeremiah had predicted *seventy years for the desolation* of the temple [cf. Jer 25:11–12; 29:10–11]. After that, the people would again return to Judea and build the temple and Jerusalem. This reality does not cause Daniel to become negligent but encourages him to pray even more, that God might, by means of their prayers, fulfill what he had promised through his own mercy, lest negligence and pride give birth to offense.[2] In fact, we also read in Genesis that before the flood came one hundred and twenty years were appointed for repentance [cf. Gen 6:3]. Since they refused to repent even within so long a time, namely, a hundred years, God does not wait for the remaining twenty years to be fulfilled, but he introduces early what he had threatened for later.[3] So also Jeremiah is told, on account of the hardness of the heart of the Jewish people: "Do not pray for this people, for I will not listen to you" [Jer 7:16]; and also Samuel: "How long will you mourn over Saul? I also have rejected him" [1 Sam 16:1]. Therefore, with *sackcloth and ashes* Daniel asks God to fulfill what he had promised. It is not that Daniel disbelieved what was coming, but he was concerned that his sense of security might give birth to negligence, and negligence to offense.

9:4b. *O Lord God, great and terrible.*
Toward those who despise your precepts.
9:4c. *Who keeps the alliance and mercy toward those who love you and keep your commandments.*

It is not therefore the case that what God promises will come to pass immediately, but he accomplishes his promises in those who *keep his commandments.*

9:5a. *We have sinned, we have committed iniquity, we have acted impiously.*

Because he is one of the people, he recounts the sins of the people in his own name.[4] This is what we read the apostle does, too, in the Epistle to the Romans [cf. Rom 5:8; 7:14–25].[5]

9:7a. *To you, O Lord, justice.*
For we are suffering justly what we deserve.
9:9a. *To you, O Lord our God, mercy and propitiation.*

The Lord is not only just but also merciful [cf. Ps 112:4; 116:5; 2 Macc 1:24]. Therefore, of the one of whom he had said above: "To you, O Lord, justice" [Dan 9:7], he now says: *To you mercy*, that he might invite him to show mercy, after the judge's sentence.

9:11a. *And the malediction and the curse has dripped down upon us.*

You have not poured out your entire wrath upon us, which we would not have been able to endure, but a drop of your fury, in order that we might return to you, after being corrected by the blow [cf. Lev 26:28].

9:11b. *The malediction and the curse that is written in the book of Moses, the servant of God.*

In Deuteronomy we read of God's *maledictions* and blessings [cf. Deut 27:15—28:68], which were afterward uttered on Mount Gerizim and Ebal upon the just and the sinners.

9:13b. *All this evil has come upon us, and we have not prayed to your face, O Lord our God, that we might turn back from our iniquities and meditate on your truth.*

Their hardness was very great, so that even in the midst of the scourges, they did not *pray to the Lord;* and even if they had prayed, they *did not pray*, because they did not *turn back from* their *iniquities.* Now to *turn back from iniquity* is to *meditate on the truth* of God.

9:14a. *And the Lord kept watch over the evil, and he brought it upon us.*

When we are corrected for our sins, God *keeps watch over* us and visits us [cf. Jer 31:28; 44:27; Exod 32:34; Lev 18:25; 26:16; Num 14:18; Ps 89:32]. But when we are abandoned by God and are not judged and are unworthy of the Lord's correction, that is when he is said to be asleep [Ps 34:20; 73:20; 121:4]. And this is why we read in the Psalms: "The Lord got up as one sleeping, and as a man drunk from wine" [Ps 78:65]. For our *evil* inebriates God. When it is corrected in us, he is said to wake up and to arise from his drunkenness, in order to awaken us to justice, we who had been drunk with sin.

9:15a. *And now, O Lord God, who brought forth your people out of the land of Egypt with a strong hand.*

Remember ancient kindness: in order to induce God to a similar clemency.

9:17b. *And show your face upon your sanctuary, which is abandoned.*

Fulfill in deed what you have promised in words: the time of desolation is nearing its fulfillment [cf. Dan 9:2].

9:18a. *Incline, my God, your ear and hear; open your eyes and see our desolation and the city upon which your name is called.*

He says these things ἀνθρωποπάθως (anthropomorphically), so that when we are heard, God seems to *incline* his *ear*;[6] when he deigns to show us regard, he appears to *open* his *eyes*;[7] but when he turns his face away,[8] we appear to be unworthy of both his *eyes* and *ears*.

9:20a. *Now while I was still speaking and praying and confessing my sins and the sins of my people, Israel.*

Therefore, as we said above,[9] he reviews not only the *sins of the people* but his own, since he is one of the people, or by way of humility, since he himself had not committed sin; and he unites himself with the sinful people, in order to obtain pardon by reason of his humility. Note what he says here: *I was confessing my sins.* For there are many passages in Holy Scripture where confession does not mean "repentance" but "praise" [cf. Ps 42:5; 95:2; 2 Macc 10:38].

9:21a. *While I was still speaking in my prayer, behold the man Gabriel, whom I had seen in the vision, at the beginning.*

He calls the preceding *vision*, which this one follows [cf. Dan 8:15–16], the *beginning*. The effect of his prayer was very great, and the promise of the Lord was fulfilled who says: "While you are yet speaking, I will say: Behold, I am at hand" [Isa 58:9 LXX]. Now Gabriel appears not as an angel or archangel, but as a man (*vir*), in order to indicate his power (*virtutis*), not his sex.

9:21b. *And flying, he touched me at the time of the evening sacrifice.*

He is said to *fly*, because he had appeared as a man; and it was *at the time of the evening sacrifice*, because the prophet's prayer had continued all the way from the morning sacrifice to the *evening sacrifice*. That is why he had turned God's mercy toward himself.

9:22a. *And he instructed me.*

The vision is so obscure that the prophet needs the angel's instruction.

9:22c. *Daniel, I have now come forth that I might instruct you and that you might understand.*

I have been sent to you *now* and *have come forth*, not from the face of God, for I do not depart from him, but to come to you.

9:23a. *From the commencement of your prayers a word went forth.*

When you began to pray, you immediately procured God's mercy, and his sentence *went forth*. I have therefore been sent to explain to you the things of which you are ignorant.

9:23c. *For you are a man of desires.*

Either "lovable" and "worthy of God's love," even as Solomon was called *Ididia* [cf. 2 Sam 12:25], or *man of desires*,[10] because in view of your desire, you deserve to hear God's secrets and to receive knowledge of the future.

9:23d. *You therefore pay attention to the word and understand the vision.*

If Daniel is told: *Pay* diligent *attention* to hear and *understand* what you are seeing, what ought we to do, whose eyes have been blinded by the darkness of ignorance?

9:24a. *Seventy weeks have been shortened upon your people and upon your holy city.*

Because the prophet had said: "You brought forth your people" [Dan 9:15], and "Your name has been invoked upon your city and upon your people" [Dan 9:19], therefore Gabriel says in the name of God: They are not God's people, but *your people*; nor is it the holy city of God, but only *your holy city*, as you say. This is similar to what we read in Exodus also, when God says to Moses: "Go down, for *your people* have sinned" [Exod 32:7]. That is, they are not my people, for they have forsaken me. And so, because you are pleading on behalf of Jerusalem and praying for the Jewish people, hear what shall befall your people and your city in *seventy weeks* of years, the things that follow. I know that highly educated men have discussed this question in various ways, and that each of them has expressed his thoughts according to the capacity of his own genius. And so, because it is risky to pass judgment upon the opinions of some teachers of the church and to prefer one over another, I will tell what each of them thought, leaving it to the reader's choice as to whose explanation he ought to follow.[11]

In the fifth book of his *Chronology*, Africanus[12] said the following about the seventy weeks (and I quote him verbatim):

> The section which we read in Daniel concerning the seventy weeks contains many admirable things which would take too long to discuss right now. Therefore, we must treat only what pertains to our present task, namely that which concerns chronology. No one doubts that this is a prediction of Christ's advent [cf. Dan 9:24–25]. He appeared to the world after the seventy weeks. After him the transgressions were finished, sin received its end, iniquity was destroyed, and eternal justice was proclaimed, which overcame the justice of the law. And the vision and the prophecy were fulfilled [cf. Dan 9:24], for "the law and the prophets were until the John's baptism" [Luke 16:16; cf. Matt 11:13], and the saint of saints was anointed [cf. Dan 9:25]. For before Christ assumed a human body, all these things were hoped for rather than held onto.
>
> Now the angel himself speaks of *seventy weeks* of years, that is, four hundred and ninety years, "from the issuing of the word that a response be given and that Jerusalem be rebuilt" [Dan 9:25 Theod.]. This period began in the twentieth year of Artaxerxes, king of the Persians [cf. Neh 2:1].[13] For as we read in the book of Ezra,[14] his cupbearer Nehemiah [cf. Neh 1:11] petitioned the king and obtained a response that Jerusalem be rebuilt [cf. Neh 2:1]. And this word [Dan 9:25] went forth which granted permission to build the city and surround it with walls. For up to that time the city lay exposed to the attacks of the neighboring nations [cf. Neh 2:5–9]. But if one points to the command of king Cyrus, who had granted authority to those who desired to return to Jerusalem, the high priest Jesus and Zerubbabel, and later on the priest Ezra, together with the others who had been willing to set out with them, attempted to build the temple and the city with its walls,

but they were hindered by the surrounding nations from completing the task, on the pretext that the king had not commanded this [cf. 2 Chr 36:22; Ezra 1–5]. And so, the task remained incomplete up to Nehemiah and the twentieth year of king Artaxerxes. At this time, a hundred and fifteen years of the Persian Empire had elapsed. Now this was the one hundred and eighty-fifth year of the captivity of Jerusalem; and at that time Artaxerxes first gave orders to build the walls of Jerusalem [cf. Neh 2:5–6].[15] Nehemiah was in charge of that task, and the street was built and the surrounding walls. Now if you want to count seventy weeks of years from that time, you can come out to the time of Christ.[16]

But if we are unwilling to take the starting point for these weeks from that time, the chronology will not concur, and we will encounter many contradictions. For if the seventy weeks are counted from Cyrus and his first decree giving permission by which the Jews were released from captivity, we will meet with a deficit of a hundred years and more short of the stated number of seventy weeks.[17] If we count from the day when the angel spoke to Daniel, the deficit would be much greater.[18] If you wish to put the beginning of the weeks at the commencement of the captivity, an even greater number of years is added. For the kingdom of the Persians endured for two hundred and thirty years until the beginning of the Macedonians; then the Macedonians themselves reigned for three hundred years. From that date until the fifteenth[19] year of Tiberius Caesar [cf. Luke 3:1], when Christ suffered, sixty years are counted.[20] All of these years added together come to the number of five hundred and ninety, so that a hundred years are left over.

But from the twentieth year of king Artaxerxes to Christ, seventy weeks are completed, if we reckon according to the lunar computation of the Hebrews, who did not number their months according to the course of the sun, but according to the moon.[21] For from the one hundred fifteenth year of the Persian kingdom, when Artaxerxes the king of the same empire was in the twentieth year of his command, and this was the fourth year of the eighty-third Olympiad, up to the two hundred and second Olympiad, and the second year of that same Olympiad was the fifteenth year of Tiberius Caesar, this comes to four hundred seventy-five years. This makes four hundred ninety Hebrew years, which are reckoned according to the lunar months, as we have said. For according to their reckoning, these years can be made up of months of twenty-nine and a half days each. Thus, the sun, during a period of four hundred ninety years, completes its orbit in three hundred sixty-five days and a quarter. This comes to twelve lunar months for each individual year, with eleven and a fourth days left over to spare.[22] And this is why the Greeks and Jews over a period of eight years insert three intercalary months (ἐμβολίμους). For if you will multiply eleven and a quarter days by eight, you will come out to ninety days,[23] that is, three months. Now if you divide the eight-year periods into four hundred seventy-five years, your quotient will be fifty-nine plus three months. These fifty-nine plus eight-year periods produce enough intercalary months to make up fifteen years, more or less; and if you will add these fifteen years to the four hundred seventy-five years, you will come out to seventy weeks of years, that is, a total of four hundred and ninety years.[24]

This is what Africanus said. We have translated him verbatim.[25]

Let us move on to Eusebius Pamphili.[26] In the eighth book of his Εὐαγγελικῆς ἀποδείξεως (*The Demonstration of the Gospel*) he conjectures something like this:[27]

It is not for nothing, it seems to me, that the division of the seventy weeks was made, so that seven was mentioned first, then sixty-two, and lastly one week was added, which is itself divided into two parts. For it is written: "And you shall know and understand, that from the going forth of the words that a response be given and that Jerusalem be built until Christ the prince [there shall be] seven weeks, and sixty-two weeks" [Dan 9:25]. And after the other things that he related in between, he records at the end: "And one week confirmed a covenant with many" [Dan 9:27]. It is clear that the angel did not answer these things for nothing and without God's inspiration.

This observation seems to require cautious and careful reasoning, so that the reader may pay diligent attention and inquire into the reasons for this division. But if it is necessary for us too to say what we think by another exposition which deals with this present reading, in that the angel says: "From the going forth of the words that a response be given and that Jerusalem be built until Christ the prince" [Dan 9:25], we think it refers to no other princes but those who had charge of the Jewish people after this prophecy and the return from Babylon—that is to say, the ἀρχιερεῖς (chief priests) and priests whom the Scripture gives the name of "christs," because they are "anointed ones" [cf. 2 Macc 1:10]. The chief of these was Jesus [Jeshua] the son of Jehozadak, the high priest [cf. Hag 1:1], and then the rest who lived until the advent of the Lord and Savior.[28] And the prophet's prediction points to them when it says: *From the going forth of the words that a response be given and that Jerusalem be built until Christ the leader, there shall be seven weeks, and sixty-two weeks*; that is, that the seven weeks, and later the sixty-two weeks, which come to a total of four hundred and eighty-three years, be reckoned from the time of Cyrus.

And lest we appear to be merely reporting a rash opinion and not putting our statements to the test, let us list those who were in charge of the people as *christs* from the time of Jesus (Jeshua), the son of Jehozadak, until the advent of the Savior, that is, the ones *anointed* for the high priesthood. First, then, as we have already said, after Daniel's prophecy, which was made under king Cyrus, after the people returned from Babylon, Jesus the son of Jehozadak was the high priest, and Zerubbabel, son of Shealtiel [cf. Hag 1:1], who laid the foundations of the temple [cf. Ezra 3; Neh 3]. And when the task was hindered by the Samaritans and the other surrounding nations [cf. Ezra 4; Neh 4], seven weeks of years were completed, that is, forty-nine years, during which the work on the temple remained unfinished. The prophecy separates these weeks from the remaining sixty-two weeks.[29] In fact, the Jews in the gospel also express this opinion when they say to the Lord: "This temple was built over forty-six years, and you will raise it up in three days?" [John 2:20]. For this was the number of years which elapsed between the first year of king Cyrus, who granted to those Jews who so desired the permission to return to their fatherland [cf. 2 Chr 36:22–23; Ezra 1:1–4], and the sixth year of king Darius, under whom the entire work of the temple was finished [cf. Ezra 6:14–15].[30] On the other hand, Josephus adds another three years as well, during which the enclosure of the temple [cf. Ezek 42:7; 1 Macc 14:48] and certain other things which remained were completed.[31] When these are added to the forty-six years, they make forty-nine years, that is, seven weeks of years.[32]

Now they count the remaining sixty-two weeks from the seventh year of the same Darius.[33] At that time Jesus (Jeshua) the son of Jehozadak, and Zerubbabel (who had already reached a mature age) were in charge of the people [cf. Ezra 3:2ff.]. Under them Haggai and Zechariah prophesied [cf. Hag 1:1; Zech 1:1]. After them came Ezra and Nehemiah from Babylon and constructed the walls of the city, during the high priesthood of Joiakim, son of Jesus, surnamed Jehozadak [cf. Ezra 7:6]. After him Eliashib succeeded to the priesthood, then Joiada and Johanan after him [cf. Neh 12:10–11]. Following him there was Jaddua, in whose lifetime Alexander, the king of the Macedonians, founded Alexandria, as Josephus tells us in his books of the *Antiquities*. "And he came to Jerusalem and offered sacrifices in the temple."[34] Now Alexander died in the one hundred and thirteenth Olympiad, in the two hundred thirty-sixth year of the Persian Empire, which had begun in the first year of the fifty-fifth Olympiad. At that time Cyrus king of the Persians conquered the Babylonians and Chaldeans. After the death of the priest Jaddua, who had been in charge of the temple during Alexander's reign, Onias received the high priesthood.[35] It was at this time that Seleucus subjugated Babylon and placed upon his own head the crown of all Asia. This was the twelfth year after Alexander's death [cf. 1 Macc 1:8–11]. Up to that time, all the years from the rule of Cyrus tally up to two hundred and forty-eight. From that age, the Scripture of the Maccabees reckons with the kingdom of the Greeks. Following Onias, the high priest Eleazar was in charge of the Jews. It was at that time that the Seventy translators are said to have

BOOK THREE 113

rendered the Holy Scriptures into the Greek language at Alexandria. After him, there was Onias II,[36] who was followed by Simon, who ruled over the people when Jesus the son of Sirach wrote the book which bears the Greek title of Πανάρετος ("All Virtuous [Wisdom]"[37]), and which is falsely attributed to Solomon by most people.[38] Another Onias succeeded him in the high priesthood.[39] It was at this time that Antiochus compelled the Jews to sacrifice to the gods of the Gentiles [cf. 1 Macc 1:43–67; 2 Macc 6:1–11]. When Onias died, Judas Maccabaeus cleansed the temple and destroyed the images of the idols [cf. 1 Macc 6:16; 4:36–58; 2 Macc 9:28—10:5]. His brother Jonathan succeeded him, and after Jonathan their brother Simon governed the people. At the time of his death, the one hundred[40] seventy-seventh year of the Syrian kingdom was fulfilled [cf. 1 Macc 16:14–16]. The First Book of Maccabees contains the history up to that time. And from the first year of Cyrus, king of the Persians, until the end of the First Book of Maccabees and the death of the high priest Simon, there is four hundred twenty-five years. After him, John [Hyrcanus] held the high priesthood for twenty-nine years.[41] When he died, Aristobulus[42] held charge over the people for one year. He was the first man, after the return from Babylon, to associate the crown, the sign of the royal power, with the office of high priesthood.[43] His successor Alexander, who likewise was high priest and king,[44] ruled the people for twenty-seven years. Up to this point, the number of years from the first year of Cyrus the king and the return of the captives who desired to come back to Judea tallies up to four hundred and eighty-three. This total is made up of the seven weeks and the sixty-two weeks, that is sixty-nine weeks altogether.

And during this whole time high priests ruled over the Jewish people. I now think that they are called christ-princes.[45] Now when the last of them, Alexander, died, the leaderless Jewish nation was harassed by seditions, this way and that, into various factions, to such an extent that Alexandra,[46] who was also called Salina, and who was the wife of the same Alexander, seized power and indeed kept the high priesthood for her son Hyrcanus. But she passed on the kingdom to her other son Aristobulus,⁴⁷ and he exercised it for ten years. But when the brothers fought with each other in civil war and the Jewish nation was drawn into various factions, then Gnaeus Pompey, the general of the Roman army, came upon the scene. He captured Jerusalem and even entered the inner shrine in the temple, which was called the Holy of Holies. He sent Aristobulus back to Rome in chains, keeping him for his triumphal procession, and then he gave the high priesthood to his brother Hyrcanus.⁴⁸ Then for the first time the Jewish nation became tributary to the Romans.⁴⁹ After him, Herod, the son of Antipater, received the kingdom of the Jews by senatorial decree, after Hyrcanus had been killed. He was the first foreigner to hold charge over the Jews.⁵⁰ When his parents died, he handed over the high priesthood too to his children, even though they were non-Jews, hardly in accordance with the law of Moses. Nor did he entrust the office to them for long, on account of favors and bribes, for he despised the commands of the divine law.

The same Eusebius records still another explanation, but if we wanted to translate it into the Latin language, we would lengthen this book.⁵¹ And so, here is the gist of his alternate interpretation:

The time from the sixth year of Darius⁵²—who reigned over the Persians after Cyrus and his son, Cambyses—when the work on the temple was completed, until Herod and Caesar Augustus numbers seven weeks plus sixty-two weeks, which make a total of four hundred eighty-three years. That was the date when the christ, that is to say, Hyrcanus [II], being the last high priest from the family of the Maccabees, was murdered by Herod,⁵³ and the succession of high priests of God in accordance with the law came to an end. It was then also that a Roman army under the leadership of a Roman general devastated both the city and the sanctuary itself. Or else it was Herod himself who by his ambition seized power illegitimately among the Jews. And as for the added words, *And he confirmed a covenant with many in one week; and in the half of the week the victim and sacrifice shall fail* [Dan 9:27], he interprets it as follows.

Christ was born while Herod was reigning in Judea and Augustus among the Romans. He preached the gospel for three years and six months, according to John the Evangelist [cf. John 2:13; 6:4; 11:55] and he *confirmed* the worship of the true God *with many,* undoubtedly meaning the apostles and believers. And then, after the Lord's passion, *the victim and sacrifice failed* again *in the half of the week.* For whatever was done in the temple after that date was not a *sacrifice* to God but the worship of the devil, since they all cried out together: "His blood be upon us and upon our children" [Matt 27:25]; and: "We have no king but Caesar" [John 19:15].

The interested reader can find a more detailed discussion of this passage in the *Chronicle* of this same Eusebius, which I translated into the Latin language many years ago.[54]

But as for his statement that the number of years to be reckoned from the completion of the temple to the tenth year of the Emperor Augustus, that is, when Hyrcanus was killed and Herod took control of Judea, amounts to seven plus sixty-two weeks, that is, four hundred eighty-three years, we can prove this as follows. The construction of the temple was completed in the first year of the sixty-sixth Olympiad, which was the sixth year of Darius. In the third year of the one hundred and eighty-sixth Olympiad, that is, the tenth year of Augustus, Herod received command over the Jews. This comes to four hundred and eighty-three years, reckoning up by the individual Olympiads and counting four years for each.

This same Eusebius gives another opinion as well, which in part is not rejected:[55]

> Most authorities extend the one week of years into seventy years, reckoning each year as a decade. They also claim that there were thirty-five years between the passion of Christ and the reign of Nero,[56] when the weapons of Rome were first raised against the Jews, and this is what the half a week of the seventy years refers to. After that, indeed, from the time of Vespasian[57] and Titus[58] and thereafter, when Jerusalem and the temple were set on fire, up to Trajan,[59] another thirty-five years elapsed. And this, they assert, was the week of which the angel said to Daniel: *And he confirmed*

a covenant with many for one week [Dan 9:27]. For the gospel was preached by the apostles all over the world, since they continued even to that time. Church historians hand down that John the Evangelist lived up to the time of Trajan.

Yet I do not know how we can understand the earlier weeks, seven and the sixty-two, to consist in seven years each, and this last one in ten years, or seventy years in all. In any case, this is what Eusebius wrote.

Now Hippolytus has conjectured about these same weeks as follows.[60] He reckons the seven weeks as prior to the return of the people [from Babylon], and the sixty-two [weeks] as subsequent to their return and extending to the birth of Christ.[61] But the chronology does not match at all: if indeed the years of the kingdom of the Persians be reckoned at two hundred and thirty, and those of the Macedonians at three hundred, and the years after these up to the birth of the Savior at thirty, that is, five hundred and sixty years from the beginning of Cyrus king of the Persians until the advent of the Savior.[62] Moreover, Hippolytus places the final week at the end of the world, which he divides into the time of Elijah and of the Antichrist.[63] Thus during the three and a half years of the last week the knowledge of God is *confirmed*, of which it was said: *He confirmed a covenant with many for one week* [Dan 9:27], and then during the other three years under the Antichrist *the victim and sacrifice will fail.* But when Christ arrives and kills the wicked one by the breath of his mouth [cf. 2 Thess 2:8], desolation shall continue all the way to the consummation and the end.

Apollinaris of Laodicea extricates himself from every question dealing with past chronology and stretches out his wishes toward the future [cf. Phil 3:13] and sets forth a view of things that is uncertain and dangerous. For if perchance those who live after us do not see these things fulfilled at the time he determined, they will be forced to seek another solution and to accuse him of being a teacher of error.[64] And so, lest I appear to be misrepresenting someone for what he never said, I will translate him word for word:

> In four hundred ninety years, sins and all the vices that arise from sins will be stopped. After this, good things shall come, and God will be reconciled with the world at the advent of Christ, his Son. For *from the going forth of the Word* [cf. Dan 9:25], when Christ was born of the Virgin Mary, to the forty-ninth year, that is, the end of the seven weeks,

Israel's repentance has been awaited [cf. Rom 11:26]. But after that, from the eighth year of Claudius Caesar,[65] the Romans took up arms against the Jews. For in the thirtieth year of his life in the flesh, according to the evangelist Luke, the Lord began to preach the Gospel [cf. Luke 3:23]. And according to the evangelist John, after this Christ completed two years over a period of three Passovers [cf. John 2:13; 6:4; 11:55]. And from that point, the six years of Tiberius are reckoned; and the four of Gaius Caesar, surnamed Caligula;[66] and the eight of Claudius.[67] This makes a total of forty-nine years, or seven weeks of years.

But when four hundred thirty-four years shall have elapsed after these things, that is to say, the sixty-two weeks, then[68] Jerusalem and the temple must be rebuilt, during three and a half years within the final week, beginning with the advent of Elijah, who according to the words of our Lord and Savior, will come "to turn back the heart of the fathers toward their children" [Mal 4:5; Sir 48:10; Luke 1:17]. And then, the Antichrist shall come, and according to the apostle, he will sit in the temple of God [cf. 2 Thess 2:4] and be killed by the breath of the Lord and Savior [cf. 2 Thess 2:8], after he has waged war against the saints. And thus it shall come to pass that in the middle of the week he shall confirm God's covenant with the saints [cf. Dan 9:27], and again in the middle of the week he will announce the cessation of sacrifices, under the authority of Antichrist. For the Antichrist shall set up the abomination of desolation, that is, an idol and statue of his own god, within the temple. Then shall ensue the final devastation and the condemnation of the Jewish people, who spurned Christ's truth and welcomed the lie of the Antichrist [cf. 2 Thess 2:11].

Now this same Apollinaris asserts that he conceived this interpretation about the chronology, because Africanus,[69] the author of the *Chronology*, whose explanation I have recorded above, attests that the final week will occur at the end of the world; and it is not possible that time periods that are conjoined be divided up. Rather, all the time periods must be united with each other, in accordance with Daniel's prophecy.

The highly educated man Clement, a priest of the church at Alexandria, gives little consideration to the number of years.[70] He says that the seventy weeks of years were completed by the span of time from the reign of Cyrus, king of the Persians, to the reign of the Roman emperors, Vespasian and Titus; that is, the four hundred ninety years,[71] adding into that same number the two thousand three hundred days of which we spoke above [cf. Dan 8:14]. He tries to calculate into these seventy weeks the times of the Persians, the Macedonians, and the Caesars, even though, according to the most careful computation, six hundred and thirty years are counted from the first year of Cyrus, king of the Persians and Medes, when Darius also was in command, up to Vespasian and the destruction of the temple.[72]

When Origen set his mind on this same section, he urged us to seek what we do not understand, and because he had no room for allegory, in which one may discuss without constraint, he was confined by the truth of history and made these brief notes in the tenth book of the *Stromata*:

> The times must be very carefully searched into, from the first year of Darius, the son of Ahasuerus [cf. Dan 9:1], up to the advent of Christ. How many years were there, and what happened during them? Then we might be able to see whether we can fit these things in with the advent of the Lord.[73]

We can learn what Tertullian had to say on the subject from the book that he wrote against the Jews.[74] His words must be set forth briefly:[75]

> How, then, do we show that Christ came within the sixty-two weeks [cf. Dan 9:25]? Let us count from the first year of Darius, since that was the time when the vision itself was shown to Daniel [cf. Dan 9:1]. For [the angel] says to him: "Understand and conjecture from the prophesying of the words for me to give you this reply" [Dan 9:25 LXX; cf. 9:23]. Hence we ought to compute from the first year of Darius, when Daniel saw this vision.
> Let us see, then, how the years are fulfilled up to the advent of Christ. Darius reigned nineteen years; Artaxerxes forty-one; Ochus who is also [called] Cyrus twenty-four years; Argus, one year; the other Darius, who was named Melas, twenty-one years.[76] Alexander the Macedonian

reigned twelve years. Then after Alexander, who had ruled over both the Medes and the Persians, whom he had conquered, and had established his rule in Alexandria, calling it after his own name, Soter reigned there in Alexandria for thirty-five years, and was succeeded by Philadelphus, reigning for thirty-eight years. After him Εὐεργέτης reigned for twenty-five years, and then Philopator for seventeen years, followed by Epiphanes for twenty-four years. Still another Εὐεργέτης ruled for twenty-eight years, and Soter for thirty-eight years; Ptolemy for thirty-seven years, and Cleopatra for twenty years and five months.[77] Now Cleopatra shared the rule with Augustus for thirteen years. After Cleopatra Augustus held command for another forty-three years. For all of the years of the empire of Augustus were fifty-six in number. Now we see that Christ was born in the forty-first year of the reign of Augustus, who held command after the death of Cleopatra. And this same Augustus went on to live another fifteen years after Christ was born. And the remaining chronology of years up to the day of Christ's birth will bring us to the forty-first year of Augustus, after the death of Cleopatra,[78] a total figure of four hundred and thirty-seven years and five months.[79] Whence are filled up sixty-two weeks and a half, which come to four hundred and thirty-seven years and six months, on the day of the birth of Christ. And "eternal justice was manifested, and the Saint of saints was anointed" [Dan 9:24], namely Christ, "and the vision and prophet were sealed," and "sins" were remitted which are granted through faith in Christ's name to all who believe in him [cf. Acts 10:43].

But what does it mean when it says: the "vision and prophecy are sealed" [Dan 9:24 Theod]? That all the prophets announced him and said that he would come and that he would have to suffer. Therefore, since the *prophecy* was fulfilled through his advent, for that reason he said that "the vision and prophecy were sealed." For he himself is the seal of all the prophets, fulfilling everything that the prophets had previously announced about him [cf. Matt 26:56]. For after his advent and his passion, there is no longer any vision or prophet to announce him as coming.

And after a little bit [Tertullian] says:

> Let us see what is the meaning of the other seven and a half weeks, which are distinguished by a separation from the preceding weeks. In what event were they fulfilled? For after Augustus, who lived on after Christ's birth, fifteen years elapsed. He was succeeded by Tiberius Caesar, and he controlled the empire for twenty-two years, seven months and twenty-eight days. In the fifteenth year of his reign, Christ suffered, being about thirty years of age when he suffered [cf. Luke 3:1, 23]. Then there was Gaius Caesar, also named Caligula, who reigned for three years, eight months and thirteen days.[80] Nero reigned for fourteen years, nine months and thirteen days. Galba ruled for seven months and twenty-eight days; Otho for three months and five days; and Vitellius for eight months and twenty-eight days. Vespasian triumphed in his war against the Jews in the first year of his reign. Thus, the years come to a total of fifty-two, plus six months. For he held command for eleven years. And so on the day of his assault [on Jerusalem], the Jews had completed the seventy weeks foretold by Daniel.[81]

What the Hebrews think about this passage, I have touched upon with a few words, leaving the question of the reliability of the statements to those who stated them. In order to make the meaning clearer, therefore, let me express this in a paraphrase:[82]

> O Daniel, know that from this day on which I now speak to you—and that was the first year of the Darius who slew Belshazzar and transferred the kingdom of the Chaldeans to the Medes and Persians [cf. Dan 9:1; 5:30–31]—unto the seventieth week of years, that is, four hundred and ninety years, the following things will happen to your people in stages (*per partes*). First, God, whom you now are vigorously praying to, will be rendered propitious to you, sin shall be blotted out, and transgression shall receive its end [cf. Dan 9:24]. For although the city at present lies deserted and the temple has been destroyed down to its foundations, and the people are beset with grief, yet after no great amount of time there shall be a restoration. And not only shall this

come to pass within these seventy weeks, that the city shall be built and the temple restored, but also the Christ, that is, eternal justice, shall be born, and the vision and the prophet shall be sealed, so that no prophet will be found in Israel, and the saint (*sanctus*) of saints (*sanctorum*) shall be anointed [cf. Dan 9:24]. We read of him in the Psalter: "Therefore God, your God, has anointed you with the oil of gladness above your fellows" [Ps 45:7]. And in another passage he says of himself: "Be ye holy (*sancti*), for I also am holy (*sanctus*)" [Lev 19:2].

Know therefore that from this day on which I now speak to you and make you the promise by the word of God that the people shall return, and Jerusalem shall be restored, sixty-two weeks shall be numbered until the Christ-prince and the perpetual desolation of the temple. And what is more, there shall be another seven weeks in which the two events shall take place in their own order, which I have already mentioned, namely that the people shall return, and the street shall be rebuilt by Nehemiah and Ezra. Therefore, at the end of the weeks, God's sentence shall be accomplished in distressing times, when the temple shall again be destroyed, and the city will be taken captive. For "after the sixty-two weeks the Christ will be killed," and the people who had the intention to deny him[83] "shall not be his"—or, as the Jews say, the empire which they thought they would retain "shall not be his."

And why do I speak of the killing of Christ, and of the people's utter forfeiture of God's help, since the Roman people were going to demolish the city and sanctuary under Vespasian, the prince who was to come [cf. Dan 9:26]? Upon his death, the seven weeks or forty-nine years were completed, and after the city of Aelia was established upon the ruins of Jerusalem, Aelius Hadrian, with his general Tinius Rufus,[84] defeated the rebellious Jews in their war. It was at that time that the victim and sacrifice failed, and the desolation will continue unto the consummation and end of the world [Dan 9:27].

And it does not trouble us, they say, that the seven weeks are numbered first, and afterward the sixty-two, and then one week divided into two parts. For this is an idiom of the Hebrew language, and of Latin speech of the ancients as well, that in counting they give lesser numbers before larger ones.[85] For instance, we ourselves, according to proper usage of our language, now say: "Abraham lived a hundred seventy-five years" [cf. Gen 25:7]. The Hebrews, on the other hand, say: "Abraham lived five years and seventy and one hundred."[86] Therefore, the fulfilment is not as it reads, but it has reached its end when the whole sum is calculated together.

We are not unaware that some [of the Jews] say that what is written about the one week: "He confirmed a covenant with many for one week" [Dan 9:27] is divided up between Vespasian and Hadrian. Thus, according to the history of Josephus, Vespasian and Titus made peace with the Jews for three years and six months.[87] But the three years and six months are reckoned to Hadrian, when Jerusalem was completely overthrown and the Jewish nation was massacred in throngs, to the point that they were even expelled from the borders of Judea.

These are the things that the Hebrews say. They are not greatly concerned that from the first year of Darius, king of the Persians, until the final overthrow of Jerusalem, which happened to them under Hadrian,[88] the amount of time comes to a hundred and seventy-four Olympiads, that is, six hundred ninety-six years, which total up to ninety-nine Hebrew weeks plus three years. This was when Cochba, the leader of the Jews, was put down and Jerusalem was leveled to the ground.[89]

Vision 10[90]

10:1a. *In the third year of Cyrus king of the Persians, a word was revealed to Daniel surnamed Belteshazzar (Balthasar).*

And how is it that we read at the end of the first vision: "And Daniel lived until the first year of Cyrus the king" [Dan 1:21]?[91] Well then, we understand that he held his former office among the Chaldeans and was clothed in purple and fine linen right up until the first year of king Cyrus, when Cyrus overthrew the Chaldeans; and later Daniel began to be with Darius, the son of Ahasuerus, of the seed of the Medes, who held command over the kingdom of the Chaldeans [cf. Dan 9:1]. Or else, it was when Darius had already died, in whose first year Daniel had learned of the mysteries of the seventy weeks [cf. Dan 9:24]. Now the narrative states that he saw these things *in the third year of king Cyrus*.[92]

10:1b. *And it was a true word and great strength.*

This refers either to the strength of the God who will do these things, or to the strength of the prophet who will understand these things.

10:2–3. *In those days I Daniel mourned during the days of three weeks. I ate no desirable bread, and neither flesh nor wine entered into my mouth, neither was I anointed with ointment, until the days of three weeks were accomplished.*

By this example we are taught to abstain from daintier foods during times of fasting—I think that this is what he calls *desirable bread* here—and not to *eat flesh* or *drink wine*, and moreover not to seek out *ointments*. This custom is kept by the Persians and Indians to the present day: they use ointments as a substitute for taking baths. Also, he afflicts his soul for *three weeks*, lest his prayer seem temporary or due to chance. Now anagogically, one should say this, that a person in mourning who laments the absence of the bridegroom *does not eat the desirable bread* "which comes down from heaven" [John 6:58–59], neither does he take in solid food, which is to be understood in the word *flesh*, nor does he *drink the wine* which "gladdens the heart of man" [Ps 104:15], or make his face cheerful with *oil*, as we read in the Psalms: "That he may make the face cheerful with oil" [Ps 104:15]. Fasting like this makes the bride's tears efficacious when the bridegroom is taken away from her [cf. Matt 9:14–15; Mark 2:18–20; Luke 5:34–35]. Daniel also rightly dares to pray to the Lord, for already in the first year of king Cyrus, the captivity of the Jews had been partly released [cf. Ezra 1].

10:4b. *I was by the great river, which is the Tigris.*

Ezekiel also saw a great vision *by a river*, the Chebar (*Chobar*) [Ezek 1:1]. And it was upon the flow of the Jordan that the heavens are opened to the Lord and Savior and to John the Baptist [cf. Matt 3:13–16; Mark 1:9–10; Luke 3:21].

10:5a. *And I lifted my eyes and saw.*

We need to lift up our eyes in order to be able to discern a mystical vision.

10:5b. *And behold a man clothed in linen.*

Instead of *linen*, as Symmachus[93] translated it, Theodotion recorded *baddin*, the Septuagint "fine linen" (*byssus*), Aquila ἐξαίρετα, that is, "exceptional." And instead of what we have rendered in accordance with the Hebrew as *Behold, a man*, Symmachus recorded: "as a man," for he was not a man, but resembled a man.

10:5c. *And his loins (renes) girded with the finest (obryzo) gold.*

The Hebrew term for this is *ophaz*, which Aquila has translated as follows: "And his loins (*lumbi*) were girded with the color of 'ephaz.'"

10:6a. *And his body was like chrysolite.*

For *chrysolite*, which is one of the twelve stones placed in the oracular breastplate of the high priest,[94] the Hebrew has *tharsis*, a word that Theodotion and Symmachus simply transliterated.[95] But the Septuagint called it "the sea," according to what we read in the Psalms: "With a violent wind (*spiritu*) you shatter the ships of tharsis," that is, "of the sea" [Ps 48:7]. Jonah, also, desired to flee [cf. Jonah 1:3], not to Tarsus, the city of Cilicia, as most people suppose, recording it letter for letter, nor to the country of India, as Josephus thinks,[96] but simply out to open sea.[97]

10:7. *And I Daniel alone saw the vision; but the men that were with me did not see it, but an exceedingly great terror fell upon them, and they fled into hiding.*

The apostle Paul also experienced something like this in the Acts of the Apostles, so that while the others did not see it, he *alone* beheld the *vision* [cf. Acts 9:7; 22:6–9].

10:10a. *And behold a hand touched me.*

An angel appears under the figure of a man and lays a human *hand* upon the prophet who is lying there, in order that he might not be terrified, when he sees a body of his own kind.

10:11a. *And he said to me, Daniel, man of desires.*

He is fittingly called *man of desires*, because by his persistent prayers, by the affliction of his body, and by the hardness of his fasts, he desires to know about the future and to learn the secrets of God. Instead of *man of desires*, Symmachus translated it as "desirable man." For every saint has a beauty of soul within himself and is loved by the Lord.

10:12. *And he said to me: Fear not, Daniel, for from the first day when you set your heart to understand that you were to afflict yourself in the sight of your God, your words have been heard; and I have entered to your words.*

On the twenty-fourth day of the first month [cf. Dan 10:4], that is, of Nisan, after three weeks or twenty-one days had elapsed [cf. Dan 10:2], he sees this vision. And he hears from the angel that *on the first day when* he had begun to pray and to *afflict himself in the sight of* the Lord, his *words were heard*. It is asked, If he is heard immediately, it is asked why the angel was not sent to him immediately. By the delay, an opportunity was given to him to pray to the Lord all the more, so that by his effort he might deserve to hear more, in proportion to his greater longing. Now as for the words: *And I have entered to your words*, it has this meaning: "After you began to call upon God's mercy by good works, tears and fasting, I too took the opportunity to *enter in the sight of God* and to pray for you."

10:13a. *But the prince of the kingdom of the Persians resisted me for twenty-one days.*

It appears to me that this is the angel to whose charge the Persians were entrusted, in accordance with what we read in Deuteronomy: "When the Most High divided the nations and scattered the sons of Adam abroad, he established the boundaries of the nations according to the number of God's angels" [Deut 32:8 LXX].[98] These are the *princes* of whom the apostle Paul also says: "Among the perfect we speak wisdom which none of the *princes* of this world have known. For if they had known it, they would not have crucified the Lord of glory" [1 Cor 2:6, 8]. Now *the prince* or angel *of the Persians resisted.* Acting on behalf of the province entrusted to him, he was trying to prevent the entire captive people from being released. And it is possible that although the prophet was heard by the Lord from the first day because he set his heart to understand, the angel was not sent at once to proclaim to him God's permission, for the reason that the *prince of the Persians resisted him for twenty-one days,* by listing the sins of the Jewish people. He claimed that they should justly be kept in captivity and ought not to be released.

10:13b. *And behold Michael, one of the premier princes, came to help me.*

While the angel of the Persians was resisting your prayers and my mission of presenting your requests to God, the angel *Michael,* who is in charge of the people of Israel, *came to help me.* Now by *premier princes* we understand the archangels.

10:13c. *And I remained there with the king of the Persians.*

He calls the angel or prince *king of the Persians* and shows that for a little while he had stayed *with* Michael, who spoke in opposition to the prince of the Persians.

10:14a. *But I have come to teach you what things will befall your people in the last days.*

Because Daniel prayed, he deserves to hear from God what would happen to the *people* of Israel, not in the short term, but *in the last days,* that is, at the consummation of the world.

10:16b. *Lord, at your vision my insides turned within me.*

Theodotion translated this in accordance with what we read in the one hundred and second Psalm: "Bless the Lord, O my soul, and all *my insides*, [bless] his holy name" [Ps 103:1]. For our *insides* must direct their gaze without before we deserve to see a *vision* of God. But when we see a *vision* of God, our *insides* are *turned* and we are wholly involved with those things concerning which it is written in another passage: "All the glory of the king's daughter is inside" [Ps 45:13].

10:19b. *And when he spoke with me, I grew strong and I said: Speak, O lord, for you have strengthened me.*

If the touch of a son of man, as it were, had not *strengthened* him and the terror left his heart, he could not have heard the mysteries of God. And that is why he now says: *Since you have strengthened me, speak, O Lord*; for you have brought it about that I can both hear and understand what you are saying.

10:20a. *And he said: Do you know why I have come to you? And now I will return to fight against the prince of the Persians.*

What he means is this: "I have" indeed "come to teach you" [Dan 10:14] that your prayers have been heard; but *I will return to* fight, in the sight of God, *against the prince of the Persians*, who is unwilling that your people be released from captivity.

10:20b. *For when I went forth, the prince of the Greeks appeared and entered.*

He says, "I myself *went forth* from God's presence to announce to you 'what will befall your people in the last days' [Dan 10:14]; and yet I am still not tranquil, since the prince of the Persians stands and speaks against your prayers and my mission [cf. Dan 10:13]. And behold, *the prince of the Greeks*, that is, of the Macedonians, came and *entered* into God's presence, in order to accuse the prince of the Medes and Persians, that the kingdom of the Macedonians might succeed in their place." The mysteries of God are truly wonderful, for when the Jewish people were released from captivity, Alexander, king of the Macedonians, killed Darius and overthrew the kingdom of the Persians and Medes, and *the prince of the Greeks* conquered the prince of the Persians.

10:21a. *Nevertheless I will announce to you what is expressed in the Scripture of truth.*

Here is the order of the reading: "The affair is still in doubt. For even though you are praying to the Lord and I am presenting your prayers, yet the prince of the Persians stands in opposition and is unwilling to see the people to be released from captivity. But because the prince of the Greeks has come, and in the meantime is fighting against the prince of the Persians, in the midst of their battle, *I*, who *have Michael there as a helper*, will *report to you the coming events that God has foretold* to me and has ordered me to tell you." And let no one raise the trivial objection that he says "the prince of the Greeks," that is Ἑλλήων, rather than "prince of the Macedonians"; for Alexander, king of the Macedonians, did not take up arms against the Persians until he had first overthrown Greece and subjected it to his power.[99]

10:21b. *And no one is my helper in all these things, except Michael, your prince.*

He says, "I am that angel who presents your prayers to God, and there is no other *who is my helper* in praying to God on your behalf, *except* the archangel *Michael*, to whom the Jewish people have been entrusted. And meanwhile, at this time the prince of the Greeks and I are battling in a common effort against the prince of the Persians." We should review ancient history and consider whether perhaps he means that time when the Persians were conquered by the Greeks.

According to the common (*vulgatam*) edition,[100] this single vision is thought to extend to the end of the book, namely, that vision which appeared to Daniel in the third year of Cyrus, king of the Persians [cf. Dan 10:1; 11:1 LXX]. On the other hand, according to the Hebrew truth, the sections that follow are separate visions, and they are written in a [chronologically] inverted order.[101] We have spoken about the reasons for this above.[102] For the things that are written here are said to have occurred in the first year of the Darius [cf. Dan 11:1] who overthrew Belshazzar (Balthasar) [cf. Dan 5:30–31], not in the third year of Cyrus [cf. Dan 10:1].[103]

11:1. *And from the first year of Darius the Mede*[104] *I stood up that he might be strengthened and confirmed.*

Daniel says: "*From the first year* of king *Darius*, who overthrew the Chaldeans and delivered me from the hand of my enemies, as far as he was able to—he even sealed the lions' den with his ring for my protection [cf. Dan 6:17], to keep my adversaries from killing me [cf. Dan 6:18]—*I stood up* before God [cf. Dan 9:3–4], and I asked for his mercy for the one who had singled me out with esteem, that either *he* or his kingdom *might be strengthened and confirmed*. And since I persevered in prayer, I learned the following things from the Lord's response." Now it is customary for the prophets to introduce personas suddenly and without any prefatory words. For example, there is the following instance of this in the thirty-first Psalm. For when the prophet had asked God and said: "You are my refuge from the tribulation which has beset me; O my Exultation, deliver me from those who now surround me" [Ps 32:7], suddenly the persona of the Lord is introduced who replies: "I will give you understanding, and I will instruct you in the way in which you shall go; I will fix my eyes upon you" [Ps 32:8]. So also here then, when the prophet reports: *From the first year of Darius the Mede, I stood up and pleaded that he might be strengthened* and that his rule *might be confirmed,* God suddenly responds:

11:2. *And now I shall proclaim the truth to you.*

And the meaning is this: "Because you want to know what shall happen to the kings of Persia, hear the order of events and listen to what you seek."[105]

11:2b. *And behold, there shall stand three more kings in Persia, and the fourth shall be enriched exceedingly above them all, and when he shall have grown mighty by his riches, he shall stir up all against the kingdom of Greece.*

He says that *four kings* shall arise *in Persia* after Cyrus: Cambyses, the son of Cyrus; and Smerdis the Magus,[106] who married Panthaptes, the daughter of Cambyses. Then, when he was killed by seven Magi and Darius had taken command in his place, the same Panthaptes married Darius; and by him she gave birth to a son, Xerxes, who was the most powerful and richest king. He led an army that could not be counted against Greece and performed those deeds which the Greek histories relate.[107] For under prince Callias[108] he set Athens on fire, and at that time he waged the war at Thermopylae and the naval battle at Salamis. This was when Sophocles and Euripides were regarded as famous,[109] and Themistocles[110] fled in exile to Persia, where he died as a result of drinking the blood of a bull. Therefore, that writer[111] is in error who records as the *fourth* king that Darius who was defeated by Alexander, for he was not the *fourth,* but the fourteenth king of the Persians after Cyrus.[112] It was in the seventh year of his empire that Alexander defeated and slew him. And one should note that after he has listed four kings of the Persians after Cyrus, he passed over nine others and moved on to Alexander. For the Spirit of prophecy was not concerned about following the historical sequence but only in touching upon all that was remarkable.

11:3–4a. *But there shall rise up a strong king, and he shall rule with great power, and he shall do what he pleases. And when he shall have stood, his kingdom shall be broken.*

He is clearly speaking of Alexander the Great, king of the Macedonians, who was the son of Philip.[113] For after he had overcome the Illyrians and Thracians, conquered Greece and destroyed Thebes, he crossed over into Asia, put Darius's generals to flight, and captured the city of Sardis. Then he captured India and founded the city of Alexandria. He died by poisoning in Babylon at the age of thirty-two, in the twelfth year of his empire [cf. 1 Macc 1:7].

11:4b. *And it shall be divided toward the four winds of heaven, but not to his posterity nor according to the power with which he ruled.*

After Alexander, his kingdom was *divided toward the four winds*, namely, to the east, the west, the south, and the north. For in Egypt, that is, toward the south, Ptolemy the son of Lagos was the first to reign; in Macedonia, that is, toward the west, the Philip who was also called Aridaeus, a brother of Alexander;[114] Seleucus Nicanor[115] was the king of Syria, Babylon, and the upper regions, that is, toward the east; Antigonus was king of Asia, Pontus, and the other provinces in that region, that is, toward the north.[116] We say this according to the regions of the entire world; but a person who is in Judea regards Syria as toward the north and Egypt as toward the south. But as for what he says: *But not to his posterity*, this means that Alexander would have no children, but rather, *his kingdom would be torn to pieces among strangers, except* [Dan 11:4c] for his brother Philip, who kept control of Macedonia. *Nor according to his power with which he ruled.* For when it was divided into four parts, the kingdom was weaker, for they constantly fought among themselves and were raving with an internal fury.

11:4c. *For his kingdom shall be torn in pieces, even among strangers, with the exception of these.*

Besides the four kingdoms of Macedonia, Asia, Syria, and Egypt, the kingdom of the Macedonians was *torn in pieces even among* other rather obscure rulers and petty kings. Now he means Perdicas,[117] Craterus,[118] and Lysimachus,[119] for Cappadocia, Armenia, Bithynia, Heracleia, Bosphorus, and other provinces withdrew from the authority of the Macedonians and set up different kings for themselves.

11:5a. *And the king of the south shall be strengthened.*

He means Ptolemy, son of Lagos, who was the first to rule in Egypt. He was very wise, courageous, and wealthy, and he possessed such great power that he was able to restore Pyrrhus, King of Epirus, to his kingdom, after he had been driven out. He also seized Cyprus and Phoenicia, and after he had conquered Demetrius, the son of Antigonus, he restored to Seleucus that portion of his kingdom which

Antigonus had taken away from him. He also took control of Caria[120] and many islands, cities, and districts. There is no need at present to write about these matters. Now he leaves the other kingdoms aside, namely, Macedonia and Asia, and only narrates about the kings of Egypt and Syria, since Judea is located in between them, and it was held now by one line of kings and now by the other, and it is not the aim of Holy Scripture to compose external history independent of the Jews, but only that which is connected with the people of Israel.

11:5b. *And one of his princes shall prevail over him, and he shall rule with great authority, for his dominion shall be great.*

This refers to Ptolemy Philadelphus, the second king of Egypt and the son of Ptolemy I.[121] It was under him that the Seventy (*septuaginta*) translators of Alexandria are said to have translated the Holy Scripture into the Greek language. He also sent many treasures to Jerusalem for the high priest Eleazar, and votive vessels for the temple.[122] Demetrius of Phalerum was in charge of his library. Among the Greeks he was regarded as an orator and philosopher. Philadelphus is said to have possessed such great power that he surpassed his father Ptolemy. For history relates that he had two hundred thousand foot soldiers, twenty thousand cavalry, two thousand chariots, and four hundred elephants, which he was the first to bring in from Ethiopia. He also had fifteen hundred longboats, which are now called Liburnians, and a thousand others to transport food for the troops. Moreover, he had a great amount of gold and silver, so that he received a yearly revenue from Egypt that came to fourteen thousand eight hundred talents of silver, as well as grain in the amount of fifteen hundred thousand *artabae*,[123] a measure that comes to three and one third pecks.[124]

11:6. *And after the end of years, they shall be in a league together* (or, as Theodotion translated it: *And after his years, they shall be mingled together*). *And the daughter of the king of the south shall come to the king of the north to make friendship; and she shall not obtain strength of arm, nor shall her seed stand. And she herself shall be handed over, and her young men who brought her and who were strengthening her in the times.*

As we said,[125] Seleucus, surnamed Nicanor, was the first to rule over Syria.[126] The second [king] was Antiochus, who was called Soter.[127] The third was Antiochus himself, who was called Θεός, that is "God."[128] He was the one who waged numerous wars against Ptolemy Philadelphus, who was the second to hold command over the Egyptians. He also fought with all the Babylonians and the men of the East.[129] And so, *after many years*, Ptolemy Philadelphus wanted to bring an end to this troublesome conflict, so he gave his daughter, named Bernice, in marriage to Antiochus, who had two sons by a previous wife named Laodice, namely, Seleucus surnamed Callinicus and the second Antiochus. And Philadelphus conducted her as far as Pelusium and bestowed countless thousands in gold and silver by way of a dowry. This is why he was called *Phernophoros* or Dowry-giver. But as for Antiochus, even though he had said he would regard Bernice as his royal consort and keep Laodice in the status of a concubine, after a long time he was overcome by love to restore Laodice to the royal palace along with her children. But she feared the wavering heart of her husband, that he might bring back Bernice, and so she killed him by means of her servants by poisoning.[130] And she handed over Bernice and the son whom she had born of Antiochus to be killed by Icadio and Genneus, princes of Antioch, and then set up her elder son, Seleucus Callinicus, as king in his father's place.

And this is what is being talked about now: *after* many *years,* Ptolemy Philadelphus and Antiochus Θεός will *make a friendship; and the daughter of the king of the south,* that is, of Ptolemy, *will go to the king of the north,* that is, to Antiochus, as she joins in *friendship* between her father and her husband. And it says: *she will not* be able *to obtain, nor shall her seed stand* in the kingdom of Syria; but instead, both Bernice herself and *the men who had brought her* shall be killed. And also the king, Antiochus, *who had strengthened her,* that is, through whom she could have prevailed, is killed by his wife's poison.

11:7–9. *And an offspring of the bud of her roots shall rise up and he shall come with an army and shall enter into the province of the king of the north, and he shall abuse them, and shall prevail. Moreover he shall carry away captive into Egypt their gods, and their graven things, and their precious vessels of gold and silver. He shall prevail against the king of the north. And the king of the south shall enter into the kingdom, and shall return to his own land.*

After the killing of Bernice and the death of her father, Ptolemy Philadelphus, in Egypt, her brother, who was also named Ptolemy and surnamed Εὐεργέτης, succeeded to the throne as the third [of his dynasty], from the *offspring* and the *bud* of the same *root* as she was, because he was her brother.[131] *He came with* a great *army* and *entered into the province of the king of the north,* that is, of Seleucus surnamed Callinicus, who, together with his mother Laodice, reigned in Syria, and he *abused them and prevailed,* to such an extent that he captured Syria, Cilicia, and the upper regions beyond the Euphrates, and nearly all of Asia as well. And when he heard that a rebellion was stirring in *Egypt*, he plundered the kingdom of Seleucus and carried off forty thousand talents of silver and also *precious vessels* and images of the *gods* to the amount of two thousand five hundred. Among them were the same images that Cambyses had carried off to Persia at the time when he captured Egypt.[132] After all, the Egyptian peoples were devoted to idolatry, for when he had brought back their gods to them after so many years, they called him Εὐεργέτην (Benefactor). And indeed, he himself *prevailed* over Syria, but he handed over Cilicia to the governance of his friend, Antiochus, and the provinces beyond the Euphrates he handed over to Xanthippus, another of his generals.

11:10. *But his sons shall be provoked, and they shall assemble a multitude of numerous armies; and he shall come with haste like a flood, and he shall return and be stirred up, and he shall join battle with his strength [12b. And his heart will be lifted up].*[133]

After the flight and death of Seleucus Callinicus, his two sons, the Seleucus surnamed Ceraunus and the Antiochus who was called the Great,[134] were *provoked* by a hope of victory and so they *assembled an army* to avenge their father, and took up arms against Ptolemy Philopator.[135] And when, through the treachery of Nicanor and Apaturius, the elder brother, Seleucus, was slain in Phrygia in the third year of his reign, the army that was in Syria summoned to the throne from Babylon his brother, Antiochus the Great. And this is why he now adds that "two" *sons* were *provoked* and *assembled a multitude of numerous armies.* But one of them, Antiochus the Great, *came* from Babylon to Syria, which at that time was held by Ptolemy Philopator, the son of Euergetes, who was the fourth king to rule in Egypt. And after he had fought against his generals, or rather had by the betrayal of Theodotius obtained possession of Syria, which had already been held by a succession of kings from Egypt, he became so emboldened by his contempt for Philopator's luxurious manner of life and for the magical arts to which he was said to be enslaved, that on his own initiative he tried to wage war on the Egyptians.

11:11–12. *And the king of the south, being provoked, shall go forth and shall fight against the king of the north; and he shall prepare an exceeding great multitude, and a multitude shall be given into his hand. And he shall capture a multitude, and his heart shall be lifted up, and he shall cast down many thousands, but he shall not prevail.*

For Ptolemy surnamed Philopator lost Syria through the betrayal of Theodotius. He gathered together a very numerous *multitude* and entered *against* Antiochus the Great, whom [Daniel] now calls *king of the north*, in accordance with the location of Egypt and the province of Judea. For owing to the nature of the country, this place is situated partly to the south and partly to the north. For instance, if we speak of Judea, it lies to the north of Egypt and to the south of Syria. And so, when he had joined battle near the town of Raphia, which is at the entrance of Egypt, Antiochus lost his entire army and was almost *captured* as he fled across the desert.[136] And when he had withdrawn from Syria, the conflict was finally concluded by means of a treaty and certain conditional terms.[137] And this is what the Scripture is speaking of here: Ptolemy Philopator *shall cast down many thousands, but he shall not prevail*, for he was unable to capture his adversary. As for what follows: 11:13–14a. *And the king of the north shall return and shall prepare a multitude much greater than before, and in the end of times and years he shall come in haste with a large army and immense resources. And in those times many shall rise up against the king of the south.*

This is signifying Antiochus the Great, who despised the sloth of Ptolemy Philopator—for the latter had fallen desperately in love with a lute player named Agathoclea and also her brother, and he kept Agathocles himself as his male concubine and afterward appointed him as general of Egypt.[138] From the upper regions of Babylon, he assembled an army that surpassed belief. And when Ptolemy Philopator died, Antiochus broke the treaty and set his army in motion against Philopator's four-year-old son, who was called Ἐπιφανὴς. For the dissoluteness and arrogance of Agathocles was so great that those provinces which had previously been subjected to Egypt rose up in rebellion, and even Egypt itself was disturbed by rebellions. Moreover, Philip, King of Macedon, and Antiochus the Great made peace with each other and engaged in a common struggle against Agathocles and Ptolemy Epiphanes, on the understanding that each of them should annex to his own dominion those cities of Ptolemy which lay nearest to them.[139] And so this is what it says, that *many shall rise up against the king of the south*, that is, against Ptolemy Epiphanes, who was just a boy.[140]

11:14b. *And the sons of the transgressors of your people shall be lifted up to fulfill the vision, and they shall fall to ruin.*

While Antiochus the Great and Ptolemy's generals were fighting against each other, Judea, which is situated in between them, was torn apart into opposing parties, some favoring Antiochus, others Ptolemy. Finally, the priest Onias fled to Egypt, taking a large number of Jews along with him. Ptolemy welcomed him honorably, and he received that region known as Heliopolis. With the king's permission, he built a temple in Egypt like the temple of the Jews.[141] It remained standing until the reign of Vespasian, two hundred and fifty years. But the city itself, which was known as the City of Onias, was leveled to the ground because of the war that the Jews waged later on against the Romans, and no trace of either the city or that temple remains. Therefore, on the occasion of Onias's high priesthood, countless swarms of Jews fled to Egypt. At that time, the land was also filled with a large number of Cyrenians, for Onias claimed that he was fulfilling the prophecy of Isaiah, who wrote: "There shall be an altar of the Lord in Egypt, and a placard of the Lord in its boundaries" [Isa 19:19].[142] And this is what he is saying now: *The sons of the transgressors of your people*—who forsook the law of the Lord and wanted to offer sacrifices to God in a place other than the one he had commanded [cf. Deut 12:5–6]—*will be lifted up* in pride and will boast that they were fulfilling the *vision*— that is, God's command—*but they shall fall to ruin*, for later on, both the temple and city shall be destroyed. And while Antiochus was in control of Judea, a leader of the Ptolemaic party called Scopas, son of Aetholus, was sent. He fought bravely against Antiochus, captured Judea, and returned to Egypt, leading the nobles of Ptolemy's party back with him.[143]

11:15–16. *And the king of the north shall come and shall cast up a mound, and he shall capture the most fortified cities; and the arms (*brachia*) of the south shall not withstand, and his chosen ones shall rise up to resist, and there shall be no strength. And he shall come upon him and do according to his own pleasure, and there shall be none to stand against his face. And he shall stand in the illustrious land, and it shall be destroyed by his hand.*

For Antiochus wanted to retake Judea, and a large number of cities of Syria. He initiated a battle with Scopas, Ptolemy's general, near the sources of the Jordan where the present-day city of Paneas was founded, and he put him to flight.[144] And with ten thousand armed men, he besieged him when he was shut up in Sidon. In order to liberate him, Ptolemy dispatched the famous generals Eropus, Menocles, and Damoxenus, but he was unable to lift the siege until Scopas was overcome by famine and surrendered.[145] He was sent away with his comrades, stripped bare.[146] As for the statement: *He shall cast up a mound*, this indicates that Antiochus would besiege the garrison of Scopas in the citadel of Jerusalem for a long time, while the Jews give their support, and also capture other *cities*, which had formerly been under the control of the Ptolemaic faction—of Syria, Cilicia, and Lycia. For at that time the cities of Aphrodisias, Soloe, Zephyrion,

Mallos, Anemurium, Selinus, Coracesium, Corycus, Andriace, Limyra, Patra, Xanthus, and lastly Ephesus were all captured. Both Greek and Roman histories tell of all these things.[147]

As for what he added: *And he shall stand in the illustrious land, and it shall be consumed* (or, accomplished) *by his hand,* the *illustrious land,* or, as the Septuagint translated it, "the land of his will," that is, which pleases God, signifies Judea, and particularly Jerusalem, to which Antiochus pursued those men of Scopas's party who had been honorably welcomed there. Instead of *illustrious land,* as Aquila translated it, the one whom we followed on this passage, Theodotion simply recorded the Hebrew word itself, *Sabir.* Instead of that, Symmachus translated it "land of force."

11:17a. *And he shall set his face in order to come and take control of all his kingdom, and he shall deal with him justly. And he shall give him the daughter of women to overthrow him (that is, Ptolemy, or else to overthrow it, that is, his kingdom).*

Antiochus not only wanted to take possession of Syria, Cilicia, Lycia, and the other provinces that had belonged to Ptolemy's party, but to extend his kingdom to Egypt too. By means of Eucles of Rhodes, he betrothed his *daughter* Cleopatra to young Ptolemy in the seventh year of his reign; and in his thirteenth year he handed her over, having given her all of Coele-Syria and Judea as a dowry.[148] But he calls her *daughter of women* by pleonasm,[149] just as the poet says: "Thus she spoke with her mouth,"[150] and: "And with these ears did I drink in her voice."[151]

11:17b–19. *And she shall not stand, neither shall she be his. And he shall turn his face to the islands and shall capture many; and she shall cause the prince of her reproach to cease, and his reproach shall be turned upon him. And he shall turn his face to the empire of his own land; and he shall stumble and fall, and shall not be found.*

For he was unable to take possession of Egypt because Ptolemy Epiphanes and his generals sensed deceit and acted very cautiously. And besides, Cleopatra inclined more to her husband's side than to her father's.[152] Consequently, he turned himself to Asia and fought a naval battle against a large number of *islands.* He *captured* Rhodes, Samos, Colophon, Phocea, and many other *islands.*[153] But he was opposed by [Lucius] Scipio Nasica and also his brother, Publius Scipio Africanus, who had defeated Hannibal.[154] For since the consul Nasica, the brother of Africanus, was rather lacking in talent, the [Roman] Senate was unwilling to entrust to him a war against an extremely powerful king [Antiochus]. Africanus offered a voluntary delegation to make up for the harm caused by his brother. Thus, Antiochus was defeated and ordered to confine his rule to within the Taurus mountains.[155] And so he took refuge in Apamia and Susa and reached the furthest cities of his realm. And during a war against the Elymaeans, he was destroyed together with his entire army.[156] And this is what the Scripture is speaking of now, when it states that he would *capture many islands*, and yet because of the Roman conqueror he would lose the kingdom of Asia; and that his *reproach shall be turned upon* that one's head; and that ultimately he would flee from Asia and turn back *to the empire of his own land*, and would *stumble and fall*, and his place *would not be found*.[157]

11:20. *And there shall stand up in his place one most vile and unworthy of kingly honor, and in a few days he shall be destroyed, not in rage nor in a battle.*[158]

He is speaking of Seleucus, surnamed Philopator, the son of Antiochus the Great, who did nothing worthy of Syria or of his father's kingdom and perished ingloriously without any battles. Porphyry, however, claims that it was not this Seleucus who is referred to, but rather Ptolemy Epiphanes, who contrived a plot against Seleucus and prepared an army to fight against him,[159] and he was killed by poisoning by his own generals because when someone asked him where he was going to get the money for the great enterprises he was planning, he answered that his wealth consisted in his friends. When this remark spread among the people, the generals became afraid that he would take their property from them and therefore killed him by the evil arts. Yet how could Ptolemy be said to *stand in the place* of Antiochus the Great, since he did nothing of the sort, especially since the Septuagint translated: "And an offspring shall stand from his root" (that is, 'from his bud and seed') "who will strike the glory of the empire, and within a few days he shall be destroyed without wrath and battle"? The Hebrews want the one *most vile and unworthy of kingly honor* to be understood of Trypho [cf. 1 Macc 12:39ff.; 13:31–32].[160] He was the boy's [Antiochus VI's] tutor and seized the throne illegally.

11:21. *And there shall stand up in his place one despised, and the kingly honor shall not be given to him; and he shall come secretly and shall obtain the kingdom by fraud.*[161]

Up to this point, the historical order is pursued, and between Porphyry and ourselves there is no controversy. But the rest that follows all the way to the end of the book, Porphyry interprets as applying to the person of the Antiochus who was surnamed Epiphanes, the brother of Seleucus and the son of Antiochus the Great, who reigned in Syria for eleven years after Seleucus, and he took possession of Judea. It was under him that the persecution of God's law and the wars of the Maccabees are reported.[162] But our people think that all these things are spoken prophetically of the antichrist, who will come at the end time. And when the following objection is seemingly raised to our people, why has the prophetic discourse left such great men behind in the interval and gone from Seleucus to the end of the world, they answer that in the earlier historical account, where mention was made of the Persian kings, he recorded only four Persian kings after Cyrus of the Persians, and many who came in the interval were simply skipped over, so as to come suddenly to Alexander, king of the Macedonians.[163] And our people say that this is the custom of Holy Scripture, not to report everything, but to set forth what seems to be more important. And although many of the things which we will read and comment upon later do fit the person of Antiochus [Epiphanes], our people want him to be regarded as a type of the antichrist, and those things which preceded in part in respect to him are to be fulfilled in full in respect to the antichrist. And they say that this is the custom of Holy Scripture, to anticipate the truth of future things in types. This accords with what is said of our Lord and Savior in the seventy-first Psalm, which is entitled "of Solomon," and yet not everything that is said about him can be made to fit Solomon. For he did not "remain with the sun and before the moon throughout all generations" [Ps 72:5]; nor did he "rule from sea to sea, or from the river unto the ends of the earth" [Ps 72:8]; nor did "all the nations serve him" [Ps 72:11], nor did "his name continue before the sun" [Ps 72:17]; nor were "all the tribes of earth blessed in him" [Ps 72:17], nor did "all nations magnify him" [Ps 72:17]. But in part and, as it were, in a shadow and image of the truth, these things were anticipated in Solomon, in order that they might be more perfectly fulfilled in our Lord and Savior. Therefore, just as the Savior has Solomon and the other saints as a type of his advent, so also one should believe that the antichrist rightly had as a type of himself the utterly wicked king Antiochus, who persecuted the saints and violated the temple. Let us therefore follow the order of the exposition and, in accordance with both ways of explaining it, make brief notes on what the words mean to our opponents, and what they mean to our people.[164] Our opponents say the following:

The one who was to *stand up in place of* Seleucus was his brother, Antiochus Epiphanes [cf. 1 Macc 1:10; 2 Macc 4:7]. The party in Syria who favored Ptolemy would *not* at first *grant him the kingly honor,* but he later *obtained the rule* of Syria by a pretense of clemency. And "the arms (*brachia*) of the fighter" [Dan 11:22] Ptolemy, as the one who devastated everything, "were overcome and broken before the face" [Dan 11:22] of Antiochus. Now *arms* refers to "strength," and this is why an army's multitude is called a "hand."[165] And not only did he conquer Ptolemy *by fraud*, but also he overcame by treachery "the leader of the covenant" [Dan 11:22], that is, Judas Maccabaeus.

Or[166] it means the following: when he had obtained peace with Ptolemy and he himself had become *the leader of the covenant*, later he contrived a plot against him. Now the Ptolemy meant here was not Epiphanes, who was the fifth Ptolemy to reign in Egypt, but Ptolemy Philometor, the son of Antiochus' sister, Cleopatra; and so Antiochus was his maternal uncle. After Cleopatra's death Eulaius, the eunuch who was Philometor's tutor, and Leneus ruled Egypt. When they attempted to regain Syria, which Antiochus had seized *by fraud*, a battle broke out between the boy Ptolemy and his uncle.[167] And when they joined battle between Pelusium and Mt. Casius, Ptolemy's *princes* were defeated.[168] But then Antiochus spared the boy and feigned *friendship*. He "went up" [Dan 11:23] to Memphis and there received the crown after the Egyptian manner. Claiming that he was looking out for the boy's affairs, he subjected all Egypt to himself "with only a small people" [Dan 11:23], and he "entered rich and plentiful cities" [Dan 11:24]. "And he did things which his fathers had never done, nor his fathers' fathers" [Dan 11:24]. For no king of Syria had so devastated Egypt and "scattered" all their wealth [cf. Dan 11:24]. And he was so shrewd that he even overcame *by his fraud* the well-laid plans of those who were the boy-king's *princes*.

This is what Porphyry says, following Sutorius.[169] He pursues his interpretation in a very tangled discourse, which we have summarized very briefly.

Now our people interpret this better and more correctly. They say that the antichrist will do these things at the end of the world. He is destined to arise from *a small* nation [cf. Dan 11:23], that is, from the Jewish *people*, and he will be so lowly and, what is more, *despised* that he will not be given *kingly honor*. But by means of treachery and fraud [cf. 2 John 7; Rev 20:8; 2 Thess 2:9–10], he will *obtain* the government [cf. Dan 11:21]; and by him shall *the arms of the fighting* Roman people be *overcome and broken* [cf. Dan 11:22]. And he will do this by pretending to be *the leader of the covenant* (*foederis*) [cf. Dan 11:22], that is, of the law and covenant (*testamenti*) of God. And *he shall enter into the richest of cities and shall do what his fathers never did, nor his fathers' fathers* [Dan 11:24]. For none of the Jews except the antichrist has ever ruled over the whole world.[170] And he shall form a design against [cf. Dan 11:25] the strongest plans of the saints and shall do everything for a time, for as long as God's will permits him to do these things.[171]

11:25–26. *And his strength and his heart shall be stirred up against the king of the south with a great army; and the king of the south shall be provoked to go to war with many exceedingly strong auxiliary forces; and they shall not stand, for they shall form designs against him. And they that eat bread with him shall destroy him; and his army shall be overthrown, and many shall fall down slain.*

Porphyry interprets this of Antiochus, who set out *with a great army* on a campaign against Ptolemy, his sister's son [cf. 1 Macc 1:18–19].[172] But *the king of the south*, that is, the generals of Ptolemy, will also be *provoked to go to war with many exceedingly powerful auxiliary forces*, but they will not be able to withstand the fraudulent *designs* of Antiochus, who feigned peace with his sister's son and ate *bread with him*, and afterward occupied Egypt.

Our people, on the other hand, interpret all these things of the antichrist, in accordance with the sense given above. He will be born of the Jewish people and will come from Babylon. He will first vanquish the king of Egypt, who is one of the three horns of which we have already spoken earlier [cf. Dan 7:8].[173]

11:27–28a. *And the heart of the two kings shall be to do evil, and they shall speak the lie at one table; and they will not succeed, because as yet the end is for another time. And he shall return into his land with much riches.*

No one doubts that Antiochus made peace with Ptolemy and feasted with him and forged ruses and did not *succeed*, since he was unable to obtain his kingdom, but was expelled by Ptolemy's soldiers.

But since Scripture now says that there were *two kings* whose *heart* was deceitful and who *did evil* mutually against each other, it cannot be proved that this was the historical fulfillment. For how could Ptolemy, a small child who was *deceived* by Antiochus's *fraud*, have devised evil against him? This is why our people insist that all these things be referred to the antichrist and to the king of Egypt whom he will first overcome.[174]

11:28b–30a. *And his heart shall be against the holy covenant (testamentum); and he shall act and shall return into his own land. At the appointed time, he shall return, and he shall come to the south, and the latter [battle] shall not be like the former. And the triremes and the Romans shall come, and he shall be struck* (or, as another has translated it, *and they shall threaten him*).[175]

Both the Greek and the Roman histories relate that after Antiochus had been expelled from Egypt and had *returned*, he came to Judea, that is, *against the holy covenant*, and that he robbed the temple and removed an immense amount of gold; and then, having stationed a garrison of Macedonians in the citadel, he *returned to his own land* [cf. 1 Macc 1:20–24; 2 Macc 5:11–21].[176] And then two years later he again gathered an army against Ptolemy and *came to the south*. And while he was besieging at Alexandria the brothers of Ptolemy and sons of Cleopatra, whose uncle he was, some Roman envoys came, one of whom was Marcus Popilius Laenas. And when he found Antiochus standing on the shore and gave the senatorial decree to him by which he was ordered to withdraw from those who were friends of the Roman people and to content himself with his own domain, then Antiochus postponed his reply in order to consult with his friends. But Laenas is said to have made a circle in the sand with the staff which he held in his hand, and to have drawn it around the king, saying, "The senate and Roman people order you to make answer in this very spot as to what your decision is." At these words, Antiochus became terrified and said: "If the senate and the Roman people have voted for this, then it is necessary to withdraw." And so he immediately moved his army. But he is said to have been *struck*, not that he perished but that he lost all the greatness of his pride.

As for the antichrist, no one doubts that he will fight *against the holy covenant*, and that when he first makes war against the king of Egypt, he will be frightened off by the assistance of the Romans on their behalf. But these things came first as images under Antiochus Epiphanes, so that this most criminal king, who persecuted God's people, prefigures the antichrist, who will persecute the people of

Christ.[177] And this is why many of our people think that the antichrist will be Domitius Nero,[178] due to the extent of [his] savagery and depravity.[179]

11:30b. *And he shall return and shall be indignant against the covenant of the sanctuary; and he shall act and return and devise plans concerning those who have abandoned the covenant of the sanctuary.*
We read of these matters in more detail in the deeds of the Maccabees.[180] For after the Romans expelled him from Egypt, he came in *indignation against the covenant of the sanctuary* and was invited by those who had *abandoned* the law of God and mingled in the religious rites of the pagans [cf. 1 Macc 1:20–28].

But this is to be more fully accomplished under the antichrist, who *shall be indignant against the covenant* of God and *shall devise plans* against those whom he wants to see forsake the law of God. And thus, Aquila has translated it in a more meaningful way: "And he shall devise plans to have the pact of the sanctuary abandoned."

11:31. *And arms (*brachia*) will rise from him and defile the sanctuary of strength; and they shall take away the continual sacrifice and shall place the abomination in the desolation.* (Instead of *arms*, another translator rendered it "seeds," so that it signified root and offspring.)

Now they claim that the persons mentioned are those who were sent by Antiochus two years after he had plundered the temple, in order to exact tribute from the Jews and to eliminate the worship of God, and to set up an image of Jupiter Olympius in the temple at Jerusalem [cf. 1 Macc 1:29–30; 2 Macc 6:1–2], and also statues of Antiochus, which he now calls *the abomination* of *desolation*.[181] This happened when the burnt offering and *continual sacrifice* were taken away.

But our people contend that all these things transpired in a preliminary way as a type of the antichrist, who will take his seat in the temple of God and make himself out as God [cf. Matt 24:15; 2 Thess 2:3–4].

The Jews, on the other hand, would have us understand these things as referring neither to Antiochus Epiphanes nor to the antichrist, but to the Romans, of whom it was said earlier: "And triremes" (or Italians) "shall come, and also Romans, and he shall be humbled" [Dan 11:30]. After a long time, it says, king Vespasian shall arise from the Romans themselves, who had come to Ptolemy's aid and threatened Antiochus [cf. Dan 11:30 lemma variant]. His *arms* and *seed* will rise up, namely, his son Titus with his army, and *they will defile the sanctuary and remove the continual sacrifice*; and they will hand the temple over to eternal desolation. For *siim* and *chethim*, which we translated as "triremes" and "Romans," the Hebrews would have us understand "Italians" and "Romans."[182]

11:32. *And ungodly men shall deceitfully feign against the covenant. But the people who know their God shall prevail and act* (faciet).

We read this also in Maccabees, that there were some who *feigned* that they were the guardians of God's law, and later they *acted* (*fecerint*) with the Gentiles; but others remained in their religion [cf. 1 Macc 1:52, 62].

I think this will also transpire in the times of the antichrist, when "the love of many shall grow cold" [Matt 24:12].[183] The Lord says of them in the Gospel: "Do you think that the Son of man, when he comes, will he find faith upon the earth?" [Luke 18:8].

11:33. *And they that are learned among the people shall teach many and they shall fall under the sword, fire, captivity, and the pillaging of days.*

The Books of Maccabees relate the great sufferings of the Jews under Antiochus and stand as a testimony to their triumph. For they endured *fire* and *sword*, slavery, and *pillaging*, and even the ultimate penalty for keeping the law of God [cf. 2 Macc 6:18–31; 7:1–42].

No one doubts that these things will happen under the antichrist, while many shall resist his authority and flee away in different directions.

The Hebrews interpret these things of the final destruction of the temple, which occurred under Vespasian and Titus. They say that there were *very many* of their people who *knew their God* and were killed for keeping his law.[184]

11:34–35. *And when they shall have fallen, they shall be relieved by a small help; and a very large number shall be joined to them deceitfully. And some of the learned shall fall, to be melted and chosen and made white even to the determined time, because there shall yet be another time.*

Porphyry is of the view that the *small help* signifies Mattathias. From the village of Modein, he rebelled against the generals of Antiochus and attempted to preserve the worship of the true God [cf. 1 Macc 2:1–70].[185] He says:

> But he calls him a *small help* because Mattathias died in battle; and later his son Judas, who was called Maccabaeus, fell fighting [cf. 1 Macc 9:17–18]; and the rest of his brothers were taken in by the deceit of their adversaries [cf. 1 Macc 12:39–40]. Read the books of Maccabees.[186] Now all these

things happened, he says, that the saints might be tested and *chosen* and *made white until the determined time.* For the victory was postponed *until another time.*

Our people think the *small help* is to be understood under the antichrist, that the saints shall be gathered together to resist him, and they shall make use of *small help* [cf. Rev 13:10; 14:12], and afterward *very many of the learned shall fall.* And this shall take place in order that they *may be melted,* as in a furnace, and *chosen and made white,* until *the determined time* comes. For the true victory shall be at the coming of Christ.

Some of the Hebrews understand these things as referring to the princes Severus[187] and Antoninus,[188] who held the Jews in very high esteem. But others understand this of the emperor Julian;[189] for when they were oppressed by Gallus Caesar[190] and had suffered much in the afflictions of their captivity, Julian rose up as one who feigned love for the Jews. He promised that he would even offer sacrifice in their temple. They would have a *small* hope of *help* from him, and *many* of the Gentiles were to *join themselves* to their party, although falsely and not in truth. For they will feign friendship with them for the sake of worshipping idols. And they will do this "in order that those who were approved might be made manifest" [1 Cor 11:19]. For the *time* of their true salvation and *help* will be the coming of the Christ, whom they wrongly await as one yet to come, though the one they will receive will be the antichrist.[191]

11:36. *And the king shall act according to his will, and he shall be lifted up, and shall be magnified against every god, and he shall speak great things against the God of gods, and shall go straight on, until the wrath be fulfilled. For the determination is made* (or as someone else translated it, *for in him there will be the consummation*).

From this passage the Hebrews think that it is talking of the antichrist, that after the "small help" [Dan 11:34] of Julian, a *king* will rise up who shall *act according to his own will and shall lift himself up* "against all that is called *god*" [2 Thess 2:4], and *shall speak great things against the God of gods,* so that he "sits in the temple of God and shall make himself out to be God" [2 Thess 2:4], and his will *shall go straight on until the wrath* of God *is fulfilled, for in him there will be the consummation.*[192] We too understand this as referring to the antichrist.

On the other hand, Porphyry and the others who follow him think that it is speaking of Antiochus Epiphanes. For he *raised himself up* against the worship of God, and became so arrogant that he commanded his own statue to be placed in the temple in Jerusalem [cf. 1 Macc 1:43; 2 Macc 6:2].[193] And as for what follows: *And he shall go straight on until the wrath be accomplished, for in him there will be a consummation*, they understand it to mean that his power will endure until such time as God becomes angry at him and orders him to be killed. For indeed Polybius and Diodorus,[194] who composed historical libraries,[195] relate that Antiochus not only *acted* against the God of Judea, but also was so inflamed with greed that he attempted to plunder the temple of Diana in Elymais because it contained so much wealth.[196] But he was put down by the temple guards and the neighboring populace [cf. 1 Macc 6:1–4; 2 Macc 1:13–14] and also beset by certain fearful apparitions, so that he became demented and finally died of illness [cf. 1 Macc 6:8–16; 2 Macc 1:13–16; 9:5–27]. And the historians record that this happened to him because he tried to rob the temple of Diana. But we maintain that even though this thing befell him, it did so because he had perpetrated great cruelty upon the saints of God and had defiled his temple. For we ought not to believe that he was punished for something he only tried to do and then left off the fulfillment of it by doing penance [cf. 1 Macc 6:12–13; 2 Macc 9:12–13], but rather for something he actually did do.[197]

11:37–39. *And he shall have no regard for the God of his fathers, and he shall be in the lusts of women* (feminarum); *nor shall he care for any of the gods, for he shall rise up against everything. But he shall venerate the god Maozim in his place, and a god whom his fathers did not know shall he worship with gold and silver and precious stone and things of great price. And he shall do this to fortify Maozim with a foreign god whom he has known. And he shall increase glory and shall give them power over many and shall divide the land as a free gift.*

Instead of our translation, *and he shall be in the lusts of women*, the Septuagint translated: "And he will not be subject to the lusts of women (*mulierum*)." And again, instead of *the god Maozim*, which is found in the Hebrew, Aquila translated it: "the God of forces (*fortitudinum*)," whereas the Septuagint says, "God most mighty (*fortissimum*)." But there was ambiguity in the Hebrew in what we recorded as: *And he shall be in the lusts of women*, since Aquila, who expresses things word for word, says: Καὶ ἐπὶ Θεὸν πατέρων αὐτοῦ οὐ συνήσει, καὶ ἐπὶ ἐπιθύμίαν γυναικῶν καὶ ἐπὶ πάντα Θεὸν οὐ συνήσει, that is, "And concerning the God of his fathers he shall not understand, and concerning the lust of women and concerning every god he shall not understand." By these words, interpreters understand that he lusted after women, and that he did not lust after them.¹⁹⁸ If we read and understand it ἀπὸ κοινοῦ (from the context)¹⁹⁹: *And he shall not understand concerning the lust of women*, then it becomes an easier interpretation to make concerning the antichrist: that he will feign chastity in order to deceive many. But if we read it as follows: *And in the lust of women*, supplying in thought "he shall be," then it will fit better the character of Antiochus. For he is said to have been utterly dissolute, and to have become such a disgrace to the dignity of kingship through his acts of sexual immorality and seduction, that he publicly had intercourse with actresses and harlots, and satisfied his lust in the presence of the people.²⁰⁰

As for the *god Maozim*, Porphyry made a fool of himself in his interpretation by saying that Antiochus's generals set up a statue of Jupiter in the village of Modein, from which came Mattathias and his sons [cf. 1 Macc 2:1, 15–28], and that he compelled the Jews to offer sacrifices to it, that is, to *the god of Modein*.²⁰¹

Now as for what follows: *and he shall worship a god whom his fathers did not know*, this fits better the antichrist than Antiochus. For we read that Antiochus held to the worship of the idols of Greece and compelled the Jews and Samaritans to venerate his own gods [cf. 1 Macc 1:41–42; 2 Macc 4:10–11; 6:1–2].

And besides, there is what he adds: *And he shall do this to fortify Maozim with a foreign god whom he has known. And he shall increase glory and shall give them power*²⁰² *and shall divide the land as a free gift.* Theodotion translated this as follows: "And he shall do these things in order to fortify garrisons with a foreign god, and he shall make a display for them, he will increase glory; and he shall cause them to lord over many and he will divide up the land freely." Symmachus translated "places of refuge" rather than *garrisons*. Porphyry explained this as follows:

> *He will do* all this *to fortify* the citadel in Jerusalem, and he will set in place *garrisons* in the rest of the cities, and he will teach the Jews to worship a *foreign god*, which doubtless refers to Jupiter, whom *he will manifest with them* and he will persuade them to worship him. Then *he will give* the deluded both honor and very great *glory*, and he *shall deal* with the rest who have lorded over Judea, and *divide up* estates unto them in return for their transgression, and shall distribute gifts [cf. 1 Macc 1:35–49; 2:18].

The antichrist too will abundantly bestow many rewards upon the deceived and *will divide up the land* to his army. And those whom he will not be able to subject to himself by intimidation, he will do so through their avarice.

11:40–41a. *And at the determined time the king of the south shall fight against him, and the king of the north shall come against him like a storm, with chariots, and with horsemen, and with a large fleet, and he shall enter into the lands and shall destroy and pass through. And he shall enter into the glorious land and many (multae) shall fall* (which Symmachus translated: *and many thousands shall fall*; Theodotion: *and many shall be weakened*). Now according to Aquila, the *many* that *fall* are to be understood as cities, countries, or provinces.

Porphyry refers these things too to Antiochus. For in the eleventh year of his reign he waged war for a second time against his sister's son, Ptolemy Philometor, who upon hearing that Antiochus had come, gathered *many thousands* of peoples. But Antiochus entered very many lands *like* a mighty *storm, with his chariots and horsemen and a large fleet,* and he devastated everything as he went through. And he came to the illustrious *land,* that is, Judea, which Symmachus translated as "land of strength." Instead of this, Theodotion recorded the Hebrew word itself, *sabai.* And Antiochus used the ruins of the wall of the city to fortify the citadel, and thus he reached Egypt [cf. 1 Macc 1:18–19].[203]

Now our people refer even these things to the antichrist. They say that he shall first *fight against the king of the south,* that is, of Egypt, and shall afterward conquer Libya and Ethiopia, for these constitute the three broken horns about which we read previously [cf. Dan 7:8]. And because he shall come to the land of Israel, and many cities or provinces shall be given into his hands.

11:41b. *And these only shall be saved out of his hands: Edom and Moab and the commencement of the sons of Ammon.*

[Porphyry's people] say that in his haste to fight Ptolemy, the king of the south, Antiochus left untouched the Idumeans, Moabites, and Ammonites, who dwelt to the side of Judea, lest he should make Ptolemy the stronger by engaging in battle elsewhere.

The antichrist too will leave Idumea untouched, and also the Moabites and the sons of Ammon, that is, Arabia, for the saints will flee there to the deserts.

11:42–43. *And he shall send his hand upon the lands, and the land of Egypt shall not escape. And he shall have power over the treasures of gold and*

of silver, and all the precious things of Egypt, and he shall pass through Libya and Ethiopia.
We do read that Antiochus did these things in part.
But as for what follows: *He shall pass through Libya and Ethiopia*, our people claim that this corresponds better with the antichrist. For Antiochus did not have control of Libya, which most writers understand to be Africa, nor of Ethiopia; unless perhaps his capture of the Egyptians troubled those provinces of Egypt which lay in the same general direction as Ethiopia, and which lay as neighbors to it, far away through the deserts. Hence, he does not say that he captured them, but that he *passed through Libya and Ethiopia.*
11:44–45. *And a report out of the east and out of the north shall disturb him; and he shall come with a great multitude to destroy and kill many. And he shall pitch his tent in Apedno, between the seas, upon an illustrious and holy mountain; and he shall come unto its summit; and no one shall help him.*
Even for this passage, Porphyry dreams up something or other about Antiochus. He says:

> While fighting against the Egyptians and passing through Libya and Ethiopia, he will hear of wars being incited against him *out of the north* and out of the *east*. Therefore he will go back and capture the Aradian[204] resistance, and lay waste the entire province along the seacoast of Phoenicia. And immediately he will proceed to Artaxias, the king of Armenia, who was stirred up from the regions of the *east*, and having slain a large number of his troops, he will place *his tent* in the place called *Apedno* which is *between* two very wide rivers, the Tigris and the Euphrates.

But after proceeding to this point, Porphyry is unable to tell us upon what *illustrious and holy mountain* he settled—though he was not even able to prove that he settled *between two seas*, and it would be foolish to interpret the *two seas* as the two rivers of Mesopotamia. That is why Porphyry skipped over the *illustrious mountain* by following the translation of Theodotion, who said: "upon the holy mountain Saba between the two seas." And even though he supposes that Saba was the name of a mountain in Armenia or Mesopotamia, he cannot tell us why it was *holy*.[205] By this same license for invention, we ourselves can add what Porphyry kept silent about, that the mountain is called *holy* because, in accordance with the error of the Armenians, it was consecrated to idols. He says:

> *And he shall come even unto the summit* of the same mountain, in the province of Elymais, which is the most remote district of the Persians eastward. When he wanted to plunder the temple of Diana that is there, which held countless sums of donated money, he was put to flight by the barbarians, who admired that shrine with a wondrous sense of worship.[206] And Antiochus was consumed by grief and died in Tabes, a town in Persia.

This is [Porphyry's] skillfully crafted discourse composed as an affront to us.[207] But even if he could have proven that these things were said of Antiochus and not of the antichrist, what is that to us? For do we not prove the advent of Christ and the lie of the antichrist based on all passages of the Scriptures? Indeed, suppose these things were spoken of Antiochus, how does that harm our religion?[208] Is it not true that in the earlier vision also [cf. Dan 11:1–20], where the prophecy culminated in Antiochus, something is said of the antichrist? And so, let [Porphyry] put aside doubtful matters and stick to what is plain. Who is that stone which was hewn from the mountain without hands, and which grew to be a great mountain and filled the earth, and which smashed to pieces the fourfold image [cf. Dan 2:34–35]? Who is that son of man who will come with the clouds and will stand before the Ancient of Days and is to be given a kingdom that shall have no end, and who will be served by all peoples, tribes, and languages [cf. Dan 7:13–14]? [Porphyry] bypasses these things, which are plain, and he claims that the prophecy refers to the Jews, whom we know are in servitude to this very day. And he claims that the person who wrote the book under the name of Daniel invented[209] these things in order to revive the hopes of his own people. Not that he was able to know the entire future history, but he records things that had already happened. Thus [Porphyry] lingers in false statements in regard to the final vision, recording rivers for the *sea*, and positing *an illustrious and holy mountain, Apedno* even though he is unable to furnish any historical source in which he has read about it.

Our people, on the other hand, explain the final section of this vision as relating to the antichrist as follows. They say that during his war against the Egyptians, Libyans, and Ethiopians, in which he shall smash three of the ten horns [cf. Dan 7:8], the Antichrist will hear that wars have been stirred up against him in the regions of the *north and east*. Then he shall come *with a great multitude to crush and kill very many people*. He will pitch his tent in *Apedno* near Nicopolis, which was formerly called Emmaus, where the mountains of the province of Judea begin to rise. Finally, arising from there to the Mount of Olives, it is in the district of Jerusalem that he ascends; and this is what the Scripture means here: *And when he has pitched his tent* at the base of the mountainous province *between two seas*. These are, of course, that which is now called the Dead Sea on the east, and the Great Sea on whose coasts Caesarea, Joppa, Ashkelon, and Gaza are situated. Then *he shall come up to the summit of its mountain*, that is, of the mountainous province, that is, to the top of the Mount of Olives, which is called *illustrious*, because from it our Lord and Savior ascended to the Father [cf. Luke 24:51; Acts 1:6–12]. And *no one* shall be able *to help* the antichrist as the Lord rages against him. Our people say that antichrist will perish in that spot from which the Lord ascended to heaven.[210]

Apedno is a compound word. If you divide it up, it can be understood to mean θρόνου αὐτοῦ, that is, "of his throne," and the meaning is that *he will pitch his tent* and his throne *between the seas upon the illustrious and holy mountain*. Symmachus translated this passage as follows: Καὶ ἐκτενεῖ τὰς σκηνὰς τοῦ ἱπποστασίου αὐτοῦ μεταξὺ τῶν θαλασσῶν εἰς τὸ ὄρος τῆς δυνάμεως τὸ ὅγιον, which means in Latin: "And he shall extend the pavilions of his cavalry between the seas upon the holy mountain of power, and he shall come even unto the top of the mountain." In fact, Theodotion renders it thus: "And he shall pitch his tent in Apedno between the seas on the holy Mount Saba, and he shall come to the region thereof." Aquila says: "And he shall plant the tent of his *praetorium* in Apedno between the seas, on the glorious and holy mountain, and he shall come even unto its end." Only the Septuagint frees itself from the problem about the name by translating: "And he shall establish his tent then between the seas and the holy mountain of [his] will, and the hour of his consummation shall come." Following the Septuagint's rendering, Apollinaris omitted all mention of the name *Apedno*. I have recorded these things somewhat prolixly both to show Porphyry's sophistry, who either was ignorant of all these things or pretended not to know them, and to show the difficulty of Holy Scripture. Men who are altogether lacking in experience lay special claim to the understanding of it, apart from the grace of God and without instruction from our elders. Moreover, one should take note that the Hebrew language has no letter *p*, but uses instead the letter *phe*, which has the sound of the Greek *phi*.²¹¹ It is simply that in this particular place, the Hebrews write the letter *phe*, yet it is to be pronounced as *p*.

But that the antichrist will come *to the summit of the holy and illustrious mountain* and perish there, Isaiah speaks of this in greater detail: "The Lord shall cast down on the holy mountain the face of the ruler of the darkness which is over all nations (and: him who rules over all peoples), and the anointing with which he was anointed against all the nations" [Isa 25:7 (Symmachus)].²¹²

12:1–3. *But at that time Michael shall rise up, the great prince, who stands for the children of your people, and a time shall come such as never was from the time that nations began to exist even until that time. And at that time your people shall be saved, every one that shall be found written in the book. And many of those who sleep in the dust of the earth shall awake, some unto eternal life, others unto reproach, to see it always. But they that are learned shall shine as the brightness of the firmament, and they that instruct many to justice, as stars for all eternity.*

Up to this point Porphyry held up as best he could, and he imposed upon the ignorant among our own and upon the poorly educated among his own. But what will he say about this chapter in which the resurrection of the dead is described, with some being raised *unto eternal life* and others unto *reproach* forever?²¹³ He cannot even tell us who the people were under Antiochus who *shone like the brightness of the firmament*, and those others who shone *like the stars for all eternity.*

But what will obstinacy not do! Like a bruised serpent [cf. Gen 3:15], he raises his head when he is about to die, and injects his venom into those who are themselves about to die, and he says:

> This too is written about Antiochus, for after he had invaded Persia, he left his army with Lysias,²¹⁴ who was in charge of Antioch and Phoenicia, for the purpose of fighting against the Jews and destroying their city of Jerusalem [cf. 1 Macc 3:31–36]. Josephus, the author of the *Hebrew History*, narrates all these things.²¹⁵ For there was such a tribulation *as had never been*, and *a time came such as had never been from the time when nations began to exist even unto that time.* But when victory was achieved, and the generals of Antiochus had been slaughtered, and Antiochus himself had died in Persia, the people of Israel were saved: *all who had been written*

in the book of God, that is, those who very bravely defended the law. And, on the other hand, those who stood forth as transgressors of the law and who had sided with the party of Antiochus were blotted out of the book [cf. Exod 32:32]. Then, he says, those who were, as it were, *sleeping in the dust of the earth* and buried under the weight of evils, and as it were hidden away in the tombs of misery, rose up *from the dust of the earth* to an unexpected victory, and lifted up their heads from the ground. The guardians of the law will rise up to *everlasting life*, and the transgressors will rise up to everlasting *disgrace*. But those masters and teachers who possessed a knowledge of the law *shall shine like the heaven*, and those who have exhorted the inferior peoples to keep the ceremonies of God *shall shine like the stars for all eternity*.

He also records the historical account concerning the Maccabees in which it is said that many Jews under the leadership of Mattathias and Judas Maccabaeus fled to the desert and hid in caves and holes in the rocks, and came forth again after the victory [1 Macc 2:28–30]. These things, then, were predicted metaphorically,[216] [says Porphyry] as a kind of resurrection of the dead.[217]

But it is understood more truly to mean that *in the time* of the Antichrist there shall be a tribulation such as *has never been since nations began to exist*. For let us suppose that Lysias, who was conquered, had conquered, and that the Jews who conquered had been completely overwhelmed. Would that tribulation have been as great as the one that occurred at the time when Jerusalem was captured by the Babylonians, the temple destroyed, and all the people led into captivity? Therefore, when the antichrist is crushed and extinguished by the breath of the Savior [cf. 2 Thes 2:8], the people *written in* God's *book shall be saved* [cf. Matt 24:29–31]; and in accordance with the diversity of merits, some shall rise up *unto eternal life* and others *unto* eternal *reproach* [cf. Luke 20:35]. The teachers shall have the likeness of heaven, and those who have *instructed* others shall be compared to the *brightness* of the *stars*. For it is not sufficient to know wisdom, unless you also instruct others; and the speech of instruction which keeps to itself and fails to edify another cannot receive a wage for being idle. This passage is expressed by Theodotion, that is, the common (*vulgata*) edition,[218] in the following way: "And those who understand shall shine forth as the brightness of the firmament, and many of the just like the stars forever and beyond." Some are accustomed to ask whether a learned saint and a simple saint shall both have the same reward and the very same dwelling-place (*mansionem*) in heaven [cf. John 14:2]. Whence it is said now in accordance with Theodotion that the learned will have the likeness of heaven, whereas the just who are without learning will be compared to the brightness of the stars. And so, the distance that separates learned holiness and holy rusticity shall be as great as that between heaven and the stars.[219]

12:4. *But you, O Daniel, shut up the words and seal the book until the time appointed; many shall pass over, and knowledge shall be manifold.*[220]

He himself who had revealed *manifold* truth to Daniel signifies that the things he has said are secrets. He instructs him to roll up the *words* and *seal the book*, so that *many* shall read it and seek the truth of the history and make diverse conjectures because of its great obscurity. For as for what he says: *Many shall pass over* or "run through," this indicates that many people will read this. For it is a familiar expression to say: "I ran through the book," or, "I have gone through an historical account." Indeed, this is what Isaiah also says concerning the obscurity of his own book:

> And the words of that book shall be like the words of a book that is sealed. But if they give it to an illiterate man, saying to him, "Read it," he will reply: "I do not know how to read." But if they give it to a man who does know how to read and say, "Read the book," he will reply, "I cannot read it, because it is sealed up." [Isa 29:11–12]

Also in the Revelation of John, a book is seen that is sealed with seven seals inside and outside [cf. Rev 5:1–3]. And when no one can break its seals, John says: "I wept exceedingly. And a voice came, saying: 'Do not weep; behold the lion of the tribe of Judah, the root of David, has conquered to open the book and break its seals'" [Rev 5:4–5]. Now that book can be broken open by one who has learned the mysteries of Scripture and who understands its αἰνίγματα (enigmatic sayings) [cf. 1 Cor 13:12] and its words shrouded in darkness because of the greatness of the secrets [cf. Prov 1:3–6], and who can interpret parables and transform the letter that kills into the spirit that gives life [cf. Rom 7:6; 2 Cor 3:6].

BOOK THREE 153

12:5–6. *And I Daniel looked, and behold as it were two others stood, one on this side upon the bank of the river, and another on that side, on the other bank of the river. And I said to the man that was clothed in linen, who stood upon the waters of the river: How long to the end of these wonders?* Daniel sees two angels standing on either side *upon the bank of the river* of Babylon. Although it is recorded here without a name, I think that in accordance with the preceding vision it would be the Tigris [cf. Dan 10:4], which is called *eddechel* in Hebrew. Yet he does not ask those who were *standing upon either bank*, but rather the one whom he had seen at the beginning [cf. Dan 8:16; 9:21], *who was clothed in linen* clothing (or *byssus*, which is called *baddim* in Hebrew). And this same angel was *standing upon the waters of the river* of Babylon, trampling upon them with his foot. From this, we understand that the former pair of angels whom he saw *standing upon the bank* and does not ask them anything or deem them worthy of inquiry were the angels of the Greeks and Persians. But this angel was the very kind one who had presented Daniel's prayers before God, during the twenty-one days while the angel of the Persians was opposing him [cf. Dan 10:4–20]. And Daniel asks him about these *wonders* spoken of in the present vision, as to the time when they should be fulfilled.

Porphyry, in his usual fashion, interprets this of Antiochus, while we refer it to the antichrist.

12:7a. *And I heard the man that was clothed in linen, who stood upon the waters of the river, when he had lifted up his right hand and his left hand to heaven, and had sworn by him who lives forever, that [it should be] unto a time, and times, and half a time.* Porphyry interprets *a time and times and half a time* to mean three and a half years, and we do not deny that this accords with the idiom[221] of Sacred Scripture. For higher up we also read that seven *times* passed over Nebuchadnezzar, that is, the seven years of his living like a wild beast[222] [cf. Dan 4:20–22]. It is also recorded in the vision of the four beasts, the lion, the bear, the leopard, and the other beast whose name is concealed, but which signified the kingdom of the Romans [cf. Dan 7:25]. And later on it is said of the antichrist:

> He will humble three kings and speak words against the Exalted One and will crush the saints of the Most High; and he will think that he can alter *times* and laws. And they [the saints] will be delivered over to his hand unto a time and times and half a time. And the judgment will sit down,

in order that power may be removed and be shattered and vanish away until the end. [Dan 7:24–26]

And [he says] clearly about the coming of Christ and of the saints: "But kingdom and power and the greatness of the kingdom which lies beneath the whole heaven shall be given to the people of the saints of the Most High, whose kingdom is an everlasting kingdom; and all the kings shall serve and obey him" [Dan 7:27].

And so, if the things higher up, which were plainly written about the Antichrist, Porphyry refers to Antiochus and to the three and a half years during which, he says, the temple was abandoned, then he ought to prove that what follows, *His kingdom is eternal, and all kings shall serve and obey him,* likewise pertains to Antiochus or, as he himself thinks, to the Jewish people. Clearly this does not stand. We read in the Books of Maccabees—and Josephus also concurs in the same opinion[223]—that the temple in Jerusalem lay defiled for three years [cf. 1 Macc 1:59; 4:52; 2 Macc 10:5]. Moreover, under Antiochus Epiphanes an idol of Jupiter stood within it; that is to say, from the one hundred forty-fifth year of the Macedonian rule from Seleucus; in the ninth month of the same year until the ninth month of the one hundred forty-eighth year, which comes to three years.[224] But under the antichrist it is not said that the desolation and overthrow of the temple shall endure for three years, but for three and a half years, that is, for one thousand two hundred and ninety days [cf. Dan 12:11].

12:7b. *And when the scattering of the band* (manus) *of the holy people shall be accomplished, all these things shall be fulfilled.*

When, he says, the *people* of God shall be *scattered*—either under the persecution of Antiochus, as Porphyry claims, or of antichrist, as our people prove to be truer—at that time *all these things shall be accomplished.*

12:8–10. *And I heard and did not understand and I said: My Lord, what shall be after these things? And he said: Go, Daniel, because the words are shut up and sealed until the time of consummation. Many shall be chosen and made white, and shall be tried as fire, and the wicked shall deal wickedly, and none of the wicked shall understand, but the learned shall understand.*

The prophet wants to *understand* what he had seen, or rather, what he had *heard,* and he desires to learn the truth of the things to come. For he had *heard* of the various wars of kings, and of battles between them, and the complex history; but he had not *heard* the names of the individuals involved [cf. Dan 11].

Now if the prophet *heard and did not understand,* what will those men do who with a presumptuous mind discourse on a book that has been *sealed* and closed up with many obscurities *unto the time of the consummation?* But, he says, when the end comes, *the wicked will not understand,* and those who are *learned* in the teaching of God will themselves be able to *understand.* "For wisdom will not enter the perverted soul, nor can it impart itself to a body which is subject to sins" [Wis 1:4 LXX].

12:11. *And from the time when the continual sacrifice shall be taken away, and the abomination unto desolation shall be set up, there shall be a thousand two hundred ninety days.*

Porphyry thinks that these *one thousand two hundred and ninety days* were fulfilled at the time of Antiochus in the *desolation* of the temple. Yet, as we have said, both Josephus and the Book of Maccabees record that it lasted for only three years [cf. 1 Macc 1:57; 4:52].[225]

From this, it is clear that the three and a half years are spoken of the time of the antichrist, who will persecute the saints for three and a half years, or for *one thousand two hundred and ninety days,* and then he will fall on the "famous and holy mountain" [Dan 11:45]. Therefore, from the time [of the removal] of the ἐνδελεχισμός,[226] which we have translated as *continual sacrifice*,[227] when the antichrist obtains possession of the world and forbids the worship of God, unto the day of his killing, three and a half years, or *one thousand two hundred and ninety days,* shall be accomplished.

12:12. *Blessed is he who waits and comes to a thousand three hundred thirty-five days.*

He says, *Blessed is he who* after the murder of the antichrist waits for forty-five days beyond the determined number, for it is within that period that our Lord and Savior will come in his majesty. But why the silence for forty-five days after the murder of the antichrist? This is a matter for the knowledge of God, unless perhaps we should say that the postponement of the kingdom of the saints is a test of their patience.

Porphyry explains this passage in the following way, that the forty-five days beyond the one thousand two hundred and ninety signify the time of the victory over the generals of Antiochus, when Judas Maccabaeus fought bravely and cleansed the temple and broke the idol to pieces and offered blood sacrifices in the temple of God [cf. 1 Macc 4:30–58]. He would have spoken correctly, if the Book of Maccabees had recorded that the temple was defiled over a period of three and a half years instead of just three years [cf. 1 Macc 1:57; 4:52].[228]

12:13. *But you, go your way until the appointed [time], and rest, and you will stand in your lot unto the end of the days.* (Instead of this, Theodotion translated it: "But you, go and rest, and you shall rise up again in your turn at the consummation of the days.")

From these words, it is shown that the entire prophecy is near the resurrection of all the dead, when the prophet also will rise.

And it is vain for Porphyry to want to refer all these things to Antiochus, which were spoken concerning the antichrist, with Antiochus being a type.[229]

As we have said, Eusebius of Caesarea, Apollinaris of Laodicea, and partially also that very eloquent man, the martyr Methodius, replied to his calumny in great detail. Anyone who wants to learn more of these things can find them in their books.[230]

[THE STORIES OF SUSANNA AND BEL]¹

I have explained to the best of my ability the things contained in the Book of Daniel according to the Hebrew. I will now briefly record what Origen said about the stories of Susanna and Bel in the tenth book of his *Stromata*. These are his words.²

13:3. *And her parents [were] just and had taught their daughter in accordance with the law of Moses.*

One should use this testimony to exhort parents to *teach* not only their sons but also *their daughters in accordance with the law* of God and the divine word.

13:5a. *And there were two of the elders of the people appointed judges that year.*

A Hebrew related that these men were Achias and Zedekiah of whom Jeremiah writes: "May the Lord make you as Achias and Zedekiah, whom the king of Babylon roasted in the fire because of the iniquity they had done in Israel and were committing adultery with the wives of their citizens" [Jer 29(36):22–23 LXX].³

13:5b. *Of whom the Lord said: Iniquity came out from Babylon from the elder judges, who seemed to govern the people.*

It is nice that he does not say of these sinful elders: "Who governed the people," but: *Who seemed to govern*. For those who preside well over the people *govern the people*, but those who merely have the name of *judges* and preside unjustly over the people only *seem to govern the people* rather than govern.

13:8b–9. *And they were inflamed with lust toward her, and they perverted their own mind and turned their eyes away that they might not look toward heaven nor remember just judgments.*

What the Greeks call πάθος we translate more correctly by "disturbance" than by "passion."⁴

Therefore, this disturbance and lustful desire aroused them, or rather, it struck the hearts of the elders. But in order that it might lay a foundation in their hearts and they might devise a way to fulfill their desires, they themselves *perverted their own mind*. And once their minds had been overthrown, *they* turned away *their eyes that they might not look toward* heavenly things *nor remember just judgments*, whether of God, of honesty, or of the nature that is implanted in all persons for the good.

13:[13–14 LXX]. *And behold Susanna walked in according to her custom.*[5]

Previously it was already said that Susanna walked in the mornings [cf. Dan 13:7]. To appease those people who look for precedent from Holy Scripture for everything we do, it is not unfitting to adopt this passage about taking walks, and to say that it is a good thing for a person to take walks to invigorate his body.

Origen says: "I have recorded this particular passage from the Septuagint version." By this statement, he shows that he discussed other things that were not in accord with the Septuagint translators.[6]

13:22. *And Susanna sighed deeply and said: I am in anguish on every side. For if I do this thing, it is death to me; and if I do it not, I shall not escape your hands.*

The one who has arrived at the summit of perfect virtue never says that danger threatens her, if she does not *escape the hands* of adulterers who say, "Consent to us and have intercourse with us; for otherwise, if you refuse, we will witness against you that a young man was with you and you sent away your maidens from you for this purpose" [Dan 13:20–21]. For it pertains to human frailty to be afraid of death that is inflicted for the sake of justice. Unless perhaps we shall interpret her *anguish* as arising not from the threat of death but from the reproach and shame that would be heaped upon her by those who accuse her and say: "A young man was with her, and that is why she sent away her maidens." *For if I do this thing, it is death to me; but if I do it not, I shall not escape your hands.* She is calling sin *death*. Therefore, just as adultery is *death* for the one who commits adultery, so one should name as *death* every sin that leads to *death*. And we are thought to die as often as we sin unto *death*. Whence on the other hand we rise again and are made alive, just as often as we do works that are worthy of life.[7]

13:23. *But it is better for me to fall into your hands without having done the deed than to sin in the sight of the Lord.*

The Greek does not have *better*, that is, αἱρετώτερον, but αἱρετὸν, which we can translate "good." Thus, she did not say eloquently: *It is better for me to fall into the hands* of the unjust elders *than to sin in the sight of the Lord,* so as not to appear to be calling something which was good *better* in comparison with sin. But she says, *It is* good *for me not* to do the wicked thing, *and to fall into your hands,* lest I sin *in the sight of the Lord.* Therefore, one should not read this sentence as a comparison: *It is better for me to fall into your hands than to sin in the sight of the Lord,* but in an absolute sense: "It is good for me not to do the wicked thing" *and fall into your hands, lest I sin in the sight of the Lord.*

13:24a. *And Susanna cried out with a great voice.*[8]

Her *voice* was *great* not from the vibration of the air and the shout that came from her throat, but from the greatness of her chastity by which she *called* out to the Lord. And this is why the Holy Scripture did not attribute a *great voice* to the outcry of the elders; for it follows: "The elders also cried out against her" [Dan 13:24].

13:42–43a. *But Susanna cried out with a great voice and said: Eternal God, who knows hidden things, who knows all things before they come to pass, you know that they have borne false witness against me.*

The sentiments of her heart, the pure confession of her mind, and her good conscience had made her voice ring out more clearly. And so, her *outcry* to *God* was *great,* which was not heard by the people.

13:45. *And as she was being led away to death, God roused the holy spirit of a young boy whose name was Daniel.*

These words show that a holy spirit did not enter into Daniel, but rather that he was within him, and was resting because of the weakness of his age, and was unable to demonstrate his works. When the opportunity came for the sake of the holy woman, the spirit was *roused* by the Lord.

13:46. *And he cried out with a great voice: I am clean of the blood of this woman.*

Because a holy spirit had been roused within him and was suggesting to the youth what he ought to say, his *voice* was *great.* And one should note down if there is any place in Holy Scripture where the *voice* of a sinner is called *great.*[9]

13:54–55, 58–59. *Say under which tree you saw them speaking with each other. He said: Under the mastic tree* (schino)*. And Daniel said to him, Well have you lied against your own head; for behold, the angel of God has received his sentence from him and shall cut* (scindet) *you in two.*[10] *And a little while later the other elder said: Under the holm oak tree* (prino)*. And Daniel said to him: Well have you also lied against your own head; for the angel of God waits with a sword to slice* (secet) *you in two.*

Since the Hebrews reject the history of Susanna and say that it is not found in the Book of Daniel, we ought to investigate carefully the names of the trees, the *schinos* and the *prinos*—which the Latins interpret as "holm-oak" (*ilicem*) and "mastic-tree" (*lentiscum*)—and see whether they exist among the Hebrews and what their derivation (ετυμολογια) is.[11] For example, in the Greek language "cleaving" (*scissio*) may be expressed from *mastic* (*schinos*), and "cutting" (*sectio*) or "sawing" (*serratio*) from *holm tree* (*prinos*).[12] But if no such derivation can be found, then we, too, are of necessity forced to agree with the verdict of those who claim that this chapter [Greek *pericope*] was originally composed in Greek, because it contains a Greek etymology not found in Hebrew. But if anyone can show that the derivation of the ideas of cleaving and cutting is also valid in Hebrew, then we may accept this Scripture also.

13:61b–62a. *And they did to them as they had maliciously dealt against their neighbor, acting in accordance with the law of Moses* [cf. Deut 19:16–19]; *and they put them to death.*

If the whole synagogue [cf. Dan 13:60] *put them to death*, the view that we mentioned earlier is apparently refuted, namely, that these were the elders Achias and Zedekiah according to Jeremiah [cf. Jer 29(36):22–23 LXX];[13] unless perhaps we interpret what is written: *They put them to death*, to mean that they handed them over to the king of Babylon to be put to death, in a manner similar to the way we say that the Jews put the Savior to death; not in the sense that they themselves struck him, but they handed him over to be killed, and they cried out and said: "Crucify him! Crucify him!" [Luke 23:21; John 19:6; cf. Mark 15:13, 14; John 19:15].

13:63. *But Helchias and his wife praised God for their daughter Susanna, with Joachim her husband, and all her relatives, because there was no base thing found in her.*

Fittingly they praise God like saints, not because Susanna was delivered from the hands of the elders—for that is not an adequate matter for praise, even if she would not have been delivered from great danger—but rather because *no base thing was found in her.*[14]

14:17 (18).[15] *And as soon as the doors were opened, the king looked at the table, and cried out with a great voice: You are great, O Bel, and there is not any deceit with you.*

What the Scripture says here: *He cried out with a great voice*, appears to undermine our observation whereby a short time ago we asserted that the expression *great voice* is found only in connection with saints.¹⁶ For it is used here of an idolater and someone who does not know God. The easy solution to this objection will be by the one who says that this story is not found in the Book of Daniel as used by the Hebrews; but if someone can prove that it is a part of the canon, then we would need to look for something necessary to say in response to this question.¹⁷

APPENDIX

Origen's epistolary reply to Julius Africanus was elicited by a letter that Julius had addressed to Origen concerning the story of Susanna that is appended to the Book of Daniel. Africanus had serious doubts as to the canonical authority of the account. Julius offers the following arguments[1] to show that the story of Susanna is not an authentic part of the prophecy of Daniel.

1. In the authentic part of the book, Daniel prophesies in many ways, but never by prophetic inspiration, as in this story (3).
2. Daniel's exposure of the two elders is ridiculous; it would not even appear in a writer of farcical stories (4).
3. The puns on the tree names are only possible in Greek, whereas Old Testament books have been translated from Hebrew (5).
4. The historical context of the story is not true to life. Captives would not have been allowed to carry out a sentence of capital punishment (6).
5. The Jews do not have this story in their texts of the book of Daniel (7).
6. In the story, Daniel cites Exod 23:7; but none of the prophets cite their predecessors the way he does (8).
7. Finally, the style of this section is different from the rest of the book of Daniel (9).

Origen replies to these objections one by one and seeks to uphold the story as both useful in itself and a genuine portion of the ancient prophetical writings. His reply to Julius's arguments can be summarized as follows:

1. Daniel's case can be compared with that of Jacob, who received revelation in various ways, including prophetic inspiration (16/10).
2. Daniel's judgment in the trial is no less ridiculous than that of Solomon in the case of the dispute between the two harlots over the dead baby (17/11).

3. The presence of plays on words can be explained by the skill of the translator.
4. The historical setting is not untrue to life. There are convincing parallels in the Bible (19/13) and also in the present condition of the Jews (20/14).
5. The church does receive this story among her canonical writings.
6. In Scripture there are many instances of one prophet citing the words of another prophet (21/15).
7. Origen does not agree that the style of this story differs from the rest of the book (22/16).

A Letter to Origen from Africanus About the History of Susanna[2]

1. Greeting, my Lord and son, most worthy Origen, from Africanus.

2. (1) In your sacred discussion with that ignorant man,[3] you referred to that prophecy of Daniel which is related of his youth. This at that time, as was fitting, I accepted as genuine. Now, however, I cannot understand how it escaped you that this part of the book is spurious. For, indeed, this section, although apart from this it is elegantly written, is plainly a more modern forgery. There are many proofs of this.

3. When Susanna is condemned to die, the prophet is seized by the Spirit and cries out that the sentence is unjust [Sus 45]. Now, in the first place, it is always in some other way that Daniel prophesies—by visions, and dreams, and an angel appearing to him, never by prophetic inspiration.[4]

4. Then, after crying out in this extraordinary fashion, he detects them in a way no less incredible, which not even Philistion the playwriter would have resorted to.[5] For, not satisfied with rebuking them through the Spirit, he placed them apart and asked them severally where they saw her committing adultery. And when the one said, "Under a holm-tree" (*prinos*), he answered that the angel would saw him asunder (*prisein*); and in a similar fashion he menaced the other, who said, "Under a mastich-tree" (*schinos*), with being rent asunder (*schisthenai*).

5. Now, in Greek, it happens that "holm-tree" and "saw asunder," and "rend" and "mastich-tree" sound alike; but in Hebrew they are quite distinct. But all the books of the Old Testament have been translated from Hebrew into Greek.

6. (2) Moreover, how is it that they who were captives among the Chaldeans lost and won at play? thrown out unburied on the streets, as was prophesied of the former captivity [cf. Tob 2:3; Jer 14:16], their sons torn from them to be eunuchs, and their daughters to be concubines, as had been prophesied [cf. Isa 39:7]; how is it that such could pass sentence of death, and that on the wife of their king Joakim, whom the king of the Babylonians had made partner of his throne? Then if it was not this Joakim but some other from the common people, whence had a captive such a mansion and spacious garden?

7. But a more fatal objection is that this section, along with the other two at the end of it, is not contained in the Daniel received among the Jews.

8. And add that, among all the many prophets who had been before, there is no one who has quoted from another word for word. For they had no need to go begging for words, since their own were true; but this one, in rebuking one of those men, quotes the words of the Lord: "The innocent and righteous you shall not slay" [Exod 23:7; cf. Sus 53].

9. From all this I infer that this section is a later addition. Moreover, the style is different.

10. I have struck the blow;[6] you give the echo; answer and instruct me. Salute all my masters. The learned all salute you. With all my heart I pray for your and your circle's health.

A Letter from Origen to Africanus[7]

1. (1) Origen to Africanus, a beloved brother in God the Father, through Jesus Christ, his holy child, greeting.

2. Your letter, from which I learn what you think of the Susanna in the Book of Daniel which is used in the churches, although apparently somewhat short, presents in its few words many problems, each of which demands no common treatment but such as oversteps the character of a letter and reaches the limits of a book. And I, when I consider, as best I can, the measure of my intellect, that I may know myself, am aware that I am wanting in the accuracy necessary to reply to your letter; and that the more, that the few days I have spent in Nicomedia have been far from sufficient to send you an answer to all your demands and queries even after the fashion of the present epistle. Wherefore pardon my little ability and the little time I had, and read this letter with all indulgence, supplying anything I may omit.

3. **(2)** You begin by saying[8] that when, in my discussion with our friend Bassus, I used the Scripture that contains the prophecy of Daniel when yet a young man in the affair of Susanna, I did this as if it had escaped me that this part of the book was spurious. You say that you praise this passage as elegantly written, but find fault with it as a more modern composition and a forgery; and you add that the forger has had recourse to something that not even Philistion the playwriter would have used in his puns between *prinos* and *prisein*, *schinos* and *schisis*, which words as they sound in Greek can be used in this way, but not in Hebrew. In answer to this, I have to tell you what it behooves us to do in the cases not only of the History of Susanna, which is found in every church of Christ in that Greek copy which the Greeks use, but is not in the Hebrew, or of the two other passages you mention at the end of the book containing the history of Bel and the Dragon, which likewise are not in the Hebrew copy of Daniel; but of thousands of other passages also which I found in many places when with my little strength I was collating the Hebrew copies with ours.

4. For in Daniel itself [with respect to the fiery furnace], I found the word *bound* [Dan 3:23 (Theodotion)] followed in our versions by very many verses that are not in the Hebrew at all, beginning (according to one of the copies that circulate in the churches) thus: "Ananiah, and Azariah, and Mishael prayed and sang to the Lord" [Dan 3:24 LXX], down to "O, all you who worship the Lord, bless the God of gods. Praise him and say that his mercy endures for ever and ever. And it came to pass, when the king heard them singing, and saw them that they were alive" [Dan 3:90–91 LXX]. Or, as in another copy, from "And they walked in the midst of the fire, praising God and blessing the Lord" [Dan 3:24 Theod.] down to "O, all you who worship the Lord, bless the God of gods. Praise him and say that his mercy endures to all generations" [Dan 3:90 Theod.]. But in the Hebrew copies the words, "And these three men, Shadrach, Misach, and Abednego fell down bound into the midst of the fire," are immediately followed by the verse, Nebuchadnezzar the king was astonished, and rose up in haste, and spoke, and said unto his counselors" [Dan 3:24 Aquila]. For so Aquila, following the Hebrew reading, gives it, who has obtained the credit among the Jews of having interpreted the Scriptures with no ordinary care, and whose version is most commonly used by those who do not know Hebrew, as the one that has been most successful. Of the copies in my possession whose readings I gave, one follows the Seventy, and the other Theodotion; and just as the History of Susanna

which you call a forgery is found in both, together with the passages at the end of Daniel, so they give also these passages, amounting, to make a rough guess, to more than two hundred verses.

5. (3) And in many other of the sacred books, I found sometimes more in our copies than in the Hebrew, sometimes less. I shall adduce a few examples since it is impossible to give them all. Of the Book of Esther neither the prayer of Mordechai nor that of Esther, both fitted to edify the reader, is found in the Hebrew [cf. Esth 4:17]. Neither are the letters; nor the one written to Amman about the rooting up of the Jewish nation [Esth 3:13], nor that of Mordechai in the name of Artaxerxes delivering the nation from death [Esth 8:12].

6. Then in Job, the words from "It is written, that he shall rise again with those whom the Lord raises," to the end, are not in the Hebrew, and so not in Aquila's edition; while they are found in the Septuagint and in Theodotion's version, agreeing with each other at least in sense.[9] And many other places I found in Job where our copies have more than the Hebrew ones, sometimes a little more, and sometimes a great deal more: a little more, as when to the words, "Rising up in the morning, he offered burnt-offerings for them according to their number," they add, "one heifer for the sin of their soul" [Job 1:5]; and to the words, "The angels of God came to present themselves before God, and the devil came with them" [Job 1:6], "from going to and fro in the earth, and from walking up and down in it" [Job 1:21]. Again, after "The LORD gave, the LORD has taken away," the Hebrew has not, "It was so, as seemed good to the Lord." Then our copies are very much fuller than the Hebrew, when Job's wife speaks to him, from "How long wilt thou hold out? And he said, Lo, I wait yet a little while, looking for the hope of my salvation," down to "that I may cease from my troubles, and my sorrows which compass me" [Job 2:9]. For they have only these words of the woman, "But say a word against God, and die" [Job 2:9]. (4) Again, through the whole of Job there are many passages in the Hebrew that are wanting in our copies, generally four or five verses, but sometimes, however, even fourteen, and nineteen, and sixteen. But why should I enumerate all the instances I collected with so much labor, to prove that the difference between our copies and those of the Jews did not escape me?

7. In Jeremiah I noticed many instances, and indeed in that book I found much transposition and variation in the readings of the prophecies. Again, in Genesis, the words, "God saw that it was good" [Gen 1:8], when the firmament was made, are not found in the Hebrew, and

there is no small dispute among them about this; and other instances are to be found in Genesis, which I marked, for the sake of distinction, with the sign the Greeks call an obelisk, as on the other hand I marked with an asterisk those passages in our copies which are not found in the Hebrew. What need is there to speak of Exodus, where there is such diversity in what is said about the tabernacle and its court and the ark and the garments of the high priest and the priests, that sometimes the meaning even does not seem to be akin [cf. Exod 35—40]?

8. And, indeed, when we notice such things, are we forthwith to reject as spurious the copies in use in our churches, and enjoin the brotherhood to put away the sacred books current among them, and to coax the Jews and persuade them to give us copies that shall be untampered with and free from forgery? Are we to suppose that that Providence which in the Sacred Scriptures has ministered to the edification of all the churches of Christ had no thought for those bought with a price [cf. 1 Cor 6:20; 7:23], for whom Christ died [Rom 14:15]; whom, although his Son, God who is love [cf. 1 John 4:9, 16], spared not, but gave him up for us all, that with him he might freely give us all things [cf. Rom 8:32]? In all these cases consider whether it would not be well to remember the words, "Thou shalt not remove the ancient landmarks which thy fathers have set" [cf. Deut 19:14; Prov 22:28; 23:10].

9. Nor do I say this because I shun the labor of investigating the Jewish Scriptures, comparing them with ours and noticing their various readings. This, if it be not arrogant to say it, I have already to a great extent done to the best of my ability, laboring hard to get at the meaning in all the editions and various readings; while I paid particular attention to the interpretation of the Seventy, lest I might be found to accredit any forgery to the churches that are under heaven and give an occasion to those who seek such a starting point for gratifying their desire to slander the common brethren, and to bring some accusation against those who shine forth in our community. And I make it my endeavor not to be ignorant of their various readings, lest in my controversies with the Jews I should quote to them what is not found in their copies, and that I may make some use of what is found there, even although it should not be in our Scriptures. For if we are so prepared for them in our discussions, they will not, as is their manner, scornfully laugh at Gentile believers for their ignorance of the true reading as they have them.

10. So far as to the History of Susanna not being found in the Hebrew. **(6)** Let us now look at the things you find fault within the story itself. And here let us begin with what would probably make anyone averse to receiving the history: I mean the play of words between *prinos* and *prisis*, *schinos* and *schisis*. You say that you can see how this can be in Greek, but that in Hebrew the words are altogether distinct. On this point, however, I am still in doubt; because, when I was considering this passage (for I myself saw this difficulty), I consulted not a few Jews about it, asking them the Hebrew words for *prinos* and *prisein*, and how they would translate *schinos* the tree, and how *schisis*. And they said that they did not know these Greek words *prinos* and *schinos* and asked me to show them the trees, that they might see what they called them. And I at once (for the truth's dear sake) put before them pieces of the different trees. One of them then said that he could not with any certainty give the Hebrew name of anything not mentioned in Scripture, since, if one was at a loss, he was prone to use the Syriac word instead of the Hebrew one; and he went on to say that some words the very wisest could not translate. "If, then," said he, "you can adduce a passage in any Scripture where the *schinos* is mentioned, or the *prinos*, you will find there the words you seek, together with the words that have the same sound; but if it is nowhere mentioned, we also do not know it." This, then, being what the Hebrews said to whom I had recourse and who were acquainted with the history, I am cautious of affirming whether or not there is any correspondence to this play of words in the Hebrew. Your reason for affirming that there is not, you yourself probably know.

11. **(7)** Moreover, I remember hearing from a learned Hebrew, said among themselves to be the son of a wise man and to have been specially trained to succeed his father, with whom I had conversation on many subjects, the names of these elders, just as if he did not reject the History of Susanna, as they occur in Jeremiah as follows: "The LORD make thee like Zedekiah and Achiab, whom the king of Babylon roasted in the fire, for the iniquity they did in Israel" [Jer 36:22–23 (Heb. 29:22–23)]. How, then, could the one be sawn asunder by an angel and the other rent in pieces? The answer is that these things were prophesied not of this world, but of the judgment of God, after the departure from this world. For as the Lord of that wicked servant who says, "My Lord delayeth his coming," and so gives himself up to drunkenness, eating, drinking with drunkards, and smiting his fellow servants, shall at his coming "cut him asunder, and appoint him his

portion with the unbelievers" [cf. Luke 12:45–46; Matt 24:48–51], even so the angels appointed to punish will accomplish these things (just as they will cut asunder the wicked steward of that passage) on these men, who were called indeed elders but who administered their stewardship wickedly. One will saw asunder him who was waxen old in wicked days, who had pronounced false judgment, condemning the innocent and letting the guilty go free; and another will rend in pieces him of the seed of Canaan and not of Judah, whom beauty had deceived and whose heart lust had perverted [Sus 52–53].

12. **(8)** And I knew another Hebrew, who told about these elders such traditions as the following: that they pretended to the Jews in captivity, who were hoping by the coming of Christ to be freed from the yoke of their enemies, that they could explain clearly the things concerning Christ...and that they so deceived the wives of their countrymen. Wherefore it is that the prophet Daniel calls the one "waxen old in wicked days" and says to the other, "Thus have ye dealt with the children of Israel; but the daughters of Judah would not abide your wickedness."

13. **(9)** But probably to this you will say, Why then is the "History" not in their Daniel, if, as you say, their wise men hand down by tradition such stories? The answer is that they hid from the knowledge of the people as many of the passages that contained any scandal against the elders, rulers, and judges as they could, some of which have been preserved in uncanonical writings (Apocrypha). As an example, take the story told about Isaiah and guaranteed by the Epistle to the Hebrews, which is found in none of their public books. For the author of the Epistle to the Hebrews, in speaking of the prophets and what they suffered, says, "They were stoned, they were sawn asunder, they were slain with the sword" [Heb 11:37]. To whom, I ask, does the "sawn asunder" refer (for by an old idiom, not peculiar to Hebrew, but found also in Greek, this is said in the plural, although it refers to but one person)? Now we know very well that tradition says that Isaiah the prophet was sawn asunder; and this is found in some apocryphal work that probably the Jews have purposely tampered with, introducing some phrases manifestly incorrect, that discredit might be thrown on the whole.

14. However, some one hard pressed by this argument may have recourse to the opinion of those who reject this Epistle as not being Paul's; against whom I must at some other time use other arguments to prove that it is Paul's.[10] At present I shall adduce from the Gospel what Jesus Christ testifies concerning the prophets, together with a

APPENDIX   171

story which he refers to but which is not found in the Old Testament, since in it also there is a scandal against unjust judges in Israel. The words of our Savior run thus: "Woe unto you, scribes and Pharisees, hypocrites because ye build the tombs of the prophets, and garnish the sepulchers of the righteous, and say, If we had been in the days of our fathers, we would not have been partaken with them in the blood of the prophets. Wherefore be witnesses unto yourselves, that you are the children of them who killed the prophets. Fill up then the measure of your fathers. You serpents, you generation of vipers, how can you escape the damnation of Gehenna? Wherefore, behold, I send unto you prophets, and wise men, and scribes; and some of them you shall kill and crucify; and some of them you shall scourge in your synagogues, and persecute them from city to city: that upon you may come all the righteous blood shed upon the earth, from the blood of righteous Abel unto the blood of Zachariah, son of Barachiah, whom you slew between the temple and the altar. Verily I say unto you, All these things shall come upon this generation" [Matt 23:29–36]. And what follows is of the same tenor: "O Jerusalem; Jerusalem, you that kill the prophets and stone them who are sent unto you, how often would I have gathered your children together, even as a hen gathers her chickens under her wings, and ye would not! Behold, your house is left unto you desolate" [Matt 23:37–39]. Let us see now if in these cases we are not forced to the conclusion that while the Savior gives a true account of them, none of the Scriptures that could prove what he tells are to be found. For they who build the tombs of the prophets and garnish the sepulchers of the righteous, condemning the crimes their fathers committed against the righteous and the prophets, say, "If we had been in the days of our fathers, we would not have been partakers with them in the blood of the prophets." In the blood of what prophets, can anyone tell me? For where do we find anything like this written of Isaiah, or Jeremiah, or any of the twelve, or Daniel? Then about Zachariah the son of Barachiah, who was slain between the temple and the altar, we learn from Jesus only, not knowing it otherwise from any Scripture. Wherefore I think no other supposition is possible than that they who had the reputation of wisdom, and the rulers and elders, took away from the people every passage that might bring them into discredit among the people. We need not wonder, then, if this history of the evil device of the licentious elders against Susanna is true but was concealed and removed from the Scriptures by men themselves not very far removed from the counsel of these elders.

15. In the Acts of the Apostles also, Stephen, in his other testimony, says, "Which of the prophets have not your fathers persecuted? And they have slain them who showed before of the coming of the Just One; of whom you have been now the betrayers and murderers" [Acts 7:52]. That Stephen speaks the truth, everyone will admit who receives the Acts of the Apostles; but it is impossible to show from the extant books of the Old Testament how with any justice he throws the blame of having persecuted and slain the prophets on the fathers of those who believed not in Christ. And Paul, in the first Epistle to the Thessalonians, testifies this concerning the Jews: "For you, brethren, became followers of the churches of God that in Judea are in Christ Jesus: for you also have suffered like things of your own countrymen, even as they have of the Jews; who both killed the Lord Jesus and their own prophets, and have persecuted us; and they please not God, and are contrary to all men" [1 Thess 2:14–16]. What I have said is, I think, sufficient to prove that it would be nothing wonderful if this history were true and the licentious and cruel attack was actually made on Susanna by those who were at that time elders, and written down by the wisdom of the Spirit but removed by these rulers of Sodom, as the Spirit would call them [cf. Isa 1:10].

16. **(10)** Your next objection is, that in this writing Daniel is said to have been seized by the Spirit, and to have cried out that the sentence was unjust; while in that writing of his which is universally received he is represented as prophesying in quite another manner, by visions and dreams and an angel appearing to him, but never by prophetic inspiration. You seem to me to pay too little heed to the words, "At sundry times, and in diverse manners, God spoke in time past to the fathers by the prophets" [Heb 1:1]. This is true not only in general, but also of individuals. For if you notice, you will find that the same saints have been favored with divine dreams and angelic appearances and (direct) inspirations. For the present it will suffice to instance what is testified concerning Jacob. Of dreams from God he speaks thus: "And it came to pass, at the time that the cattle conceived, that I saw them before my eyes in a dream, and behold, the rams and he-goats that leaped upon the sheep and the goats, white-spotted, and speckled, and grizzled. And the angel of God spoke to me in a dream, saying, Jacob. And I said, What is it? And he said, Lift up your eyes and see, the goats and rams leaping on the goats and sheep, white-spotted, and speckled, and grizzled: for I have seen all that Laban does to you. I am God, who appeared to you in the place

APPENDIX   173

of God, where you anointed a pillar to me and vowed a vow there to me: now arise, go out from this land, and return unto the land of your kindred" [Gen 31:10–13]. And as to an appearance (which is better than a dream), he speaks as follows about himself: "And Jacob was left alone; and there wrestled a man with him until the breaking of the day. And he saw that he prevailed not against him, and he touched the breadth of his thigh; and the breadth of Jacob's thigh grew stiff while he was wrestling with him. And he said to him, Let me go, for the day breaks. And he said, I will not let you go, unless you bless me. And he said to him, What is your name? And he said, Jacob. And he said to him, Your name shall be called Jacob no more, but Israel shall be your name: for you have prevailed with God, and are powerful with men. And Jacob asked him, and said, Tell me your name. And he said, Why do you ask my name? And he blessed him there. And Jacob called the name of the place Vision of God: for I have seen God face to face, and my life is preserved. And the sun rose, when the vision of God passed by" [Gen 32:25–32]. And that he also prophesied by inspiration is evident from this passage: "And Jacob called his sons and said, Gather yourselves together, that I may tell you what shall befall you in the last days. Gather yourselves together, and hear, sons of Jacob; and hearken unto Israel your father. Reuben, my first-born, my might, and the beginning of my children, hard to be born, hard and stubborn. You were wanton, do not boil over like water; because you went to your father's bed; then defiled the couch to which you went" [Gen 49:1–4]. And so with the rest: it was by inspiration that the prophetic blessings were pronounced [cf. Gen 49:5–27]. We need not wonder, then, that Daniel sometimes prophesied by inspiration, as when he rebuked the elders sometimes, as you say, by dreams and visions, and at other times by an angel appearing to him.

17. (11) Your other objections are stated, as it appears to me, somewhat irreverently, and without the becoming spirit of piety. I cannot do better than quote your very words: "Then, after crying out in this extraordinary fashion, he detects them in a way no less incredible, which not even Philistion the playwriter would have resorted to. For, not satisfied with rebuking them through the Spirit, he placed them apart and asked them severally where they saw her committing adultery; and when the one said, 'Under a holm-tree' (*prinos*) he answered that the angel would saw him asunder (*prisein*); and in a similar fashion threatened the other, who said, 'Under a mastich-tree' (*schinos*), with being rent asunder." You might as reasonably compare

to Philistion the playwriter a story somewhat like this one, which is found in the third Book of Kings, which you yourself will admit is well written. Here is what we read in Kings: "Then there appeared two women that were harlots before the king and stood before him. And the one woman said, To me, my Lord, this woman and I dwell in one house; and we were delivered in the house. And it came to pass, the third day after I was delivered, that this woman was delivered also: and we were together; there is no one in our house except us two. And this woman's child died in the night, because she laid on it. And she arose at midnight, and took my son from my arms. And your handmaid slept. And she laid it in her bosom, and laid her dead child in my bosom. And I arose in the morning to give my child suck, and he was dead; but when I had considered it in the morning, behold, it was not my son which I did bear. And the other woman said, No; the dead one is your son, but the living is my son, And the other said, No; the living is my son, but the dead is your son. Thus they spoke before the king. Then said the king, You say, This is my son that lives, and your son is dead: and you say, No; but your son is dead, and my son is living. And the king said, Bring me a sword. And they brought a sword before the king: And the king said, Divide the living child in two, and give half to the one, and half to the other. Then said the woman whose the living child was with the king (for her bowels yearned after her son), and she said, To me, my Lord, give her the living child, and do not slay it. But the other said, Let it be neither yours or mine, but divide it. Then the king answered and said, Give the child to the one who said, Give her the living child, and do not slay it: for she is the mother of it. And all Israel heard of the judgment which the king had judged; and they feared the face of the king: for they saw that the wisdom of God was in him to do judgment" [1 Kgs 3:16–28]. For if we were at liberty to speak in this scoffing way of the Scriptures in use in the churches, we should rather compare this story of the two harlots to the play of Philistion than that of the chaste Susanna. And just as the people would not have been persuaded if Solomon had merely said, "Give this one the living child, for she is the mother of it," so Daniel's attack on the elders would not have been sufficient had there not been added the condemnation from their own mouth, when both said that they had seen her lying with the young man under a tree, but did not agree as to what kind of tree it was. And since you have asserted, as if you knew for certain, that Daniel in this matter judged by inspiration (which may or may not have been the case), I would have you notice that there seem to me to be some analogies in the story of Daniel to the judgment of Solomon, concerning whom the Scripture testifies that the people saw that the wisdom of God was in him to do judgment. This might be said also of Daniel, for it was because wisdom was in him to do judgment that the elders were judged in the manner described.

18. **(12)** I had nearly forgotten an additional remark I have to make about the *prino-prisein* and *schino-schisein* difficulty; that is, that in our Scriptures there are many etymological fancies, so to call them, that in the Hebrew are perfectly suitable, but not in the Greek. It need not surprise us, then, if the translators of the History of Susanna contrived it so that they found out some Greek words derived from the same root that either corresponded exactly to the Hebrew form (though this I hardly think possible), or presented some analogy to it. Here is an instance of this in our Scripture. When the woman was made by God from the rib of the man, Adam says, "She shall be called woman, because she was taken out of her husband" [Gen 2:23]. Now the Jews say that the woman was called "Essa," and that "taken" is a translation of this word as is evident from "*chos isouoth essa,*" which means, "I have taken the cup of salvation" [Ps 116:13]; and that "*is*" means "man," as we see from "*Hesre ais,*" which is, "Blessed is the man" [Ps 1:1]. According to the Jews, then, "*is*" is "man," and "*essa*" "woman," because she was taken out of her husband (*is*). It need not then surprise us if some interpreters of the Hebrew "Susanna," which had been concealed among them at a very remote date and had been preserved only by the more learned and honest, should have either given the Hebrew word for word, or hit upon some analogy to the Hebrew forms, that the Greeks might be able to follow them. For in many other passages we can find traces of this kind of contrivance on the part of the translators, which I noticed when I was collating the various editions.

19. **(13)** You raise another objection, which I give in your own words: "Moreover, how is it that they, who were captives among the Chaldeans, lost and won at play, thrown out unburied on the streets, as was prophesied of the former captivity, their sons torn from them to be eunuchs, and their daughters to be concubines, as had been prophesied; how is it that such could pass sentence of death, and that on the wife of their king Joakim, whom the king of the Babylonians had made partner of his throne? Then, if it was not this Joakim, but some other from the common people, whence had a captive such a mansion and spacious garden?" Where you get your "lost and won

at play, and thrown out unburied on the streets," I know not, unless it is from Tobit [cf. Tob 2:3]; and Tobit (as also Judith), we ought to notice, the Jews do not use. They are not even found in the Hebrew Apocrypha, as I learned from the Jews themselves. However, since the churches use Tobit, you must know that even in the captivity some of the captives were rich and well to do. Tobit himself says, "Because I remembered God with all my heart; and the Most High gave me grace and beauty in the eyes of Nemessarus, and I was his purveyor; and I went into Media, and left in trust with Gabael, the brother of Gabrias, at Ragi, a city of Media, ten talents of silver" [Tob 1:12–14]. And he adds, as if he were a rich man, "In the days of Nemessarus I gave many alms to my brethren. I gave my bread to the hungry, and my clothes to the naked: and if I saw any of my nation dead and cast outside the walls of Nineveh, I buried him; and if king Sennecherib had slain any when he came fleeing from Judea, I buried them in secret (for in his wrath he killed many)" [Tob 1:16–18]. Think whether this great catalogue of Tobit's good deeds does not betoken great wealth and much property, especially when he adds, "Understanding that I was sought for to be put to death, I withdrew myself for fear, and all my goods were forcibly taken away" [Tob 1:19–20]. And another captive, Dachiacharus, the son of Ananiel, the brother of Tobias, was set over all the exchequer of the kingdom of king Acherdon; and we read, "Now Achiacharus (Ahikar) was cupbearer and keeper of the signet, and steward and overseer of the accounts" [Tob 1:21–22]. Mordecai, too, frequented the court of the king, and had such boldness before him, that he was inscribed among the benefactors of Artaxerxes [cf. Esth 2]. Again, we read in Esdras, that Nehemiah, a cupbearer and eunuch of the king, of Hebrew race, made a request about the rebuilding of the temple and obtained it; so that it was granted to him, with many more, to return and build the temple again [cf. Neh 1:11; 2:6]. Why then should we wonder that one Joakim had garden, and house, and property, whether these were very expensive or only moderate, for this is not clearly told us in the writing?

20. (14) But you say, "How could they who were in captivity pass sentence of death?" asserting, I know not on what grounds, that Susanna was the wife of a king, because of the name Joakim. The answer is that it is no uncommon thing, when great nations become subject, that the king should allow the captives to use their own laws and courts of justice. Now, for instance, that the Romans rule, and the Jews pay the half-shekel to them, how great power by the concession

of Caesar the ethnarch has; so that we, who have had experience of it, know that he differs in little from a true king! Private trials are held according to the law, and some are condemned to death. And though there is not full license for this, still it is not done without the knowledge of the ruler, as we learned and were convinced of when we spent much time in the country of that people. And yet the Romans only take account of two tribes, while at that time besides Judah there were the ten tribes of Israel. Probably the Assyrians contented themselves with holding them in subjection, and conceded to them their own judicial processes.

21. (15) I find in your letter yet another objection in these words: "And add, that among all the many prophets who had been before, there is no one who has quoted from another word for word. For they had no need to go begging for words, since their own were true. But this one, in rebuking one of these men, quotes the words of the Lord, "The innocent and righteous shall thou not slay" [Sus 53; Exod 23:7]. I cannot understand how, with all your exercise in investigating and meditating on the Scriptures, you have not noticed that the prophets continually quote each other almost word for word. For who of all believers does not know the words in Isaiah? "And in the last days the mountain of the LORD shall be manifest, and the house of the LORD on the top of the mountains, and it shall be exalted above the hills; and all nations shall come unto it. And many people shall go and say, Come, and let us go up to the mountain of the LORD, unto the house of the God of Jacob; and he will teach us his way, and we will walk in it: for out of Zion shall go forth a law, and a word of the LORD from Jerusalem. and he shall judge among the nations and shall rebuke many people; and they shall beat their swords into ploughshares, and their spears into pruning-hooks: nation shall not lift up sword against nation; neither shall they learn war anymore" [Isa 2:2–4]. But in Micah we find a parallel passage, which is almost word for word: "And in the last days the mountain of the LORD shall be manifest, established on the top of the mountains, and it shall be exalted above the hills; and people shall hasten unto it. And many nations shall come, and say, Come, let us go up to the mountain of the LORD, to the house of the God of Jacob; and they will teach us his way, and we will walk in his paths: for a law shall go forth from Zion, and a word of the LORD from Jerusalem. And he shall judge among many people, and rebuke strong nations; and they shall beat their swords into ploughshares, and their spears into pruning-hooks: nation shall not lift up a sword against

nation, neither shall they learn war anymore" [Mic 4:1–3]. Again, in First Chronicles, the psalm that is put in the hands of Asaph and his brethren to praise the Lord, beginning, "Give thanks to the LORD, call upon His name" [1 Chr 16:8], is in the beginning almost identical with Psalm 105, down to "and do my prophets no harm" [Ps 105:15], and after that it is the same as Psalm 96, from the beginning of that psalm, which is something like this, "Praise the Lord all the earth," down to "For he comes to judge the earth" [1 Chr 16:23; Ps 96:1]. (It would have taken too much time to quote more fully; so I have given these short references, which are sufficient for the matter before us.) And you will find the law about not bearing a burden on the Sabbath day in Jeremiah, as well as in Moses [Jer 17:21–22; Exod 35:2; Num 15:32]. And the rules about the Passover, and the rules for the priests, are not only in Moses, but also at the end of Ezekiel [Lev; Ezek 43–46]. I would have quoted these, and many more, had I not found that from the shortness of my stay in Nicomedia my time for writing you was already too much restricted.

22. **(16)** Your last objection is that the style is different. This I cannot see.

23. This, then, is my defense. I might, especially after all these accusations, speak in praise of this history of Susanna, dwelling on it word by word, and expounding the exquisite nature of the thoughts. Such an encomium, perhaps, some of the learned and able students of divine things may at some other time compose.[11]

24. This, however, is my answer to your strokes, as you call them. Would that I could instruct you! But I do not now arrogate that to myself. My Lord and dear brother Ambrosius, who has written this at my dictation, and has, in looking over it, corrected as he pleased, salutes you. His faithful spouse, Marcella, and her children also salute you. Also, Anicetus. Do you salute our dear father Apollinarius, and all our friends.

NOTES

Introduction to St. Jerome

1. The year of Jerome's birth is contested, but I am leaning increasingly toward 331.
2. *Acta Apostolicae Sedis* 12:385–420.
3. November 7 and 14, 2007, https:// www.vatican.va/ content/ benedict-xvi/ en/ audiences/ 2007/ documents/ hf _ben -xvi _aud _20071107 .html; https:// www.vatican.va/ content/ benedict-xvi/ en/ audiences/ 2007/ documents/hf_ben-xvi_aud_20071114.html.
4. Pope Francis, Apostolic Letter *Scripturae Sacrae Affectus*; https:// www.vatican.va/ content/ francesco/ en/ apost _letters/ documents/ papa -francesco-lettera-ap_20200930_scripturae-sacrae-affectus.html. The quote is from Jerome's *Ep* 52.7.
5. See the familiarity with it that he displays in *De viris illustribus*, "On Famous Men." I grant that Jerome was not personally acquainted with many of the works he listed here but was dependent on Eusebius as his source of information. See P. Courcelle's study, *Late Latin Writers and their Greek Sources*, trans. H. E. Wedeck (Cambridge, MA: Harvard University Press, 1969), chap. 2.
6. This list was formally ratified by Pope Boniface VIII on September 20, 1295.
7. *Scripturae Sacrae Affectus*, introduction.
8. Desiderius Erasmus, *Patristic Scholarship: The Edition of St. Jerome*, ed. J. Olin, CWE 61 (Toronto: University of Toronto Press, 1992), 53–54.
9. For instance, John P. O'Connell begins his thorough and admirable study of Jerome's eschatology with the unfortunate claim: "[Jerome] was not a theologian but an exegete and a polemicist." *The Eschatology of Saint Jerome*, Dissertationes ad Lauream 16 (Mundelein, IL: Pontifical Theological Faculty of the Seminary of St. Mary of the Lake, 1948), i.
10. Cf. Alan D. Booth, "The Date of Jerome's Birth," *Phoenix* 33, no. 4 (1979): 346–52.
11. See the allusion to him under Dan 11:17a.
12. Cf. *Ep* 48.20 to Pammachius (NPNF2 6:87); *Ep* 7.4 to Chromatius, Jovinus, and Eusebius (NPNF2 6:9)
13. See Jerome's interaction with Hilary in *Ep* 34 to Marcella.
14. They are found in NPNF2, 6.299–318.
15. See St. Jerome, Origen, *Commentary on Isaiah*; Origen *Homilies 1–9 on Isaiah*, trans. Thomas P. Scheck (Mahwah, NJ: Newman Press, 2015);

Origen, *Homilies on Jeremiah, Homilies on 1 Kings 28*, trans. John Clark Smith (Washington, DC: Catholic University of America Press, 1998); Origen, *Homilies 1–14 on Ezekiel*, trans. Thomas P. Scheck (Mahwah, NJ: Newman Press, 2010). There is now a second translation of *Origen's Homilies on Isaiah* by E. A. Dively Lauro, *Origen: Homilies on Isaiah*, FOTC 142 (Washington, DC: Catholic University of America Press, 2021).

16. See Origen, *The Song of Songs, Commentary and Homilies*, trans. J. Mierow, R. P. Lawson (Mahwah, NJ: Newman Press, 1956).

17. See Jerome, *Commentary on Ecclesiastes*, trans. Richard J. Goodrich and David J. D. Miller (Mahwah, NJ: Newman Press, 2012).

18. See Jerome, *Dogmatic and Polemical Works*, trans. John N. Hritzu (Washington, DC: Catholic University of America Press, 1965).

19. See: Robert C. Hill, *Didymus the Blind: Commentary on Zechariah*, FOTC 111 (Washington, DC: Catholic University of America Press, 2006); *Jerome, Commentaries on the Twelve Prophets*, vol. 2, ed. Thomas P. Scheck, Ancient Christian Texts (Downers Grove, IL: Intervarsity Press, 2017).

20. Elizabeth Clark, *The Origenist Controversy: The Cultural Construction of an Early Christian Debate* (Princeton, NJ: Princeton University Press, 1992); J. N. D. Kelly, *Jerome: His Life, Writings, and Controversies* (New York: Harper & Row, 1975).

21. *Commentary on Ezekiel*, preface.

22. M. Hale Williams, *The Monk and the Book: Jerome and the Making of Christian Scholarship* (Chicago: University of Chicago Press, 2006), 110.

23. A. Kamesar, "Jerome," in *The New Cambridge History of the Bible*, vol. 1, *From the Beginnings to 600*, ed. J. C. Paget and J. Schaper (Cambridge: Cambridge University Press, 2013), 653–75 (quote on 672–73).

24. For a more precise description of Jerome's practice with the biblical lemmata in his commentaries on the prophets, see M. Hale Williams, *The Monk and the Book*, 119n62.

25. St. Jerome, *Commentary on Isaiah*, trans. Scheck, 506.

26. Cf. M. Hale Williams, *The Monk and the Book*, 112, 192–94.

27. Cf. *Epp* 28.2; 36.12; A. Kamesar, *Jerome, Greek Scholarship, and the Hebrew Bible: A Study of the Quaestiones Hebraicae in Genesim*, Oxford Classical Monographs (Oxford: Clarendon, 1993), 67.

28. *HE* 6.16ff.

29. *Vir ill* 54.

30. H. Swete, *An Introduction to the Old Testament in Greek*, rev. R. R. Ottley (Peabody, MA: Hendrickson, 1989; orig. pub. Cambridge University Press, 1914), 43, thinks that this date under Commodus is too late.

31. *Vir ill* 54.

32. *Adv haer* 3.21.2.

33. Vulgate Preface to the Books of Solomon; cited by R. Courtray, "Les Maccabées chez Jérôme: de la liberation juive à la véritable victoire dans le Christ," in M.-F Baslez and O. Munnich, eds., *Le mémoire des persécutions. Autour du livre des Maccabées*, Collection de la Revue des Études juives 56 (Paris-Louvain, 2014), 385–97 (386).

34. S. R. Driver, *Notes on the Hebrew Text...of Samuel,* 2nd ed. (Oxford, 1913, repr. 1960), xliii; cited by S. Jellicoe, *The Septuagint and Modern Study* (Oxford: Clarendon, 1968), 102–3.
35. Cf. K. Jobes and M. Silva, *Invitation to the Septuagint* (Grand Rapids: Baker, 2000), 148.
36. Williams, *The Monk and the Book,* 142.
37. Kamesar, *Jerome, Greek Scholarship, and the Hebrew Bible,* 56.
38. See St. Jerome, *Exegetical Letters,* FOTC 147, 148, trans. Thomas P. Scheck (Washington, DC: Catholic University of America Press, 2023–24). *Ep* 106 will appear in vol. 148. There is also a comprehensive new monograph: *Jerome, Epistle 106 (On the Psalms),* introduction, translation, and commentary by Michael Graves (Atlanta: SBL Press, 2022).
39. James A. Montgomery, *A Critical and Exegetical Commentary on the Book of Daniel,* International Critical Commentary (Edinburgh: T&T Clark, 1927), 56.
40. J. Braverman, *Jerome's Commentary on Daniel: A Study of Comparative Jewish and Christian Interpretation of the Hebrew Bible* (Washington, DC: Catholic Biblical Association, 1978).
41. See Jerome's *Ep* 34 to Marcella where he expounds Ps 127. I have included a new translation of this epistle in: St. Jerome, *Exegetical Letters.*
42. Courcelle, *Late Latin Writers and Their Greek Sources,* 111–12.
43. See R. Courtray, "Nabuchodonosor, figure du diable chez Jérôme," *Connaissance des Pères de l'Église* 120 (2010): 18–26.
44. My conjecture is that Didymus the Blind may be one of these many who followed Origen in this speculation.
45. Cf. Jerome, *Ep* 14.5; 123.8; *Adversus Helvidium de Mariae virginitate perpetua,* 20.
46. Jerome, *Commentary on Jonah* 3:6–9; trans. Daniel Whitehead and Thomas P. Scheck, in *Commentaries on the Twelve Prophets,* vol. 1, ed. Thomas P. Scheck, Ancient Christian Texts (Downers Grove, IL: Intervarsity Press, 2016) 266–67. I believe that some of Jerome's polemic here is directed (unfairly) against Rufinus of Aquileia.
47. *The Christian Doctrine of Apokatastasis: A Critical Assessment from the New Testament to Eriugena* (Leiden: Brill, 2013), 20.
48. *Christian Doctrine of Apokatastasis,* 639.
49. Cf. *Adv Jov* 1.33.
50. *The Catechism of the Catholic Church,* 2nd ed. (Vatican City: Libreria Editrice Vaticana, 1997), 391–93 speaks of the "irrevocable" character of the choice of the fallen angels and of the impossibility of their future conversion. Quoting John Damascene, *De Fide Orth.* 2.4, CCC 393 says: "There is no repentance for the angels after their fall, just as there is no repentance for men after death." This point of dogma was not clear to Origen (d. 254 CE).
51. Courtray, "Nabuchodonosor, figure du diable chez Jérôme," 26.
52. Cf. Adela Yarbro Collins, "The Influence of Daniel on the New Testament," 90–123 (90) in John J. Collins, *Daniel: A Commentary on Daniel* (Minneapolis: Augsburg/Fortress 1993).
53. Yarbro Collins, "The Influence of Daniel," 90.

54. Cf. *Porphyry's Letter to His Wife Marcella Concerning the Life of Philosophy and the Ascent to the Gods*, trans. Alice Zimmern, intro. David Fideler (Grand Rapids: Phanes Press, 1986).

55. For a summary of its content, see: M. V. Anastos, "Porphyry's Attack on the Bible," in *Studies in Honor of H. Caplan*, ed. L. Wallach (Ithaca, NY: Cornell University Press, 1966), 421–50.

56. "Porphyry and the Origen of the Book of Daniel," *JTS* 27, no. 1 (1976): 16–33 (16). The internal quote is from A. Cameron, *C.Q.* lxi (N.S. xvii) (1967): 382.

57. Cf. L. G. Patterson, *Methodius of Olympus: Divine Sovereignty, Human Freedom, and Life in Christ* (Washington, DC: Catholic University of America Press, 1997).

58. J. N. D. Kelly, *Jerome: His Life, Writings, and Controversies*, 301.

59. Casey, "Porphyry and the Origins of the Book of Daniel," 15.

60. E. J. Young, *The Prophecy of Daniel: A Commentary* (Grand Rapids: Eerdmans, 1949), 320.

61. See Robert C. Hill, trans., *Theodoret of Cyrus: Commentary on Daniel* (Leiden: Brill 2006).

62. Montgomery, *A Critical and Exegetical Commentary on the Book of Daniel*, 469.

63. Joyce G. Baldwin, *Daniel*, Tyndale Old Testament Commentaries 23 (Downers Grove, IL: InterVarsity, 1978), 193, writes similarly: "The historical interpretation is surely correct in seeing a primary fulfilment of Daniel's prophecy in the second century BC, but to confine its meaning to that period is to close one's eyes to the witness of Jesus and of the New Testament writers in general that it also had a future significance."

64. See the contestation of this view by Joyce G. Baldwin, "Is There Pseudonymity in the Old Testament?," *Themelios* 4.1 (1978): 6–12.

65. J. Collins, *Daniel*, 26. Italics added.

66. See his comments under Dan 2:1b; 2:48.

67. Hartman and Di Lella, *The Book of Daniel*, 219, write: "The question why Jesus used the term [Son of Man] in regard to himself is solely a New Testament problem, treated in commentaries on the Gospels…and need not concern us here."

68. Baldwin's view resembles the conclusion of E. J. Young, *The Prophecy of Daniel*, 25: "It is one thing to issue a harmless romance under a pseudonym; it is an entirely different thing to issue under a pseudonym a book claiming to be a revelation of God…the usage of the NT shows that the NT writers did not look upon this book as a romance. It was none other than our Lord, the incarnate Son of God, Who spoke of Himself in terms taken from the book of Daniel. In the light of the decisive and authoritative usage of the NT, one is compelled to reject the idea that Daniel is a mere romance."

69. I realize that a very plausible case can be made for dating the Book of Revelation just prior to the destruction of Jerusalem in early 70 CE. See: G. Edmundson, *The Church in Rome in the First Century* (New York: Longmans, Green, 1913).

70. This survey of New Testament allusions to Daniel was gleaned from Baldwin, *Daniel*, 194.

71. C. H. Dodd, "The Fall of Jerusalem and the 'Abomination of Desolation,'" *Journal of Roman Studies* (1947): 47–54.
72. Baldwin, *Daniel*, 48–49.
73. Cf. J. Bergsma and B. Pitre, "Daniel," 875–906 in *A Catholic Introduction to the Bible*, vol. 1: *The Old Testament* (San Francisco: Ignatius, 2018).
74. Bergsma and Pitre, *Catholic Introduction to the Bible*, 896.
75. P. P. Saydon, "Daniel," 621–43 in *A Catholic Commentary on Holy Scripture*, ed. B. Orchard et al. (New York: Thomas Nelson, 1953).
76. D. Block, *The Book of Ezekiel*, 2 vols., New International Commentary on the Old Testament (Grand Rapids: Eerdmans, 1997, 1998), 1:449. See also: J. Day, "The Daniel of Ugarit and Ezekiel and the Hero of the Book of Daniel," *VT* [*Vetus Testamentum*] 30 (1980): 174–84.
77. John J. Collins, *Daniel, First Maccabees, Second Maccabees, with an Excursus on the Apocalyptic Genre* (Wilmington, DE: Michael Glazier, 1981), 149 says: "In sharp contrast to the highly symbolic language of Daniel, 1 Maccabees makes the impression of a straightforward historical account. In fact, it is universally recognized as a major source of historical information, although it is not without errors. Yet, no historical account is entirely objective."
78. *Ant* 10.266.
79. Aline Canellis, ed., *Jérôme: Préfaces aux livres de la Bible, textes latins des éditions de R. Weber et R. Gryson et de L'Abbaya Saint-Jérôme (Rome)*, Revus et Corrigés, SC 592 (Paris: Cerf, 2017). The original version is found in *Biblia Sacra iuxta Vulgatam Versionem*, ed. R. Weber, 3rd ed. (Stuttgart: Deutsche Bibelgesellschaft, 1969), 1341–42.
80. Swete, *An Introduction to the Old Testament in Greek*, 47.
81. It is found in Codex Alexandrinus, Codex Vaticanus, Codex Marchalianus; cf. Swete, *Introduction to the Old Testament in Greek*, 165ff.
82. Swete, *Introduction to the Old Testament in Greek*, 260.
83. Swete, *Introduction to the Old Testament in Greek*, 260. The mention of Julius Africanus and Origen concerns their famous exchange of letters. See ANF 4.385–92. I have included a revised version of this older translation by Dr. Frederick Crombie in an appendix of the present volume.
84. See: R. H. Charles, ed., *The Apocrypha and Pseudepigrapha of the Old Testament*, vol. 1 (Oxford: Oxford University Press, 1913), 625–64.
85. Dan 1:1—2.4a and 7–12 are written in Hebrew, whereas 2:4b—6:29 are written in Aramaic. The additions (3:24–45, 46–90; 13; 14) survive in Greek.
86. See my explanatory note *ad loc* that clarifies this.
87. Cf. R. Courtray, "Jérôme, traducteur de Livre de Daniel," *Pallas* 75 (2007): 105–24 (108).
88. *Apology against Jerome* 2.33 (NPNF2, 3.475).
89. NPNF2 3.516–17.
90. Cf. *Nova Vulgata Bibliorum Sacrorum editio* (1986), 1601–32.
91. Courtray, "Jérôme, traducteur de Livre de Daniel," 122–23. My translation.
92. G. Archer, trans., *Jerome's Commentary on Daniel* (Grand Rapids: Baker, 1958).

93. For convenience, I have adapted this chart from J. Baldwin, *Daniel*, 81.
In the endnotes below, I have also provided repeated reminders of the dates of rulers, drawing on various scholarly sources. There is not always perfect agreement on the dates, which may introduce some inconsistencies.

JEROME'S PREFACE ON THE PROPHET DANIEL

1. My new translation of this preface is based on Aline Canellis, ed., *Jérôme: Préfaces aux Livres de la Bible, Textes Latins des Éditions de R. Weber et R. Gryson et de L'Abbaya Saint-Jérôme (Rome), Revus et Corrigés*, SC 592 (Paris: Cerf, 2017), 450–64. An earlier version is in *Biblia Sacra Vulgatam Versionem*, ed. R. Weber, 3rd ed. (Stuttgart: Deutsche Bibelgesellschaft, 1969), 1341–42.

2. Lit.: "Lord Savior."

3. For Theodotion, see introduction.

4. A. Kamesar, *Jerome, Hebrew Scholarship, and the Hebrew Bible: A Study of the Quaestiones Hebraicae in Genesim* (Oxford: Oxford University Press, 1993), 7 explains: "By the time of Jerome, however, [for the Book of Daniel] the version of Theodotion had replaced that of the LXX in ecclesiastical usage." S. Jelicoe has suggested that Origen was responsible for this transition since all of Origen's citations of Daniel agree with Theodotion and he says (as preserved by Jerome, *Comm. in Dan.* 1 on 4:5a) that he would follow that version in his commentary on Daniel from chapter 4. Kamesar (*Jerome*, 7) goes on to say: "If Origen was in favor of replacing the LXX version with that of Theodotion, it is likely that his grounds for this were the fact that the former version contained too many deviations from the Hebrew."

5. Jerome uses the terms *Chaldee* and *Syriac* to refer to the language we call Aramaic. Dan 2:4—7:28; Ezra 4:8—6:8; 7:12–26; Jer 10:11 were written in Aramaic.

6. For a concise delineation of Aramaic words in Job, see S. R. Driver and G. B. Gray, *A Critical and Exegetical Commentary on the Book of Job* (Edinburgh: T&T Clark, 1921), xlvi–xlvii.

7. Quintilian (35–100 CE) was a Roman rhetorician and teacher from Spain whose *Institutio Oratoria* (*Education of an Orator*) survives complete.

8. Marcus Tullius Cicero (106–43 BCE) was the most famous Latin prose writer.

9. Canellis, *Jérôme: Préfaces aux Livres de la Bible*, SC 592, 453n7 indicates the grindstone (or the mill) is a punishment reserved for slaves, well known in the comedies of Plautus and Terence. Cf. Terence, *And* 199, 214; Plautus, *Pseud* 434; Cicero, *De Or* 1.11.46.

10. He means Hebrew.

11. An autobiographical passage from *Ep* 125.12 to Rusticus (411 CE) is similar to this one: "In my youth when the desert walled me in with its solitude I was still unable to endure the promptings of sin and the natural heat of my blood; and, although I tried by frequent fasts to break the force of both, my mind still surged with [evil] thoughts. To subdue its turbulence I betook myself to a brother who before his conversion had been a Jew and asked him to teach me Hebrew. Thus, after having familiarized myself with the pointedness of Quintilian, the fluency of Cicero, the seriousness of Fronto

NOTES   185

and the gentleness of Pliny, I began to learn my letters anew and to study to pronounce words both harsh and guttural. What labor I spent upon this task, what difficulties I went through, how often I despaired, how often I gave over and then in my eagerness to learn commenced again, can be attested both by myself the subject of this misery and by those who then lived with me. But I thank the Lord that from this seed of learning sown in bitterness I now cull sweet fruits." NPNF2 6.248.

12. Jerome uses the image of walking through an underground passage in his *Commentary on Ezekiel* 12 at 40:5–13. Canellis, *Jérôme: Préfaces aux Livres de la Bible*, SC 592, 454n1 calls this an astonishing parallel.

13. Virgil, *Georgics* 1.145–146.

14. Jerome uses this word (*sciolus*) in *Ep* 48.18; 58.5; 125.16.

15. An obelus (†) indicates words or lines that were lacking in the Hebrew. It comes from ὀβελός and refers to a critical mark shaped like a spit or small dagger placed opposite suspect passages.

16. Given in Greek.

17. This letter exchange is found in ANF 4.385–92. Because of the importance of Origen's discussion as essential background to Jerome's comments, and for the reader's convenience, I have included a slightly revised version of Frederick Crombie's nineteenth-century translation in an appendix to the present volume. Daniel twice makes a sinister wordplay based upon the Greek names of these two trees. The Hebrew's objection to the authenticity of Susanna (and the objection of Julius Africanus) is that a similar pun could not be made out from the Hebrew names, if any, of these trees; therefore, the story itself could never have been composed in Hebrew. In his reply to Africanus, Origen says that the Hebrew Bible testifies to the use of similar puns. Origen conjectures that this story could have originated in a Hebrew version, and he piercingly asks Julius Africanus, what was the basis of his confidence that the puns could not work in Hebrew. Modern scholars believe that Susanna was probably originally composed in Hebrew.

18. *Ilico* is an adverb and means "on the spot, immediately." It resembles *ilex, ilicis* f. holm oak. Jerome has successfully translated the Greek word play into Latin.

19. Lentil is a leguminous plant with flattened seeds and leafy stalks used as fodder.

20. Jerome also refers to this play on words in *Commentary on Jeremiah* Bk 1 on Jer 1:11–12. He finds Jeremiah's play on "nut-tree" and "watch" similar to Daniel's pun.

21. Julius Africanus makes a similar objection.

22. In his *Commentary on Ezekiel* Bk 3 on Ezek 8:3, and *Commentary on Hosea* Bk 1 Pref, Jerome says that Ezekiel's translation to the inner shrine of the temple was a visionary experience of the prophet that was done without the prophet's physical presence in that location.

23. As mentioned in the introduction, Rufinus of Aquileia reprimanded Jerome for his seeming preference of the Jewish canon over the Christian one. Jerome's response recorded above seems to imply that he personally disagreed with the contemporary Jewish rejection of the Greek additions to Daniel. Braverman, *Jerome's Commentary on Daniel*, 133 thinks that Jerome has

certainly given a weak answer to Rufinus here: "The truth is that he [Jerome] never did later make time to defend the canonicity of these sections of Daniel, even in his *Commentary on Daniel* (407). In fact, he there indicates the opposite."

24. Jerome is referring to contemporary Jews. (The Jews who compiled the LXX version placed Daniel among the Major Prophets immediately after Ezekiel.) In rabbinic Judaism, Jewish sacred writings were described with the acronym *TaNaKh*. The Law, or *Torah*, contains five books: Genesis, Exodus, Leviticus, Numbers, and Deuteronomy. The Prophets, *Nevi'im*, comprise eight books subdivided into the Former Prophets, containing the four historical works Joshua, Judges, Samuel, and Kings; and the Latter Prophets, the oracular discourses of Isaiah, Jeremiah, Ezekiel, and the Twelve (Minor) Prophets—Hosea, Joel, Amos, Obadiah, Jonah, Micah, Nahum, Habakkuk, Zephaniah, Haggai, Zechariah, and Malachi. The Twelve were all formerly written on a single scroll and thus reckoned as one book. The Holy Writings, Ketuvim, consist of religious poetry and wisdom literature—Psalms, Proverbs, and Job, a collection known as the "Five Megillot" ("scrolls"; i.e., Song of Songs, Ruth, Lamentations, Ecclesiastes, and Esther, which have been grouped together according to the annual cycle of their public reading in the synagogue)—and the Books of Daniel, Ezra and Nehemiah, and Chronicles. This summary has been adapted from https://www.britannica.com/topic/Tanakh.

25. In *Vir ill* 83, Jerome reports that Methodius was bishop of Olympus in Lycia and afterward of Tyre. He was martyred in the reign of Decius and Valerianus at Chalcis in Greece. His writings against Porphyry are not extant.

26. Eusebius of Caesarea (d. 340), also known as Eusebius Pamphilii, was a famous bishop, scholar, and church historian, who assumed the cognomen "of Pamphilus" in honor of his beloved mentor, the priest-martyr Pamphilus. See Jerome, *Vir ill* 81.

27. In *Vir ill* 26, Jerome reports that Apollinaris was bishop of Hierapolis in Asia. He flourished in the reign of Marcus Antoninus Verus, to whom he addressed a notable volume on behalf of the faith of the Christians. He also wrote against Montanus. His work against Porphyry does not survive. In *Ep* 84.3, Jerome said that he had learned biblical interpretation from Apollinaris, though he distanced himself from Apollinaris's heterodox understanding of the incarnation.

28. For Porphyry, see introduction.

29. St. Paula (347–404) was a noble Roman lady of great wealth, the mother of four daughters and one son. In 382, during the synod held at Rome that followed on the council of Constantinople, she hosted in her house the bishops Epiphanius of Salamis and Paulinus of Antioch (the bishop who had ordained Jerome). Through them, Jerome became intimately acquainted with her. After her husband's death in 384, she accompanied Jerome to Palestine in 385 and lived the rest of her life in Bethlehem. In *Ep* 108 to Eustochium, which is a consolatory letter written to her daughter, Jerome gives the chief facts of Paula's life. In *Vir ill* 135 he testifies that he does not know how many letters he has written to her, because he writes every day either to her or to her daughter Eustochium.

30. St. Eustochium (370?–418) was the third daughter of Paula who accompanied her mother to Palestine and presided over the hospice and convent in Bethlehem after Paula's death. She had taken a vow of perpetual virginity. Jerome wrote his famous *Ep* 22 to confirm her in this resolution.

[JEROME'S COMMENTARY] ON THE PROPHET DANIEL: PREFACE

1. My English translation is from the new critical text edited by Régis Courtray, *Jérôme, Commentaire sur Daniel*, SC 602 (Paris: Cerf, 2019).
2. In Jerome's *Commentary on Matthew* Bk 4, on Matt 24:18, he reports that Porphyry wrote against Daniel in the *thirteenth* volume of his work. Since Porphyry's work is not extant, it is not possible to determine in which volume of Porphyry the allegations occur.
3. Antiochus IV Epiphanes ascended to the throne of the Seleucid Empire in 175 BCE and died in 164 BCE. His surname Epiphanes means "illustrious" or "manifest." He attempted to Hellenize the Jews of Palestine, conquered Jerusalem, desecrated the temple and persecuted the Jews severely, as is recorded in the Books of Maccabees. A revolt against his measures was led by the priest Mattathias and his five sons, among whom Judas Maccabeus was the military leader. In 164 BCE Judas Maccabeus retook Jerusalem and cleansed and rededicated the temple, thereby inaugurating the festival of Hanukkah. Cf. 1 Macc 1:10–15; 2 Macc 4:7–20. For Christian interpreters (beginning with Jesus and Paul), Antiochus IV Epiphanes became a type of the antichrist, who will persecute the church prior to the second coming.
4. All three of the treatises against Porphyry mentioned here have been lost.
5. See Jerome's comments at Dan 7:17; 9:24–27; 11:21–45; 12:13.
6. This would refer chiefly to Dan 11.
7. Courtray, SC 602, 127n3 comments: "Jerome's point is ironic: he means that Porphyry's opinion has been accepted as truth by the enemies of Christians."
8. St. Pammachius (d. 410) was a senator of the family of Furii, fellow student and friend of Jerome. Jerome dedicated some works to him and wrote him many letters (*Epp* 48, 49, 57, 66, 83, 84, 97). He married Paulina, daughter of the Roman matron Paula and, widowed in 397, entered monastic life. When Jerome wrote his books against Jovinian in 392, Pammachius rebuked Jerome for his excessively violent language. Later he sided with Jerome during the Origenist controversies. Jerome dedicated to him his commentaries on Obadiah and Daniel. Pammachius spent his fortune to assist the poor and built a hospice for pilgrims at Porto in Rome. He died in 410 during the invasion of the Goths.
9. Jerome uses the Greek superlative: φιλομαθεστατε. Lampe PGL 1479 provides only the adverb φιλομαθῶς, "with zeal for knowledge, learnedly." The word is used in Origen's *Contra Celsum* 2.55.
10. St. Marcella was a wealthy Roman lady descended from the illustrious family of the Marcelli. Widowed after seven months of marriage, she refused a marriage offer by the distinguished and wealthy Cerealis, despite

pleas from her mother Albina. She became a friend of Jerome and adopted a strict ascetic lifestyle while continuing to live with her mother in the palatial residence on the Aventine, the southernmost of Rome's seven hills.

11. These would be (using the LXX enumeration) Pss 4—6, 8—13, 18—20, 22, 30, 35, 38—41, 43—46, 48, 50—61, 63—69, 74—76, 79, 80, 83, 84, 108, 138, 139. Add one to match the English. The RSV renders this: "To the choirmaster."

12. For Aquila, see the introduction.

13. For Symmachus, see the introduction.

14. Reaburn, "St. Jerome and Porphyry Interpret the Book of Daniel," *Australian Biblical Review* 52 (2004): 3–4 finds this passage noteworthy: "Thus, he sets the tone, a battle is about to begin, a battle of words. Amongst the unnamed adversaries is Porphyry."

15. Jerome uses the Greek ἐτυμολογίαν which means "etymology" or "analysis of a word to find its origin."

16. See his comments under 1:3–4a.

17. Note this proof that Jerome had finished his Vulgate translation of Daniel well before he wrote his commentary on the book. A new translation of this preface is provided above.

18. Obelus comes from ὀβελός and refers to a critical mark shaped like a spit or small dagger placed opposite suspect passages. In his Hexapla, Origen marked with an obelus (†) words or lines that were lacking in the Hebrew.

19. Jerome is criticizing Porphyry for his inability to distinguish the textual traditions found in Daniel. Based on the Greek wordplays found in the Story of Susanna, the Neoplatonist scholar seems to have thought that the whole Book of Daniel was an original Greek composition and thus a forgery that does not belong to the Hebrew Scriptures. See M. Reaburn, "St. Jerome and Porphyry," 4.

20. Jerome uses the Greek μεμψιμοίρους. The allusion is to Rufinus, *Apology against Jerome* 2.39, who had reproached Jerome for altering Scripture and notably suppressing Susanna and the Song of the Three Youths.

21. Cf. Origen, *Epistle to Julius Africanus* 2, 6, 11–12 (ANF 4.386–91); Eusebius, *Contra Porphyry* 18–20; Apollinaris, *Contra Porphyry* 26. It is noteworthy, however, that Origen defended the authenticity of the story of Susanna in his letter to Julius Africanus. See the appendix.

22. See the note above on Theodotion.

23. Asterisk comes from ἀστερίσκος and refers to a small star used as diacritical mark placed before imperfect, deficient passages.

24. Cf. Origen, *Epistle to Julius Africanus* 2–4.

25. I believe he means, since the Greek Origen did not despise the effort of Theodotion the Jew.

26. Apart from Rufinus of Aquileia, one of Jerome's strongest critics in this respect was Augustine of Hippo. In *Ep* 56.2 (Aug. *Ep* 28), Augustine pleaded with Jerome not to translate Scripture into Latin from the Hebrew but from the Hexaplaric revision of the Greek Septuagint, preserving the critical marks. Augustine writes (in 394 CE): "But with respect to the sacred canonical books, I would not want you to exert yourself in the work of translating them into the Latin language, unless you do so in the manner in which

you have translated Job, namely, with the addition of symbols to let it be seen plainly what differences there are between your translation and that of the Septuagint, the authority of which weighs the most. But I cannot express my surprise adequately over the idea that anything is still found in the Hebrew manuscripts that escaped the notice of so many extremely experienced translators of that language. I say nothing of the fact that there were Seventy of them, whose concord in counsel and spirit is greater than that of one man. In no way do I dare pronounce a definitive judgment about this, except to say that it is beyond question, in my judgment, that in this task [of translation] preeminent authority must be granted to them. Those other translators [Symmachus, Theodotion, Aquila] disturb me all the more who, it is reported, held rather tenaciously to the way and rules of Hebrew words and expressions, even though they translated later in time. Yet they not only failed to agree among themselves, but have left many things that, even after so long a time, remained to be elicited and brought to light. For if these things are obscure, it is believed that you too could be mistaken in them; if they are clear, it is not believed that the Seventy could possibly have been mistaken in them." Jerome replied vehemently and sarcastically to this criticism in *Ep* 112.20.

27. Courtray, SC 602 133n6 observes how Jerome uses his polemic against Porphyry as a plea on behalf of his own translation.

28. In the introduction, I cited at length Jerome's *Commentary on Isaiah*, Preface to Bk 11, where he reports that this deviation from his normal commentary method for the Book of Daniel generated new complaints from readers, who wanted him to treat every verse. So he says that for his final commentaries on Isaiah, Ezekiel, and Jeremiah, he will revert to the more comprehensive approach used on the Twelve Prophets according to which every single verse is treated.

29. He means chaps. 10–12.

30. Sutorius Callinicus was a Syrian author who wrote a history of Alexander the Great ca. 270 BCE. The work does not survive.

31. Diodorus Siculus of Agyrium, Sicily is the author of the *Library*, a universal history from mythological times to 60 BCE.

32. Hieronymus of Cardia was an historian in the court of Antigonus the One-eyed after Eumenes's death at Gabiene in 316 BCE. He was a primary source for Diodorus Siculus's history of Greek affairs.

33. Polybius (200–118 BCE) was a Greek statesman and historian, active in the Achaean League against the Romans. After the Greek defeat in the Battle of Pydna in 168 BCE, he was brought to Rome and became a friend of Scipio Aemilianus. He wrote a universal history covering the events in Roman history from 220 BCE to the destruction of Carthage and Corinth in 146 BCE. The first five books and fragments of the rest survive. He was an important source for Porphyry's historical criticism of the Book of Daniel.

34. Posidonius was a writer, philosopher, and Greek physician ca. 135–50 BCE.

35. Little is known of Claudius Theon and of Andronicus Alypius, third-century-BCE historians.

36. H. Hagendahl, *Latin Fathers and the Classics*, 225–26 comments: "While making a show of learning Jerome in reality got his knowledge of

Callinicus Sutorius, Polybius and Diodorus from Porphyrius." Moreover, Courcelle has shown that Jerome's knowledge of Porphyry's Κατὰ Χριστιανῶν was not direct but derivative from Methodius of Olympus, Eusebius of Caesarea, Apollinaris of Laodicea, as well as Origen. Cf. *Late Latin Writers and their Greek Sources*, 75. Yet despite this heavy reliance on his predecessors, Jerome's service to posterity in preserving this material from Porphyry was immense.

37. Flavius Josephus (37–100 CE) was a first-century Jewish writer who fought in the Jewish war in Galilee against the Romans. He was captured and became a court historian, writing *Antiquities of the Jews*, *Jewish War*, and *Against Apion*. Jerome knew these Greek works well. Cf. Courcelle, *Late Latin Writers and their Greek Sources*, 83–85.

38. Livy (59 BCE–17 CE) is the most famous writer of Roman history. Pompeius Trogus is a Roman historian who dates to the reign of Augustus and is known only through the epitome of the historian Justin, a second-century-BCE writer.

39. I believe Jerome is referring to his vow to renounce secular literature made in a dream recorded in *Ep* 22.30 to Eustochium. Rufinus had ridiculed him for not keeping his word, spoken in a dream, by continuing to consult secular literature. Cf. Rufinus, *Apology against Jerome* 2.6.

40. M. Reaburn, "St. Jerome and Porphyry," 4–5 summarizes Jerome's prefatory remarks: "The Prologue makes plain the fact that Jerome understands that Porphyry's interpretation threatens the standing of Daniel as prophecy and indirectly threatens the Gospel which places Daniel amongst the prophets (Matt 24:15). Porphyry does this not so much through the Maccabean interpretation of much of Daniel but by his claim that Daniel is *ex eventu*. He believes that by demonstrating that Porphyry's historical interpretation is not the only way to understand the book, the claim that Daniel is *ex eventu* will be defeated."

BOOK ONE

1. Jerome consistently uses the LXX form Nabuchodonosor. C. Lattey, *The Book of Daniel* (Dublin: Richview Press, 1948), 121 provides the following commencement dates for the rulers of the Second Babylonian Empire: Nabopolassar 625 BCE; Nebuchadnezzar 605; Amel-Marduk (= Evil-Merodach) 562–61; Nergal-Sharezer (= Neriglissar) 560; Labashi-Marduk 556; Nabuna'id (= Nabonidus) 554–38.

2. Cf. Hippolytus, *In Dan* 1.1–2 (ANF 5.177–78); Josephus, *Ant* 10.5.2–8.

3. Lit. "moved their feet."

4. Cf. Jerome *Nom Hebr* 3.18; 25.6; 48.11; 63.13–14; 72.20; 80.15.

5. Jerome gives the Greek ἀναγωγὴν which refers to the spiritual, mystical or tropological meaning of the text that transcends the literal level of interpretation. In Lampe's *Patristic Greek Lexicon*, the first meaning given to ἀναγωγή is "elevation, ascent." The noun ἀναγωγεύς means "one who guides upward." In the spiritual sense, the ascent occurs from sense perception and images to divine realities. The anagogical interpretation of Scripture leads the hearer upward from human realities to the divine Logos.

6. Plato of Athens (429–347 BCE), under the major philosophical influence of Socrates (d. 399 BCE), founded a philosophical school called the Academy.
7. Cf. Plato, *Timaeus* 34c–36e.
8. Zeno of Citium (335–263 BCE) taught in the Stoa Poecile ("Painted Colonnade"), which gave its name to Stoicism. Cf. Lactantius, *Div Inst* 7.7.13.
9. H. Hagendahl, *Latin Fathers and the Classics: A Study on the Apologists, Jerome and Other Christian Writers* (Gothenburg: Almquist & Wiksell, 1958), 227 thinks these references derive from Origen. See also Lactantius, *Div inst* 3.18.5.
10. *Tyrannorum*. G. Archer, *Jerome's Commentary on Daniel* (Grand Rapids: Baker, 1958), 20 indicates that this is Jerome's rendering of the Hebrew *partemim*, "nobles."
11. Cf. R. Courtray, "Daniel et Ashpenaz: sur quelques lectures contemporaines de Daniel 1, 7 et 9," *Anabases* 13 (2011): 55–78.
12. Normally in Jerome's usage "common version" refers to the LXX. Courtray, SC 602, 143n3 helps to clarify Jerome's remark by pointing to *Ep* 106.2, where Jerome explains that there are two versions of the Septuagint in circulation: one that the Greek authors with Origen call the common and current edition, also known as the Lucian edition; this is the old edition, corrupted over the years by the whims of copyists. The other is that found in the Hexapla manuscripts, and it is, according to Jerome, the true version of the Septuagint, the scholarly edition, maintained in its primitive purity. Kamesar comments on this passage in *Ep* 106 and says that Jerome's Hexaplaric revision must be understood not in terms of a LXX versus Hebrew opposition, but rather in the context of the rivalry between the recensions of the LXX. There were three competing recensions of the LXX in the East, and the Hexaplaric recension had not attained universal recognition. Jerome's Hexaplaric recension was his attempt to extend in the West the influence of the recension of the LXX he believed to be correct. "That this was his view is evident from *Ep* 106.2, where he describes the Hexaplaric LXX as 'incorrupta et inmaculata septuaginta interpretum translatio' and compares it with the corrupt κοινή, which he identifies with the recension of Lucian....Jerome therefore took a firm position regarding the rivalry between the recensions, and maintained that position throughout his life." A. Kamesar, *Jerome, Greek Scholarship, and the Hebrew Bible: A Study of the Quaestiones Hebraicae in Genesim* (Oxford: Oxford University Press, 1993), 56.
13. The Parthians were a Scythian people, situated to the northeast of the passes of the Caspian and south of Hyrcania. They were famous in antiquity as roving warriors and skillful archers.
14. He gives the Greek: κατὰ ἀκρίβειαν.
15. See Talmud, Sanhedrin 93b, Rab; Seder Elia R., 24; Pirqe R. Eliezer 52.52. Jerome also mentions this tradition in *Commentary on Isaiah* Bk 11 on Isa 39:7.
16. The dominant tradition in rabbinic literature is that Daniel and his associates were literally eunuchs. Cf. Braverman, *Jerome's Commentary on Daniel: A Study of Comparative Jewish and Christian Interpretation of the Hebrew Bible* (Washington, DC: Catholic Biblical Association, 1978), 54–55. Josephus

confirms it in *Ant* 10.10.1–2. Origen refers to this tradition in *Commentary on Matthew* 15:5; *Sel in Ezek* 14:16, and *Hom 4 on Ezekiel*. Jerome himself was the translator of the latter. Jerome also refers to this tradition in *Adversus Jovinianum* 1.25.

17. In the Preface to Book 1, Jerome says that Daniel and the three youths descended from the tribe of Judah.

18. The passage in Philo has not been identified. Philo of Alexandria (ca. 20 BCE–ca 50 CE) was a Jewish public official and philosopher and a prolific writer whose books were known intimately by Origen. Philo wrote a large number of commentaries on the Pentateuch, making use of Middle Platonism to interpret Scripture. See David T. Runia, "Philo of Alexandria," 169–71 in *The Westminster Handbook to Origen*, ed. John A. McGuckin (Louisville, KY: Westminster John Knox, 2004). Courcelle, *Late Latin Writers and their Greek Sources*, 81 says that Jerome's remarks on Philo in *De vir ill* 11 are pure plagiarism from Eusebius.

19. Heb.: *Zaphenath-paaneah*.

20. *Boanerges* corresponds to the Greek text of Mark 3:17. Archer, *Jerome's Commentary on Daniel*, 21 indicates that Jerome's conjectural spelling has no manuscript support but would be the Hebrew for "sons of thunder." Cf. *Nom Hebr* 66. Jerome discusses scriptural name changes in a passage based in Origen in his *Commentary on Philemon* 1–3.

21. Jerome moves from the singular to the plural to include Daniel's three companions.

22. This may be a subtle jab at Macarius and Rufinus of Aquileia. With Rufinus, who was his former friend, Jerome engaged in strident controversy on the subject of Origen's book *On First Principles*. In his *Apology against Jerome* 1.11–12 (NPNF2, 3.439–40), Rufinus claims that his project to translate Origen's *On First Principles* into Latin was inspired in part by a request for theological assistance from Macarius, who was writing a book entitled *Mathesis*, or *Against the Mathematicians*, directed against astrologers who negated free will and endorsed the idea of positive and negative astral influences upon human beings. Rufinus replied that Origen had touched on some of these matters in *Princ*. See my translation: St. Pamphilus, *Apology for Origen*; Rufinus, *On the Falsification of the Books of Origen*, trans. Thomas P. Scheck, FOTC 120 (Washington, DC: Catholic University of America Press, 2010).

23. Notice how Jerome seems to say that God gave his grace in response to Daniel's worthiness. Augustine would later accuse this idea of being heresy in respect to Pelagius, but it was quite a common view in pre-Augustinian writers. See Ali Bonner's discussion, *The Myth of Pelagianism*, British Academy Monographs (Oxford: Oxford University Press, 2018), 134–39. On the other hand, under 2:23 Jerome says that Daniel did not procure God's help due to his own merit, but he refers it to the justice of his forefathers. There seem to be different senses of the terms *merit* and *worthiness*.

24. The word *corpulentia* is used in Tertullian, *Carn. Chr.* 3.

25. Cf. Hippolytus, *In Dan* 1:12 (ANF 5.186): "Thou hast seen the incorruptible faith of the youths, and the unalterable fear of God. They asked an interval of ten days, to prove therein that man cannot otherwise find grace with God than by believing the word preached by the Lord."

26. Courtray, SC 602, 153n1 observes that by *verbum* Jerome translates the Hebrew word *dabar*, which also means "point, matter, thing." He is following the translations of the LXX (λόγος) and Theodotion (ῥῆμα).

27. In classical antiquity, sophists were itinerant professors of higher education who provided rhetorical training for aspiring politicians. Some viewed them as subversive to morality and tradition and disapproved of their argumentative techniques. Plato viewed them negatively and as partially responsible for the death of Socrates.

28. Cf. Diogenes Laertius, *De vir ill*, prol.; Origen, *Contra Celsum* 1.58.

29. Lattey, *The Book of Daniel*, 121 gives the following commencement dates for the rulers of the Persian Empire: Cyrus, 538 BCE; Cambyses 529; Darius I (Hystaspis) 522; Xerxes I (= Ahasuerus) 485; Artaxerxes I (Longimanus) 464; Xerxes II 424; Darius II (Nothus) 423; Artaxerxes II (Mnemon) 404; Artaxerxes III (Ochus) 359; Darius III (Codomannus) 338–1. Compare this with the list from Eusebius's *Chronicle* cited under Dan 11:2b.

30. Josephus, *Ant* 10.10.3. Braverman, *Jerome's Commentary on Daniel*, 72–73 comments: "Both Jerome's source as well as Josephus give the same essential answer, which Jerome adopts, offering no alternatives: the 'second year' of Nebuchadnezzar's reign does not refer to his reign over Judea alone; instead it refers to the time he subsequently enlarged his empire by conquering other nations."

31. Cf. Hippolytus, *In Dan* 2:2–5 (ANF 5.186); Jerome, *Commentary on Jeremiah* 4.59.2 on Jer 23:25–27.

32. This is Lampe's suggested meaning, PGL 510. See Origen, *Princ* 3.3.3.

33. Lampe PGL 309 suggests the meaning "casting of nativities, astrology" for the noun γενεθλιαλογία. It is found in Origen, *Contra Celsum* 6.80.

34. Or "mathematicians," as Archer rendered it by transliteration.

35. For the expression "so to speak" (*ut ita dicam*) in Jerome, see P. Antin, "'Ut ita dicam' chez saint Jérôme," *Latomus* 25 (1966): 299–304.

36. Dan 2:4b—7:28 is preserved in Aramaic (except for the Song of the Three Youths in 3:24–90, which survives in Greek). Jerome uses the term *Syriac* to designate Aramaic.

37. Cf. Hippolytus, *In Dan* 2:3 (ANF 5.186): "The dream, then, which was seen by the king was not an earthly dream, so that it might be interpreted by the wise of the world; but it was a heavenly dream, fulfilled in its proper times, according to the counsel and foreknowledge of God. And for this reason it was kept secret from men who think of earthly things, that to those who seek after heavenly things heavenly mysteries might be revealed."

38. Braverman, *Jerome's Commentary on Daniel*, 77 reports that the Jewish interpretations mentioned here by Jerome cannot be found in extant rabbinic literature nor in medieval commentaries, but the explanation of Jepheth ibn Ali is similar to the first answer brought by Jerome.

39. See under 2:49.

40. This rare word, *subostendo*, is used by Tertullian, *Adv Marc* 4.38.

41. The speaker in the lemma is Arioch, captain of the guard of King Nebuchadnezzar.

42. Jerome finds the idea that Daniel was a priest, mentioned also in the Preface to the commentary, as evidence against the authenticity of the story of Bel, since priests came from the tribe of Levi (cf. Exod 29; Num 1). Braverman, *Jerome's Commentary on Daniel*, 70 thinks that the tradition that Daniel was a priest may be based on identifying him with the priest named Daniel in Neh 10:7. A Daniel is also recorded as a member of the priestly family of Ithamar in Ezra 8:2. The names Mishael, Azariah, and Hananiah appear in Neh 8:4; 10:3, 24 respectively as contemporaries of this priest Daniel.

43. Archer, *Jerome's Commentary on Daniel*, 29 inserts "sic!" here since this portion of the book is preserved in Aramaic. Jerome may simply be referring to the Hebrew alphabet in which the Aramaic is written.

44. Archer, *Jerome's Commentary on Daniel*, 29 adds: "actually the Aramaic word is *gazerin*."

45. Cf. Lampe PGL 608.

46. Cf. Tertullian, *De Anima* 15.1–6.

47. Courtray, SC 602, 170 says that the passage in Plato has not been identified. The Stoics use the term ἡγεμονικόν to describe the governing part of the soul. Plato describes this as the rational part of the soul (*Pol* 4.439c–d) and locates it in the brain and in the head, which is the most divine part of us and master of all the other parts (*Tim* 44d). In his *Commentary on Matthew* Bk 2 on Matt 15:19, Jerome says: "'Out of the heart,' he says, 'come evil thoughts.' Therefore, the master faculty of the soul (*animae principale*) is not in the brain, as Plato claims, but according to Christ it is in the heart." Cf. Jerome, *Ep* 64.1 to Fabiola.

48. According to Courtray, SC 602, 172n1, Jerome has no particular target in this statement about the belief that was prevalent in antiquity in the eternity of the world. It is known that Philo of Alexandria wrote a book entitled *On the Eternity of the World*.

49. Courtray, SC 602, 172n2 admits that Jerome's target is difficult to identify with precision, citing: B. Jeanjean, *Saint Jérôme et l'hérésie* (Paris, 2019), 216. Valentinian Gnosticism posited three different kinds of inborn natures, spiritual, animal, and earthly, and claimed that one kind is saved, another perishes, the third is between the two. Gnostics believed that free will and good or evil works play no role in salvation for those in the first and third categories. See Jerome, *Commentary on Galatians* Bk 1 on Gal 1:15–16; *Commentary on Matthew* Bk 1, on Matt 7:18. In *Princ* 2.9.5 Origen speaks similarly of those who come from the school of Marcion, Valentinus, and Basilides.

50. See his comment under Dan 4:7–8 (10–11) where Ps 37:35 LXX is cited.

51. Jerome does not mean that Nebuchadnezzar had an unchangeably evil nature in the gnostic sense, but that his actions had been evil.

52. This is from the Greek ἀνδριάς, ὁ, gen. ἀντος, image or statue of a man. Following Vallarsi's proposed correction, Courtray's SC 602 text alters Glorie's CCSL reading of ἀνδριάνθε (which had substituted a Latin *e* for Greek epsilon as the final letter of the Greek word). Courtray says that such a practice does not correspond to Jerome's habits.

53. Courtray, SC 602, 177n3 indicates that he chose the reading of most manuscripts *calcantes* (to tread, go through) rather than Glorie's reading

NOTES 195

adcantantes ("to sing at.") This is justified insofar as Jerome will actually "go through" verses 31–45, adding to the exposition of the vision (vv. 31–35) the explanations given below (vv. 37–45), and its own historical reading.

54. Cf. Hippolytus, *In Dan* 2 (ANF 5.186–87).

55. Cf. Cicero, *Brutus* 46, 171. Jerome, *Commentary on Ezekiel* Bk 12 on Ezek 40:1–4 writes: "For this material [bronze] is more capable of producing sound than all metals, and resounds with a ringing noise for a long time. And this is why in Daniel, in the image that was made out of gold, silver, bronze, and iron, the kingdom of Alexander and of the Greeks is shown in the likeness of bronze [cf. Dan 2:38–40], in order that the eloquence of the Greek language would be signified."

56. Cf. Jerome, *Commentary on Isaiah* Bk 11 Prol.

57. Cf. Origen, *Hom Cant* 2.3; *Hom Ex* 6.12.

58. E. J. Young, *The Prophecy of Daniel: A Commentary* (Grand Rapids: Eerdmans, 1949), 79 comments: "According to Jerome, Porphyry and the Jews refer the stone to the people who will become a great nation. Jerome himself sees the fulfillment in the Virgin Birth....Essentially this view is held by Justin Martyr, Tertullian, Irenaeus and Ephraim of Syria."

59. See under 2:23a.

60. Cf. Josephus, *Ant* 10.11.5.

61. According to Neh 12:22 he was a priest about the time of the Persian king Darius III Codomannus (336–331) (who was the Persian ruler who fell to Alexander the Great). Cf. Josephus, *Ant* 11.8.4–5; Eusebius, *Demon Evang* 8.2:67.

62. Cf. Hippolytus, *In Dan* 2:48 (ANF 5.187): "For as he had humbled himself, and presented himself as the least among all men, God made him great, and the king established him as ruler over the whole land of Babylon. Just as also Pharaoh did to Joseph, appointing him then to be ruler over the whole land of Egypt."

63. Cf. Hippolytus, *In Dan* 2:49 (ANF 5.187): "For as they had united with Daniel in prayer to God that the vision might be revealed to him, so Daniel, when he obtained great honor from the king, made mention of them, explaining to the king what had been done by them, in order that they also should be deemed worthy of some honor as fellow-seers and worshippers of God."

64. For brief studies of this chapter, see J. P. K. Kritzinger, "St. Jerome's Commentary on Daniel 3," *Acta Patristica et Byzantina* 16 (2005): 54–69; M. Dulaey, "Les trois Hebreux dans la fournaise (Daniel 3) dans l'interpretation de l'Eglise ancienne," *Revue des Sciences Religieuses* 71 (1997): 33–59.

65. As Kritzinger, "St. Jerome's Commentary on Daniel 3," 55 points out, this forgetting is in contrast with Daniel. See under 2:49a.

66. Cf. Minucius Felix, *Octavius* 24.10.

67. Origen discusses the sense of duty engraved on the hearts of all people by the finger of God that teaches them that human made objects should not be considered as gods. See *Contra Celsum* 1.5.

68. Lampe PGL 1062 cites Origen, *Contra Celsum* 6.80.

69. In English we have: "The bigger they are, the harder they fall."

70. Refers to a triangular stringed instrument of a very sharp, shrill tone.

71. Archer, *Jerome's Commentary on Daniel*, 36 inserts: "actually there are many instances; cf. Brown-Driver-Briggs, *Hebrew Lexicon*, 1005." My suspicion is that Jerome is incorporating a comment of Origen here.

72. See under 3:4–6.

73. See under 3:1.

74. Singular.

75. Archer, *Jerome's Commentary on Daniel*, 37 inserts: "i.e., Chaldee."

76. *Pulchre*. Courtray, SC 602, 192n1 cites Duval who has shown that the adverb *pulchre* constitutes a frequent appreciation in Jerome aimed at emphasizing the precision of the Scriptures. I have tried to render it "nice" or "nicely" in this translation.

77. Archer, *Jerome's Commentary on Daniel*, 39 inserts: "This is a literal rendering of the Septuagint's erroneous translation of the Hebrew title *'al shoshanni'm*, which occurs in Psalm 45 and Psalm 69, and signifies: 'Upon anemonies.'"

78. Cf. Jerome, *Ep* 65.3; *Commentary on Ezekiel* Bk 14 on Ezek 48:16.

79. Courtray, SC 602, says the source has not been identified.

80. The Greek word is found in Herodotus 5.49; 7.61; Xenophon *Anab* 1.5.8.

81. Archer, *Jerome's Commentary on Daniel*, 39 inserts: "apparently erroneous information; the lexicons give only 'trousers' or, preferably, 'mantle.'"

82. Jerome gives the Greek ὁμωνύμως.

83. Archer, *Jerome's Commentary on Daniel*, 39 inserts: "actually the Aramaic is *karbela*, 'cap.'"

84. Virgil, *Aeneid* 7.247.

85. Archer, *Jerome's Commentary on Daniel*, 39–40 inserts at this point in his translation: "Since tiara does not appear in the Aramaic original at all, the comment upon it seems quite misleading to a public not having access to the original. Two other comments ought to be made about Jerome's treatment of this verse: a) he puts 'turbans' (*caps*) before 'footgear' (*pattish*) instead of after it as the original does; b) he has nevertheless consulted the original carefully, since he avoids the variant reading of the LXX, which later substitutes 'upon their heads' for the word 'footgear.'"

86. Cf. Josephus, *Ant* 10.11.5; Hippolytus, *In Dan* 2:23.

87. Archer, *Jerome's Commentary on Daniel*, 40 inserts: "i.e. the Aramaic." Sixty-eight verses are inserted between vv. 23 and 24 of the Aramaic text.

88. He seems to be responding to Rufinus's criticism in *Apology against Jerome* 2.37. See: Jerome, *Apology against Rufinus* 2.33.

89. Since some Bibles versify the *Song of the Three Children* separately, I have provided this versification in ().

90. This material probably comes from Origen, *Stromata* 9.

91. Kritzinger, "St. Jerome's Commentary on Daniel 3," 61, cites as a parallel Jerome's *Commentary on Ephesians* (*Ad Ephesios* PL 26, 549, 477) where he mentions the three youths in one breath with the prophets Ezekiel, Daniel, Haggai, and Zechariah and says that they were led into exile, not because they deserved it, but to be a comfort to the captives.

92. Archer, *Jerome's Commentary on Daniel*, 40 translates this "as representatives of." *Persona* first means "a mask, or false face used by players on the stage, which covered the whole head, and was varied according to the different characters to be represented." In a transferred sense, it means a personage, character, part, represented by an actor.

93. Jerome interprets this section of Romans in *Ep* 121.8 to Algasia. I have produced a new translation of this letter in: St. Jerome, *Exegetical Letters*, 2 vols., trans. Thomas P. Scheck, FOTC (Washington, DC: Catholic University of America Press, 2023–24). Jerome's exegesis resembles Origen's, *Commentary on Romans* 6.9.12. Augustine's exegesis of Romans 7 is at variance with Jerome's and Origen's. See: Thomas F. Martin, *Rhetoric and Exegesis in Augustine's Interpretation of Romans 7:24–25a* (Lewiston, NY: Edwin Mellen, 2001).

94. A textual variant has "confusion." Courtray, SC 602, 201n1 comments that the reading "confusion" is tempting and has been followed by previous editors, but most of the manuscripts read "confession" and the sense may be that this earth is the place where souls admit their faults.

95. I believe Jerome is alluding to Origen's speculations, possibly found in *Stromata* 9, that may have discussed the preexistence and fall of souls into this earthly existence in connection with this passage.

96. Cf. Origen, *Stromata* 9?; *Princ* 3.3.5–4.1; 8.1–4; *Contra Celsum* 5.47; *Commentary on Romans* 7.1–2; *Commentary on Matthew* 13.2; Tertullian, *de Anima* 14.2ff.

97. Courtray, SC 602, 201n2 cites Crouzel and Simonetti's edition of Origen's *Princ* (SC 269, 85–86, n. 3) to explain this. The opinion Jerome is arguing against is found in Noumenios, who distinguished two souls in the world and two souls in each person as a result of the distinction between God and matter; there was in the human person a vital principle deriving from matter and a rational principle deriving from God. They add that the ancient Persians also believed in the existence of two souls for each individual, one good, the other bad; this belief is still found among the Gnostics and the Basilidians. This same idea is attested among the Christians Tatian, Tertullian, and Clement.

98. Cf. Sallust, *Hist* 4, frag 61. Sallust was a celebrated Roman historian. Cf. Tacitus, *Agricola* 3, 30; Quintilian, 2, 5. 19; 10, 1, 101.

99. Courtray, SC 602, 202 n. 1 clarifies that Jerome establishes an erroneous etymological link between πύρινος (from πῦρ, fire) and πυρὴν (the pit or stone of an olive, *ossa*). Strabo, *Geogr* 16.1.15 speaks of the incendiary power of naphtha but without any link to olive pits.

100. This section is located further down in Glorie, CCSL. Courtray, SC 602, reports that all the manuscripts locate it here before v. 57a.

101. Cf. 3:23.

102. Cf. Irenaeus, *Haer* 4.20.11; 5.5.2; Hippolytus, *In Dan* 2.30.3; 2.32.5–9; 2.33.4; Tertullian, *Adv Marc* 4.10.12; Prax 6.6.

103. It seems noteworthy that Jerome distances himself from Christian interpreters who see the fourth figure in its historical sense as the preincarnate Christ. Jerome admits that in the spiritual sense it applies to Christ.

104. Ambrosiaster says that Nebuchadnezzar recognized the Son of God "not on his own merit, but on the merit of his royal rank," *Quaestiones Veteris et*

Novi Testamenti, PL 35, 2234); cited by Kritzinger, "St Jerome's Commentary on Daniel 3," 64.

105. For Jerome's understanding of Christ's descent to hell, see J. O'Connell, *The Eschatology of St. Jerome*, Dissertationes ad Lauream 16 (Mundelein, IL: Pontifical Theological Faculty of the Seminary of St. Mary of the Lake, 1948), 134–35.

106. Cf. Origen, *Stromata* 9?; *Princ* 1.6.2–5; R. Courtray, "Nabuchodonosor, figure du diable chez Jérôme," *Connaissance des Pères de l'Église* 120 (2010): 18–26.

107. Jerome followed Epiphanius and Theophilus of Alexandria in condemning this speculation attributed to Origen. I have briefly discussed Jerome's interaction with Origen's speculation about the *apokatastasis* in the introduction.

108. Courtray, SC 602, 212n1 says: "In the sense of 'governor.'"

109. Courtray, SC 602, 212 says the source has not been identified. Cf. Strabo, *Geogr* 16.1.4.15; Plutarch, *Life of Alexander* 35.1–2, 13.

110. The Hebrew Bible continues chap. 3 up through what is 4:3 in the English Bible.

111. In classical jargon, a *sycophant* is a habitual prosecutor. (It is not known how the word acquired its modern sense of "flatterer.") The Greek word literally means: "one who reveals figs," perhaps in connection with the denunciation of those who smuggled figs or who stole figs from consecrated fig trees. As an epithet for Porphyry, it means "slanderer," since Porphyry claimed that the Book of Daniel was written after the events it alleges to predict. The term *sycophant* is found in the plays of Plautus and Terence, which Jerome still used (cf. Jerome, *Apology against Rufinus* 2.33).

112. M. Reaburn, "St Jerome and Porphyry Interpret the Book of Daniel," *Australian Biblical Review* 52 (2004): 6 says that it may seem "quaint" today for Jerome to use such an argument against a Maccabean date for the writing of Daniel. According to Webster, "quaint" means: "pleasingly or strikingly old-fashioned or unfamiliar."

113. An important study of this chapter has been made by R. Courtray, "Le roi Nabuchodonosor changé en bête (Dn 4). Du récit biblique à quelques lectures chrétiennes anciennes," in: V. Adam and C. Noacco, eds., *La metamorphose et ses metamorphoses* (Albi: Presses du Centre universitaire Champollion, 2010), 49–64. Jerome interprets the story literally: For offending God, Nebuchadnezzar was affected by a fit of madness that lasted seven years and became like a wild beast. The chief lesson of the story is the condemnation of human pride. Modern scholarship recognizes that there is no external evidence for Nebuchadnezzar's temporary insanity, yet P. P. Saydon defends the plausibility of the story in "Daniel," *A Catholic Commentary on Holy Scripture*, ed. B. Orchard et al. (New York: Thomas Nelson, 1953), 621–43. Other scholars such as Louis F. Hartman think that the background of Daniel's story is found in the *Prayer of Nabonidus*, a first-century-BCE text written in Aramaic and discovered among the Dead Sea Scrolls, which depicts the Babylonian king Nabonidus (556–539 BCE) as having been afflicted with a bad inflammation that caused him to separate himself from human society for seven years. He prayed, confessed his sins, and a Jewish priest was sent from the Babylonian

exiles to him and furnished an interpretation of the ailment. See: "Daniel," 446–60 in *The Jerome Biblical Commentary*, ed. R. E. Brown, J. A. Fitzmyer, and R. E. Murphy (Englewood Cliffs, NJ: Prentice-Hall 1968), 453. R. K. Harrison, *Introduction to the Old Testament* (Grand Rapids: Eerdmans, 1969) as well as Pitre and Bergsma, *A Catholic Introduction to the Bible*, vol. 1: *The Old Testament* (San Francisco: Ignatius, 2018) think that Dan 4 and the *Prayer of Nabonidus* are entirely separate historical traditions.

114. Cf. Origen, *Stromata* 9?; *Princ* 4.3.9; *Hom in Num* 11.4.3; *Hom in Ezek* 13.1; *Hom in Josh* 1.6; *Cels* 6.43.

115. It appears that Origen is the unnamed commentator who questioned the historical viability of Dan 4. He thought that because the episode could not be defended historically, an allegorical interpretation is required that the Holy Spirit intended as the primary spiritual lesson from this chapter.

116. See R. Courtray, "Le roi Nabuchodonosor changé en bête (Dn 4)," 49–64; Courtray, "Nabuchodonosor, figure du diable chez Jérôme," 18–26.

117. Scylla was a hound-girt sea monster with six heads living in the Straits of Messina opposite Charybdis. She devastated Odysseus's crew. Cf. Virgil, *Aen* 3.420ff.; 5.122; 6.286; Ovid, *Met* 8.90ff.; 14.52ff.; 730ff.; *Trist* 2:393; Homer, *Od* 12:75ff.

118. The Chimaera was a fire-breathing monster of Lycia, killed by Bellerophon. In the front, it was a lion, behind a serpent, and in the middle a goat. Cf. Virgil, *Aen* 5.118; 6.288; Cicero, *Nat Deor* 2:5; Horace, *Odes* 1:27, 24; Homer, *Il* 6.181.

119. The Hydra was the many-headed monster living by Lake Lerna in the Peloponnese, which Heracles had to destroy as one of his labors. The difficulty was that when one head was cut off, two others grew. Cf. Virgil, *Aen* 6.287, 576; Horace, *Odes* 4.4.61; Lucretius, *Nat Rer* 5.27; Cicero, *Nat Deor* 2:114.

120. Centaurs were wild creatures, half human, half horse, living on the wooded mountains in Thessaly. Cf. Virgil, *Aen* 5.122; 6.286; 10.195; Horace, *Epodes* 13.11.

121. For instance, Niobe was turned into a bird; cf. Ovid, *Met* 6.155; Daphne into a laurel tree. Courtray's edition has a much more exhaustive apparatus of classical references.

122. There is a passage in Jerome's *Commentary on Jonah* 2:2–3a quite similar to this one, addressed to those who disbelieve the story that Jonah was swallowed by a whale. Jerome's argument is that while the pagans do not question the reality of their mythological tales, unbelievable as they are, why do Christians not place faith in biblical tales for what they are? Do they contain anything extraordinary? Courtray, "Le roi Nabuchodonosor changé en bête," 61–62, summarizes Jerome's intention in the present passage (Dan 4): "The argument may sound weak and specious; however, Jerome does not put the two domains [pagan and biblical] on the same level. On the one hand, there are incredible tales in which he does not believe because they concern pagan metamorphoses; on the other, there is the historically acceptable account of an easy-to-believe transformation: the sudden madness of a king. To these two opposing domains, Jerome adds a third one: ancient histories also relate incredible tales that one accepts without saying a word: one therefore slips from the historical domain to the mythological domain, as if to better show

the absurdity of those who deny a reality to the biblical text while they accept the reality of secular stories. However, in the biblical account, the extraordinary comes from elsewhere: not from the metamorphosis of the king, but from the divine omnipotence which brings about this change. The mythological argument, therefore, comes to show how much the biblical story is much more admissible than the pagan fables, but at the same time it reminds us of the superiority of the biblical God over the pagan gods: the metamorphosis of Nebuchadnezzar is neither gratuitous nor inspired by perverse feelings; it simply comes to affirm the power of God and to lower the pride of kings."

123. Referring to vv. 6–9.

124. Since *collega* is absent from all known texts, Courtray, SC 602, 220n2 endeavors to explain Jerome's translation as a misreading of the manuscript he had in front of him. He thinks that Jerome confused a manuscript reading that said *heteros* ("another") with *hetairos* ("companion, colleague").

125. I believe Jerome is defending his own endeavor to transcend the LXX and render his exegesis directly from the original Hebrew, for the church itself, in the case of Daniel, has preferred Theodotion to the LXX. His practice is thus in harmony with the mind of the church. Such an argument would be directed against critics such as Rufinus and Augustine who faulted him for setting aside the LXX.

126. See Kamesar's explanatory comment cited in a note above in the Preface to Jerome's Vulgate Version of Daniel.

127. Jerome is combatting Origen here.

128. Cf. Origen, *Stromata* 9?

129. The initial *h* stands for a rough breathing mark.

130. Ezekiel's vision of the cherubim compares their brightness with the rainbow; cf. Jerome, *Commentary on Ezekiel* Bk 1 on Ezek 1:27—2:1a. Courtray, SC 602, 225 n. 1 explains that Jerome uses a false etymology by bringing together words with similar sounds: *hir* [the Chaldean word for "watcher" cited under 4:10b] and *iris* ["rainbow"]. Jerome thinks that this connection corresponds to a similarity in reality, that the angel, like the rainbow, descends from heaven to earth.

131. Lit.: "ensavagement." My translation was not intended to be taken literally.

132. Cf. Origen, *Stromata* 9?

133. A. Bonner, *The Myth of Pelagianism*, 146, makes some valuable comments on this passage that enlighten Jerome's view of free will and human merit. She says that in Jerome's view, God listens to the prayers of the righteous, so that their prayers are more efficacious than the prayers of people who are not righteous. In support of such a view, she cites *Commentary on Matthew* Bk 3 on Matt 17:19–20 and *Commentary on Isaiah* 14.18 on Isa 52:7–8. Jerome's comments under Dan 9:3 seem to fit to this as well. Bonner further shows how Jerome rejects any notion of predestination understood as God's foreordaining of events in a way that negates effective and autonomous human will (123–34; 155–56). She summarizes the sense of Jerome's *Commentary on Ezekiel* Bk 2 on Ezek 2:4–5 (a passage that bears a resemblance to the present one in Daniel): "In Jerome's account, God's 'state of mind' (*affectus*) was described as 'undecided' (*ambigens*) and waiting on man's autonomous freely

willed choices. It is noticeable that in this passage he did not use the word 'predestination' and opted instead for 'foreknowledge.'" See also my recent article: "Election as Foreknowledge from Justin Martyr to Jerome," chapter 6 in *T & T Clark Companion to Election*, ed. Edwin Chr. van Driel (London: T&T Clark/Bloomsbury, 2023), 111–31.

134. From his classical Reformed Protestant perspective, Young, *The Prophecy of Daniel*, 108 takes Jerome to task here theologically: "It is a gross perversion of the text to force it to teach salvation by the merit of good works. Jerome gave classic expression to this false view." Young also faults Jerome's translation here as inaccurate.

135. This passage is important in showing that for Jerome, Nebuchadnezzar was not physically but only mentally transformed into a wild beast. Courtray, SC 602, 235n1, indicates that over the centuries it was a debated question whether Nebuchadnezzar lost his human physique.

136. The critical editions of Glorie and Courtray cite over twenty-five OT passages that use this phrase.

137. Archer, *Jerome's Commentary on Daniel*, 53 inserts: "The original for 'from generation to generation' is *im dar wedar*, i.e., 'with generation and generation,' which Jerome renders as *in generatione et generatione* or 'in generation and generation.' Undoubtedly the idea of the original is distributive or successive: 'unto each successive generation.' Jerome's explanation of this characteristic Semitic phrase as an occult reference to the two dispensations of the Old and New Testaments seems very farfetched." Cf. Jerome, *Commentary on Isaiah* Bk 17 on 60:15–16; *Commentary on Joel* 3:20–21.

138. These are apparently Origen's speculations.

Book Two

1. The Latin spelling in the Vulgate, which followed the Greek versions, is the same as for Daniel's name above (cf. Dan 4:19). The RSV distinguishes the names.

2. The description of Belshazzar as "king" is considered one of the major historical difficulties of the book. According to cuneiform records, it was Nabonidus, father of Belshazzar, who was actually the ruler of the Neo-Babylonian empire before it fell to Cyrus in 539 BCE. Harrison comments: "This difficulty has been resolved by archaeological discoveries that have shown that for much of the reign of Nabonidus, his eldest son Belshazzar acted as coregent. When Nabonidus took up residence in Teima, Belshazzar exercised sole rule in Babylonia and for this reason was represented as the last king of Babylon in Daniel (Dan 5.30). The reference in Dan 5.18 to Belshazzar as a son of Nebuchadnezzar is also correct according to Semitic usage, where the term 'son' could also mean 'grandson' for which there was no separate word, or simply 'descendant,' 'offspring.'" R. K. Harrison, *Introduction to the Old Testament* (Grand Rapids: Eerdmans, 1969), 1107.

3. Berosus was a distinguished Babylonian priest, historian, and astronomer of the time of Ptolemy Philadelphus (ca. 283 BCE). His work *Chaldaica*, or *Babyloniaca*, has been lost; the only fragments that have come down

to us have been preserved by Flavius Josephus, Clement of Alexandria, and Eusebius of Caesarea.

4. Evil-Merodach was son and successor of Nebuchadnezzar II as king of Babylon in 562 BCE. Cf. Josephus, *Ant* 10.11.2; *Contra Apionem* 1.5; Eusebius, *Praep Eu* 9.40.3–11.

5. G. Archer, *Jerome's Commentary on Daniel* (Grand Rapids: Baker, 1958), 55, inserts: "actually his brother-in-law."

6. Archer, *Jerome's Commentary on Daniel*, 55, "the cuneiform spelling is Labashi-Marduk."

7. Archer, *Jerome's Commentary on Daniel*, 55, inserts, "note that Jerome is not aware of Belshazzar's father, Nabonidus."

8. Courtray SC 602, 241n1 recognizes that this "Darius the Mede" is simply unknown in history. After reviewing some historical evidence that seems to suggest his identification with Cyrus the Great, Joyce Baldwin, *Daniel*, Tyndale Old Testament Commentaries 23 (Downers Grove, IL: InterVarsity, 1978), 32, concludes minimally that "it will no longer do to dismiss him as a fiction and to build on this fiction the theory that the writer believed that there was a separate Median empire."

9. Xenophon was a celebrated Greek historian and philosopher, born ca. 445 BCE. He was a pupil of Socrates who features in his *Memoirs* and *Symposium*. He was also a military leader of the Greek mercenaries in the army of Cyrus the Younger, a campaign that he documents in his most famous work, the *Anabasis*. Xenophon also wrote a book on the *Education of Cyrus the Great* in which he described Cyrus the Great's taking of Babylon by diverting the channel of the river that passed under the city walls. His soldiers marched into Babylon on the riverbed. In *Cyropaedia* 7.5, Xenophon reports that as Cyrus's soldiers were digging the alternate channel, the citizens of Babylon were drinking and making merry the whole night long. P. Courcelle *Late Latin Writers and their Greek Sources*, trans. H. E. Wedeck (Cambridge, MA: Harvard University Press, 1969), 81, observes that Jerome knew Xenophon's *Cyropedia* intimately, citing among other passages Jerome's *Commentary on Isaiah* 12.45.

10. Pompeius Trogus is a Roman historian who dates to the reign of Augustus and is known only through the epitome of Justin.

11. Astyages was king of Media, father of Mandane, and grandfather of Cyrus the Great, by whom he was deprived of his throne.

12. Archer, *Jerome's Commentary on Daniel*, 55 inserts: "The latter rendering seems to be the only one justified by the Aramaic original."

13. Braverman, *Jerome's Commentary on Daniel: A Study of Comparative Jewish and Christian Interpretations of the Hebrew Bible* (Washington, DC: Catholic Biblical Association, 1978), 79–80 explains that the basic chronological problem is in which year to begin the seventy-year period indicated by Jeremiah. He notes that the tradition Jerome cites here agrees with *Megillah* 11b, where Raba explains that Belshazzar began his count with the first year of Nebuchadnezzar's reign (605 BCE). He calculated forty-five years of Nebuchadnezzar, twenty-three of Evil-Merodach, and two of his own, totaling seventy. This was when he brought out the vessels of the temple. Braverman, 80 writes: "The Talmudic source in Megilla 11b–12a explicitly states that Belshazzar erred in his calculation, a point not mentioned but implied by Jerome. The source

of his error...was that the seventy-year computation should not have begun with Nebuchadnezzar's first year, but rather his second year (605/4), when he subjugated Jehoiakim (2 Kgs 24:1). Thus another year after Belshazzar's feast was needed to complete the seventy-year period, and this took place with the one-year reign of Darius the Mede. He was succeeded by his son-in-law, Cyrus, who combined the Persian, Median, and Babylonian Empires and issued a proclamation that the Jews of Babylonia were free to return to Israel (Ezra 1:2ff.). This therefore constituted the fulfillment of Jeremiah's seventy-year prophecy."

14. Jerome discusses this Hebrew title in *Ep* 65.3 to Principia. See my new translation of the latter: St. Jerome, *Exegetical Epistles*, vol. 1, trans. Thomas P. Scheck, FOTC 147 (Washington, DC: Catholic University of America Press, 2023). Archer, *Jerome's Commentary on Daniel*, 57 inserts: "'For those who will suffer alteration' is a remarkable interpretation of the Hebrew (*al-shoshannim*)—'according to lilies' (RSV)—rendered in the Authorized Version as 'upon Shoshannim.' The Vulgate rendering, following that of the Septuagint, is based upon a very implausible vowel pointing: *al-sheshonim*."

15. Jerome cites the feminine form *torques aurea* [golden chain] three times in his translation of Daniel: 5:7; 5:16; 5:29. Cf. H. Hagendahl, *Latin Fathers and the Classics: A Study on the Apologists, Jerome and Other Christian Writers* (Gothenburg: Almquist & Wiksell, 1958), 226n8.

16. Courtray, SC 602, 247n2 conjectures that Jerome is speaking of Rufinus, but there is no mention of this issue in his works.

17. The text of this passage raises many difficulties, which has led to conjectural emendations by the editors. First, in no surviving manuscripts does Cicero use the word *torques* in the feminine, nor does Virgil offer an example of *torques* in the feminine. Second, the manuscripts offer the two main variants as Maro and Mario. The reading *in Mario* is meaningless, leading F. Glorie, *S. Hieronymi Presbyteri Commentariorum in Danielem Libri III* <IV>, CCSL 75A (Turnholt: Brepols, 1964), to propose in his edition to read *in Manlio*, seeing here an allusion to Manlius Torquatus mentioned in *De off* 3.31.112. Courtray proposes the text *Cicero et Varro*, assuming, on the one hand, that Jerome had indeed read a manuscript of Cicero presenting the feminine spelling *torque detracta* and, on the other hand, that the scribes had deformed the name Varro into Maro or Mario. See R. Courtray, "Questions critiques autour du *Commentaire sur Daniel* de Jérôme," in *L'exégèse de saint Jérôme*, ed. É. Ayroulet and A. Canellis (Saint-Étienne: Publications de l'Université de Saint-Étienne, 2018), 201–20.

18. Archer, *Jerome's Commentary on Daniel*, 58 inserts: "A *tristates* is one who stands next in rank to the king and queen, i.e., a vizier." Jerome uses the term in his *Commentary on Ezekiel* Bk 7 on Ezek 23:22–27.

19. Cf. Josephus, *Ant* 10.11.2.
20. Cf. Origen, *Stromata* 9?
21. See under Dan 5:2.
22. Notice how Jerome places the emphasis on human culpability and free will rather than on divine foreordination and control of events.
23. Cf. Origen, *Stromata* 9?.
24. Cf. Josephus *Ant* 10.11.3.

25. Cf. Jerome, *Nom Hebr* 56.17; 6.19; 18.21; 32.18–19; 61.20.
26. See under Dan 5:1.
27. This variant matches the LXX.
28. Cf. Josephus, *Ant* 10.11:2.
29. According to Courtray SC 602, 261n2, Darius the Mede in the Book of Daniel is a nonhistorical personage. The book's author tells us in Dan 9:1 that he was a "son of Xerxes" (LXX) or "son of Assuerus" (Theodotion). His identity is one of the great historical difficulties in the book. See Baldwin, *Daniel*, 26–32, who is quoted under Dan 9:1.
30. Archer, *Jerome's Commentary on Daniel*, 62 inserts: "this rendering differs from the Hebrew original and the Septuagint, and seems altogether unjustified."
31. See under Dan 5:30–31.
32. Astyages was King of Media, father of Mandane, and grandfather of Cyrus the Great, by whom he was deprived of his throne.
33. Josephus, *Ant* 10.11:4.
34. Archer, *Jerome's Commentary on Daniel*, 64 used "liaison officers."
35. Jerome referred to the Jewish tradition that Daniel and his companions were eunuchs under 1:3. A medieval Jewish source, Midrash Megillah, may witness to the tradition to which Jerome refers here in 6:4. It relates that Daniel and his friends subjected themselves to castration in order to remove suspicion of immorality. Cf. Braverman, *Jerome's Commentary on Daniel*, 81–82. Braverman thinks that Jerome's description of the Jewish practice of "composing long tales on the pretext of a single word" may suggest that he did not agree that Daniel was a eunuch.
36. Cf. Euripides, *Med* 116.
37. Cf. under Dan 6:1–2a. J. Bergsma and B. Pitre, "Daniel," 875–906 in: *A Catholic Introduction to the Bible*, vol. 1: *The Old Testament* (San Francisco: Ignatius, 2018), 896 confirm Jerome's insight that the Book of Daniel itself repeatedly speaks of "the one kingdom of 'Medes and Persians' (Dan 5:28; cf. 6:8, 12; 15; 8:20)."
38. Cf. Jerome, *Commentary on Ezekiel* 12.41; *Ep* 106.63.
39. Jerome commonly interprets Jerusalem to mean "vision of peace." See his *Commentary on Ezekiel* 4:16–17; 13:16; 16:1–3; 16:32–34.
40. Referring to 9:00 a.m., 12:00 p.m., and 3:00 p.m. Cf. Tertullian, *Or* 25; Origen, *PEuch* 12.2; Jerome *Ep* 22.37; 108.20; 130.15.
41. Cf. Josephus, *Ant* 10.11.6.
42. See under 6:1–2a; 6:8a.
43. The modern Garda near Verona.
44. Now Lake Como, one of the largest of the great lakes of Northern Italy.
45. Cf. *Commentary on Ezekiel* Bk 10 on Ezek 32:17–32.
46. Cf. Jerome, *Commentary on Matthew* Bk 3, on Matt 16:16: "He calls him a living God in comparison with those gods that are thought to be gods but are dead. This refers to Saturn, Jove, Ceres, Liberus, Hercules, and the rest of the portents of the idols." Cf. Lactantius, *Div Inst* 1.11.18–19; Minucius Felix, *Oct* 21; 23; 13; Eusebius, *Praep Eu* 3.3.15–17; Tertullian, *Apol* 10.3; 11.1.

47. Notice again how Jerome's theological emphasis is not on the gratuitous and undeserved nature of divine grace but on its being fittingly and justly paid out to the worthy.

48. See above under Dan 4:1a; Origen, *Strom* 9?; *Princ* 1:5.5; 1:6.2–3; 4.2; Tertullian, *Adv Marc* 5.11:17; Eusebius, *Comm in Ps* 118.

49. *Quaerit utrum.* Jerome is essentially recognizing that Origen's discussion had been speculative and investigative, not dogmatically assertive. J. N. D. Kelly, *Jerome: His Life, Writings, and Controversies* (New York: Harper & Row, 1975), 303 commented on the "fanatical hostility" Jerome felt for Origen after the first Origenist controversy in Palestine. "When condensing his ideas in his own words, he almost invariably distorts them or presents them in an unfavorable light. For example, when Origen had canvassed alternative solutions (e.g. on the nature of the resurrection body), without coming down on one side or the other, Jerome depicts him as dogmatically defending the more unpalatable option." It seems to me that this type of criticism could be made of Jerome's reporting of Origen's views of Nebuchadnezzar as a figure of the devil.

50. Jerome situates Visions 7 (Dan 7) and 8 (Dan 8) as chronologically prior to Visions 5 (Dan 5) and 6 (Dan 6).

51. Cf. Jerome, *Commentary on Jeremiah* Bk 4.29.3 (Jer 21:1–2): "It should be noted that in the prophets, and above all in Ezekiel and Jeremiah, the order of kings and times is often not preserved, but, with the order reversed, what took place later according to *historia* is mentioned earlier, and that which happened earlier is mentioned later." M. Graves, trans., *Jerome: Commentary on Jeremiah*, Ancient Christian Texts (Downers Grove, IL: InterVarsity, 2011), 125–26. Also in *Commentary on Ezekiel* Bk 9 on Ezek 29:17–21, Jerome writes that times are described in inverted order, both in Jer 21—22 and Ezek 29—40.

52. Jerome survived to complete his *Commentary on Ezekiel* but not his *Commentary on Jeremiah* in its entirety (though the promised explanation is preserved in his comments on Jer 21:1–2, cited in the previous note).

53. Visions 1–6 (Dan 1—6) are presented in the form of narratives organized according to a chronological framework.

54. Visions 7–10 (Dan 7—12) relate to the genre of the visions, also ordered chronologically.

55. Jerome observes here that in Dan 7—12, it is no longer the prophet Daniel who interprets the visions of a pagan king, but it is the prophet himself who receives revelation in dreams that an angel explains to him.

56. Archer, *Jerome's Commentary on Daniel*, 72 inserts: "Actually Jerome errs in rendering *'aryeh* as 'lioness,' for it is the regular masculine form for 'lion' in Aramaic, 'lioness' being *'aryuta.'* Perhaps Jerome mistook the *he* in the unpointed text before him as the common feminine ending—*ah.* Or else he simply relied uncritically upon the Septuagint, which commits the same error." Courtray SC 602, 284 n. 1 agrees that Jerome has erred.

57. Cf. Hippolytus, *Treatise on Christ and Antichrist* 23, 28 (ANF 5.209–10).

58. Cf. Pliny, *Nat Hist* 8.42; Aristotle, *History of Animals* 6.17–18. Courtray SC 602, 285 n. 2 cites Jerome, *Commentary on Jeremiah* Bk 3 on Jer 24:3, where Jerome quotes this same expression about mares and then alludes to

a passage from Aristotle *HA* 6.18. But the idea Jerome offers here about lionesses is not actually found in Aristotle or in Pliny the Elder, which nevertheless seem to be the sources he used. Jerome appears to have confused the mores attributed to lions in Aristotle (6.17) and the next paragraph dealing with female animals being in heat, but there is no question of lionesses.

59. Cf. Hippolytus, *In Dan* 4.7.3; *De Antichristo* 28.

60. This word is used in Jerome, *Adv Jovin* 2.13, where the point is frugality: "Xenophon in eight books narrates the life of Cyrus, King of the Persians, and asserts that they supported life on barley, cress, salt, and black bread."

61. Cf. Xenophon, *Cyropaedia* 1.2.8.11.

62. After surveying the rabbis, Braverman, *Jerome's Commentary on Daniel*, 88 concludes: "We cannot find, however, any positive rabbinic statements concerning the Persians specifically derived from the phrase 'standing on one side' in Dan 7:5, or referring to the Persians' never perpetrating any cruelty against Israel, as does Jerome's Hebrew tradition. It seems quite plausible, however, that such a tradition could have been prevalent in Jerome's time in Palestine, during the end of the fourth and beginning of the fifth centuries."

63. For convenience and comparison I will record here the commencement dates for the rulers of the Persian Empire provided in the appendix of C. Lattey, *The Book of Daniel* (Dublin: Richview Press, 1948), 121: Cyrus, 538 BCE; Cambyses 529; Darius I (Hystaspis) 522; Xerxes I (= Ahasuerus) 485; Artaxerxes I (Longimanus) 464; Xerxes II 424; Darius II (Nothus) 423; Artaxerxes II (Mnemon) 404; Artaxerxes III (Ochus) 359; Darius III (Codomannus) 338–1.

64. Cyrus II was king of Persia from 558 to 530 BCE. By 550 he had established Ecbatana as a Persian royal residence.

65. Cambyses II was successor to his father Cyrus II as king of the Achaemenid Empire 529–522 BCE.

66. Archer, *Jerome's Commentary on Daniel*, 74 inserts: "The plural seems unwarranted, since there was but one brother involved, namely, Smerdis."

67. Darius I was king of Persia 522–486 BCE. He organized a Persian military expedition against the Greeks and was defeated at Marathon in 490. He supported the efforts of the Jews to rebuild the temple and Ezra recounts how, despite returning to Jerusalem under Cyrus, work on the temple in Jerusalem did not begin in earnest until the second year of Darius's reign, ca. 520 (Ezra 4:24).

68. Xerxes I was the Achaemenid king of Persia 486–465 BCE. He succeeded to the throne upon the death of Darius I, his father. He is noted for his invasion of Greece and burning of Athens.

69. Archer, *Jerome's Commentary on Daniel*, 74 inserts, "actually only the assassin of Xerxes; he never became king." He had been one of Xerxes's generals.

70. Artaxerxes I Longimanus ruled Persia 465–424 BCE. He was son and successor to Xerxes I. Some have seen the mission of Nehemiah against the background of his reign.

71. Sogdianus was one of the illegitimate sons of Artaxerxes I Longimanus. He acquired the throne on the death of his father (425 BCE) by the murder

of his legitimate brother Xerxes II. Sogdianus, however, was murdered in his turn, after a reign of seven months, by his brother Ochus.

72. Darius II (Ochus) ruled Persia 424–404 BCE. He was one of Artaxerxes I's bastard sons.

73. Artaxerxes II Mnemon ruled Persia 404–359 BCE. He was son and successor to Darius II. His claim to the throne was challenged in battle by Cyrus the Younger, as narrated in Xenophon's *Anabasis*. Cyrus's defeat returned control over the West to Artaxerxes.

74. Artaxerxes III Ochos ruled Persia 359–338 BCE. He was one of Artaxerxes II's sons and reconquered Egypt.

75. Arses is the throne name of Artaxerxes IV who ruled Persia 338–336 BCE. He was one of Artaxerxes III's sons.

76. This is the Persian king Darius III who was twice defeated by Alexander and died in 330 BCE at the hands of his own soldiers.

77. Ptolemy I Soter began rule in Egypt in 323 BCE. Seleucus I (Nicator) began to rule in 312.

78. Archer, *Jerome's Commentary on Daniel*, 75 inserts: "Philip Arrhidaeus, an illegitimate brother of Alexander, who was proclaimed king upon Alexander's death, but never exercised genuine power, and died after seven years."

79. Archer, *Jerome's Commentary on Daniel*, 75 identifies Antigonus as "the precursor of Seleucus in the rule of the Asiatic portion of Alexander's empire."

80. Cf. Hippolytus, *In Dan* 4.5.1; 4.7.4; *De Christo et Antichristo* 28.

81. Braverman, *Jerome's Commentary on Daniel*, 90–94 confirms that there is much rabbinic evidence for linking Dan 7:7 with Ps 80:13.

82. Archer, *Jerome's Commentary on Daniel*, 76 inserts: "A more accurate rendering of the Hebrew would be: '…and the moving creatures (or 'swarms') of the field do feed upon her.'"

83. For Jerome, the Roman Empire will be destroyed by being broken up into ten smaller kingdoms. These will then be conquered by or subjected to the antichrist.

84. This is the "true meaning" according to E. J. Young, *The Prophecy of Daniel: A Commentary* (Grand Rapids: Eerdmans, 1949), 148.

85. John P. O'Connell, *The Eschatology of St. Jerome*, Dissertationes ad Lauream 16 (Mundelein, IL: Pontifical Theological Faculty of the Seminary of St. Mary of the Lake, 1948), 25, comments on this passage: "Jerome does not subscribe to the opinion that Antichrist will be the Devil or a demon. He will be a man…in whom the Devil will dwell and in whom the Devil will work. Elsewhere he calls Antichrist the son of the Devil. Nor was Nero the Antichrist, as some Christians thought. Nero showed in part what Antichrist will be. But since the Roman Empire will end before the time of Antichrist, Nero could not have been he. Antichrist will be born of Jews, but will come from Babylon. He is the man of sin and the son of perdition spoke of by Saint Paul."

86. Cf. Jerome, *Commentary on Ezekiel* Bk 9 on Ezek 28:11–19.

87. Ten thousand (10,000) times one hundred thousand (100,000) equals one billion (1,000,000,000). Archer, *Jerome's Commentary on Daniel*, 79 inserts: "The Aramaic original is more conservative: 'A million were ministering unto Him, and a hundred million were standing (in His presence).'"

88. Cf. Jerome, *Commentary on Zephaniah* 1:10.

89. He repeats the challenges to Porphyry under 11:44–45 and 12:1–3. Porphyry seems to have understood the "one like a son of man" as referring to Judas Maccabeus. Yet J. Collins, *Daniel: A Commentary on the Book of Daniel*, Hermeneia (Minneapolis: Augsburg Fortress, 1993), 114 is cautious about Porphyry's alleged identification: "Most scholars have inferred from this that Porphyry identified the one like a son of man as Judas [Maccabeus], but Casey has argued, plausibly enough, that the use of the subjunctive shows that Porphyry had not explicitly made the identification. It does not follow, however, that Porphyry held a corporate interpretation of the figure, as Casey claims. If he had, Jerome could scarcely have overlooked the fact and would not have had to speculate on what he meant. In fact, Jerome again challenges Porphyry to give his interpretation of the figure on the clouds at Dan 11:44–45 and accuses him of ignoring 'these things that are so very clear.' Porphyry evidently understood both chaps. 7 and 11 to refer to the struggle of the Jewish people with Antiochus [IV Epiphanes], but he apparently did not offer a specific identification of the 'one like a son of man.'"

90. See under Dan 7:2–8.

91. Even though it had been very widespread among Christian interpreters of the earlier centuries, Jerome was strongly opposed to all forms of chiliasm, or millennialism, the belief that Christ would reign for a thousand years upon the earth when he returns. See O'Connell, *The Eschatology of St. Jerome*, chap. 4; M. Dulaey, "Jérôme, Victorin de Poetovio et le millénarisme," in *Jérôme entre l'Occident et l'Origent. XVIe centenaire du depart de saint Jérôme de Rome et de son installation à Bethléem*, ed. Y.-M. Duval, Actes du Colloque de Chantilly (September 1986), EAA 122, 1988, 83.

92. See under 11:44–45.

93. O'Connell, *The Eschatology of St. Jerome*, 30 summarizes Jerome's views: "The exaltation of Antichrist to which the Pauline text makes reference is his subjection of all religion to himself. Interdicting the worship of God, and promising to his followers escape from the punishments of hell and possession of the kingdom of heaven, he will attempt even to change the laws of God. Although Antichrist will be a Jew and a political leader, he seems also to be one of the members of the Church or at least to usurp a place therein. For when Jerome applies to him the phrase, *sedeat in templo Dei*, the temple is understood as the Church. Again, Antichrist seems to be identified with a heretic within the Church."

94. This rare word is used in Lactantius, 6, 20; Cyprian, *Ep* 2, 3.

95. Archer, *Jerome's Commentary on Daniel*, 81 inserts: "The Aramaic original here, according to the Massoretic [*sic*] vowel pointing, has the plural ending *-iyn*, not the dual ending *-ayin*. To be sure, the consonantal text could also be pointed as dual."

96. This would refer to Vision 10 (Dan 10:1—12:13).

97. See below under Dan 12:7a.

98. *Elymais* is the Greek term for the western part of ancient Elam, which is modern Khuzistan in SW Iran. The main city, Susa, constituted an important administrative and economic region under the Achaemenids and Seleucids.

99. Josephus, *Ant* 10.11.7.

100. Archer, *Jerome's Commentary on Daniel*, 83–84 inserts: "Actually the Hebrew word *'uwbal* is a common noun meaning 'canal'; the proper translation would be: 'I was by the Ulai Canal.'"

101. The West-gate of Troy, cf. *Iliad*, 3.145; 6.237; 11.170.

102. This adjective means: pertaining to Carmentis, a Roman goddess of prophecy and the mother of Evander, who went with him from Arcadia to Latium. There was a gate at Rome, near the temple of Carmentis, in the eighth district, through which the Fabii famously marched.

103. Courtray SC 602, 317n2 comments that the verb *succrescere* means "to grow under," but also "to succeed"; the meaning agrees here well with the idea of the succession of Cyrus at the head of the Medes and the Persians.

104. Cf. Josephus, *Ant* 10.11.7. Astyages was king of Media, father of Mandane, and grandfather of Cyrus the Great, by whom he was deprived of his throne.

105. Cf. Xenophon, *Cyropaedia* 1.5.2. Courtray SC 602, 317 n. 4 comments: "King Cyaxares II of whom Xenophon speaks doubtless did not exist; he is identified by Jerome as 'Darius the Mede,' also unknown to history."

106. That is, Darius III (380–330), defeated by Alexander the Great at the Battle of Gaugamela in 331 BCE and later assassinated by his own soldiers in 330.

107. Cf. Diodorus, *Bibl* 17.66.1; 71.1; Plutarch, *Life of Alexander* 21.6; 36.1–2; Justin, *Ep* 11.10.1; Quintus Curtius, *Hist* 3–5.

108. Ptolemy I Soter ([323]305–282 BCE) was the founder of the Ptolemaic dynasty. He wrote a history of Alexander's conquests that served as the basis of the most reliable account extant, that of Arrian. Shortly after Alexander's death, he established himself in Egypt.

109. See the note that cites Archer at 7:6 about this illegitimate brother of Alexander.

110. Seleucus Nicator was one of Alexander's generals whose rule dates 312–281 BCE.

111. Antigonus was one of Alexander's generals who was killed in 302 BCE.

112. Jerome also asserts this in 8:13b; 8:14; 11:31; 12:7a. E. Lucas, *Daniel*, Apollos Old Testament Commentary 20 (Downers Grove, IL: InterVarsity, 2002), 245 comments: "There is no reference to this prior to Jerome, and it does not fit well with the account in 1 Macc. 1:54."

113. Courtray SC 602, 325 n. 1 explains: "Jerome borrows this Greek word not from Dan 8:11 (which uses the word θυσία), but probably from Dan 11:31 and 12:11 (Theodotion)."

114. Cf. Josephus, *Ant* 12.5.4–5, but he records "fifth year."

115. Courtray SC 602, 327n1 clarifies: "It should be understood that these three years of the defiling of the Temple are part of the six years of the devastation of Jerusalem."

116. Archer, *Jerome's Commentary on Daniel*, 87 inserts: "Actually, however, 2200 days would come out to only six years and nine days; the reasoning here seems obscure." Courtray SC 602, 327n2 admits to this being a confused

text: "It is indeed to the 6 years that it is necessary to add 3 months to obtain approximately 2300 days; and 2200 days is not exactly 6 years."

117. Cf. Josephus, *Ant* 12.7.3–4.

118. Cf. Josephus *Ant* 12.9.1.

119. Braverman, *Jerome's Commentary on Daniel*, 95 says that there are no extant rabbinic traditions linking the anonymous "voice of a man" in Dan 8:16 with the angel Michael. However, there is a midrashic tradition that links the holy one who spoke in Dan 8:13 with Michael.

120. Cf. Jerome, *Nom Hebr* 64, 24/25.

121. Braverman, *Jerome's Commentary on Daniel*, 96 comments: "Jerome's characterization of Gabriel as the angel of war is borne out by rabbinic tradition which ascribes to this angel the annihilation of Sennacherib's camp, the destruction of Sodom, and the burning of the Temple in Jerusalem." We also note that Origen had ascribed to Gabriel the conduct of wars in *Princ* 1.8.1.

122. Archer, *Jerome's Commentary on Daniel*, 88 inserts the comment: "The point of this quotation seems to be that the Hebrew word for 'mighty' is *gibbowr*, from the root of which comes the *gabri-* of Gabriel."

123. Cf. Origen, *Princ* 1.8.1; Jerome, *Nom Hebr* 39, 24.

124. Jerome reports in the prologue to the Book of Tobit that the Hebrews had removed this book from their canon and had relegated it to the apocryphal writings. See Canellis, *Jérôme: Préfaces aux Livres de la Bible*, SC 592, 368–72.

125. Cf. Origen, *Princ* 1.8.1; Jerome, *Nom Hebr* 19, 7/8; 56, 17; 73, 20; 80, 27.

Book Three

1. Because no such name is mentioned in Xenophon's or Herodotus's account of Cyrus's conquest of Babylon, the identification of this Darius (also mentioned in Dan 5:1 and 6:1–2) has puzzled modern scholars. Courtray SC 602, 336n1 and many others believe that this Darius is a nonhistorical character. On the other hand, some conservative scholars have posited that "Darius the Mede" could be another name for Cyrus the Great (559–530 BCE) or an alternate name for Gubaru (Greek Gobryas), Cyrus's general who invaded and defeated Babylon. J. Baldwin, *Daniel*, Tyndale Old Testament Commentaries 23 (Downers Grove, IL: InterVarsity, 1978), 182 seems to favor the former solution and writes: "To some commentators these facts have seemed to prove conclusively that the writer had confused his history, but their judgment may be premature, for 'it is...now recognized that Xerxes (Ahasuerus) may be an ancient Achaemenid royal "title."' W. F. Albright has argued that the name Darius may be an old Iranian title, and while this remains a theory, it is in keeping with known history for a monarch to have more than one name, as, for example, in the case of Tiglath-Pileser, who is also called Pul (2 Kgs 15:19, 29; 1 Chr 5:26). Whatever the identity of Darius, the writer has in mind the first year of the Persian empire, 539 BCE, referred to in Ezra 1:1 as "the first year of Cyrus king of Persia."

2. J. Braverman, *Jerome's Commentary on Daniel: A Study of Comparative Jewish and Christian Interpretations of the Hebrew Bible* (Washington, DC: Catho-

lic Biblical Association, 1978), 97–98 helpfully summarizes the sense of this passage: "Jerome's basic exegetical problem is: Why did Daniel pray to God to restore Jerusalem and its Temple (Dan 9:3–19, especially 9:17, 18) when God had already promised, through his prophet Jeremiah (Jer 25:12 and 29:10ff.) that after seventy years Israel would be restored to the place whence it had been previously carried away into captivity? Jerome's answer stresses that God's promise of restoration was not automatic but was dependent upon the proper attitude of those to be redeemed. This answer is supported by Jer 29:12 which required Israel to 'call upon me, and go, and pray unto me, and I will hearken unto you,' even though two verses earlier Israel was specifically promised 'I will remember you, and perform my good word toward you, in causing you to return to this place' (Jer 29:10)." See also the note under Dan 4:24 (27) where Bonner's comment is recorded.

3. Jerome means that God shortened the period of repentance by twenty years as a punishment for humanity's unwillingness to repent. This interpretation is also found in his *Quaestiones Hebraicae in Genesim* 6:3. G. Archer, *Jerome's Commentary on Daniel* (Grand Rapids: Baker, 1958), 90–91 provides an alternate explanation of the discrepancy: "[Jerome's] deduction seems to have been based upon the fact that Gen. 5:32 mentions that Noah was five hundred years old when he had begotten Ham, Shem, and Japheth, and therefore was still the same age when God appointed the one hundred twenty years in Gen. 6:3. Since the Flood dried up in the six hundred and first year of Noah (8:13), therefore the waiting period could not have been more than a hundred years. Yet it could also have been that the age given in Gen. 5:32 was the age when, within the one hundred twenty year period, Noah's family was complete, the youngest son being born within that period, and being old enough to be married by the time the Flood itself actually occurred." According to Archer's explanation, there was no shortening of the period.

4. Lit. "from his own persona."

5. See above under 3:29 and Jerome, *Ep* 121.8 to Algasia. I have provided a new translation of the latter epistle in: *St. Jerome, Exegetical Epistles*, vol. 2, trans. Thomas P. Scheck, FOTC 148 (Washington, DC: Catholic University of America Press, 2024).

6. Courtray SC 602, 344 cites instances of this expression: 2 Kgs 19:16; Ps 17:6; 31:2; 71:2; 86:1; 88:2; 102:2; 116:2.

7. Courtray SC 602, 344 cites: 2 Kgs 6:17, 20; 19:16; 2 Chr 6:20, 40; Isa 37:17.

8. Courtray SC 602, 344 cites: 2 Chr 30:9; Ps 10:11; 13:1; 30:7; 44:24; 88:14; Ezek 7:22.

9. Cf. under Dan 9:5a.

10. Cf. Jerome, *Nom Hebr* 38, 4/5; 46, 8/9; *Commentary on Ezekiel* Bk 14 on Ezek 48:16.

11. In the introduction, I cited from Jerome's *Commentary on Isaiah* Bk 11 Pref., where he reports on the criticism he received for his exegetical method employed here, of citing various interpretations without deciding between them. He says that this recording of views does not in any way mean that he gives the same value to all the views mentioned, especially since they are sometimes contradictory. What made him decide to cite old opinions was

his desire to stand out from Porphyry and Flavius Josephus, who argued a lot about the meaning of the seventy weeks.

12. Julius Africanus (170–240?) was a learned ante-Nicene father whose great work entitled *Chronology* is a comparison of sacred and profane history from the creation of the world. It survives only in fragments, some of which appear in ANF 6.130–39. Cf. Jerome, *Vir Ill* 63; *Ep* 83 to Magnus; Socrates, *HE* 2.35. The general character of Julius's work can be assessed from the extant *Chronicon* of Eusebius (translated by Jerome), which was based upon it, and which undoubtedly incorporates much of it. Eusebius himself mentions Africanus among his authorities for Jewish history subsequent to OT times. Africanus's only complete work now extant is his letter to Origen on the authenticity of Susanna (ANF 4.385) which is referred to by Eusebius, *HE* 6.31 and Jerome, *Vir Ill* 63. Origen's reply is found in ANF 4.386–92. I have included this letter exchange in an appendix to this volume, as it has great relevance to Jerome's interpretation of Daniel. Not less celebrated is the letter of Africanus to Aristides on the discrepancy in the genealogies of Matthew and Luke. A considerable portion of this explanation has been preserved by Eusebius (*HE* 1.7).

13. The reference is clearly to Artaxerxes I Long-Hand (465–424); the twentieth year of his reign corresponds to the year 445 BCE. Again, for the purpose of convenience and comparison, here are the commencement dates for the rulers of the Persian Empire provided in the appendix of C. Lattey, *The Book of Daniel* (Dublin: Richview Press, 1948), 121: Cyrus, 538 BCE; Cambyses 529; Darius I (Hystaspis) 522; Xerxes I (= Ahasuerus) 485; Artaxerxes I (Longimanus) 464; Xerxes II 424; Darius II (Nothus) 423; Artaxerxes II (Mnemon) 404; Artaxerxes III (Ochus) 359; Darius III (Codomannus) 338–1.

14. The Vulgate reckons Nehemiah as 2 Esdras.

15. Archer, *Jerome's Commentary on Daniel*, 96 inserts: "Actually only 141 years, the interval between 587 B.C. and 446 B.C." Courtray SC 602, 353n3 concurs that there is confusion here in Africanus's chronology: "According to Africanus, Artaxerxes would have commenced his reign in 510 BCE (the twentieth year of his reign would correspond then with the year 490 BCE), the Persian domination would have started in 605 BCE and the captivity of Jerusalem in 675 BCE. Today we locate the beginning of the reign of Artaxerxes in 465 BCE, the capture of Jerusalem in 598 and the Persian domination in 538 BCE (when Cyrus allowed the Jews of Babylon to return to Jerusalem)."

16. Courtray SC 602, 354n1 explains that according to Africanus, the seventy weeks extend from the reconstruction of the temple in 445 BCE (twentieth year of Artaxerxes) to the passion of Christ in 30 CE (fifteenth year of Tiberius): the 475 elapsed solar years correspond to 490 Jewish lunar years, as he indicates later.

17. Archer, *Jerome's Commentary on Daniel*, 96 inserts: "Only seventy-eight years, by more recent computation, for Cyrus's decree was given in 538 B.C."

18. Archer, *Jerome's Commentary on Daniel*, 97 inserts: "Actually not more than a few months or a year."

19. Eusebius cites this as "sixteenth."

20. Archer, *Jerome's Commentary on Daniel* 97, inserts: "Reckoning from the death of Cleopatra, the last of the Macedonian Ptolemies."

NOTES   213

21. Courtray SC 602, 355n3 says that this note was added by Jerome.
22. The calculation is 365.25—(29.5 x 12) = 11.25.
23. 11.25 x 8 = 90.
24. Courtray SC 602, 357n3 notes that this final phrase is a new addition of Jerome.
25. Jerome will complete the explanation of Africanus below under the witness of Apollinaris.
26. See the note introducing Eusebius in the Preface to Jerome's Vulgate translation of Daniel.
27. Courtray SC 620, 358n2 remarks: "Jerome's translation is free: he omits certain passages, the formulas are sometimes shortened; however, Eusebius's ideas are not betrayed."
28. According to Eusebius, the prophecy of the seventy weeks concerns the "christs" or "anointed ones" who are the high priests. Therefore one needs to count the weeks from Jeshua, the first "christ" to Jesus Christ, the Lord and Savior.
29. Courtray SC 602, 361n3 clarifies: "According to the remark he made earlier, Eusebius separates the first seven weeks from the following sixty-two weeks. These forty-nine years extend according to him from the 1st year of Cyrus to the 6th year of Darius."
30. Archer, *Jerome's Commentary on Daniel*, inserts: "Actually the two dates involved are 538 B.C. and 516 B.C., an interval of only twenty-two years."
31. Cf. Josephus *Ant* 11.4.7.
32. While the Gospel speaks of the rebuilding of the temple in forty-six years, according to Josephus this ended in the ninth year of Darius and therefore lasted forty-nine years.
33. Courtray SC 602, 363n2 explains: "The following 434 years are counted from the 6th year of Darius, under the pontificate of Jeshua, until the entry of Pompey in Jerusalem, under the pontificate of Alexander. Eusebius takes stock of his calculations three times: up to Onias, he counts 248 years; until Simon, 425 years; finally he enumerates the duration of the last pontificates (29 years for John, 1 year for Aristobulus and 27 years for Alexander). The total is therefore 482 years; it lacks 1 year to reach the 483 years of the 69 weeks of years: the troubled events which follow the pontificate of Alexander make it possible to fill this year, even if it is in a more vague way."
34. Josephus, *Ant* 11:8.5.
35. This is Onias I, the son of Jaddua, who served in the priesthood with his brother Manasses during the early reign of Alexander the Great. Cf. Josephus *Ant* 11.8.7. Onias I ascended to the high priesthood sometime after the death of both his father and Alexander the Great in 323.
36. Onias II was son of Simon and grandson of Onias I. According to Josephus *Ant* 12.4 both his uncle Eleazar and his great uncle Manasses preceded his priestly tenure. Josephus notes his conflict with Ptolemy III Euergetes over taxes and characterizes Onias II as avaricious.
37. According to R. Charles, ed., *The Apocrypha and Pseudepigrapha of the Old Testament*, vol. 1 (Oxford: Oxford University Press, 1913), we must supply Σοφία, "Wisdom" here. Sirach is so named in Eusebius's *Chron*.

38. The Book of Sirach is also called Wisdom of Ben Sira, or the Latin title, Ecclesiasticus, "the church book." It was written in Hebrew in 180 BCE and translated into Greek by the author's grandson ca. 130 BCE.

39. Onias III was son of Simon II and grandson of Onias I. 2 Macc 3:1 speaks of his piety and hatred of wickedness. He healed Heliodorus, minister of Seleucus, from a mysterious illness, by his prayers and sacrifices to God. He was forced to make a trip to Antioch to defend himself against Simon's accusations where, upon his arrival in 175 BCE, Onias learned that Heliodorus murdered Seleucus and that Seleucus's brother, Antiochus IV Epiphanes, was now king. Meanwhile, in Onias's absence, his brother Jason purchased the position of high priest from the financially strapped Antiochus. Some think he fled to Egypt and established a Jewish temple in Leontopolis. Others associate Onias III with the Teacher of Righteousness mentioned in the Dead Sea Scrolls.

40. Courtray accepted Glorie's correction of the manuscripts which read "two hundred."

41. John Hyrcanus was Hasmonean high priest and ethnarch of Judea 135–104 BCE. He was son of Simon Maccabeus, grandson of Mattathias.

42. He was the eldest son of John Hyrcanus, who held the positions of high priest and king for only one year, 104–103 BCE.

43. Cf. Josephus *Ant* 13.11.1; 20.10.3.

44. This is Alexander Janneus, Hasmonean king and high priest of Judea (103–76 BCE), successor to his brother Aristobulus. Cf. Josephus *Ant* 20.10.4.

45. Cf. Josephus *Ant* 14.4.1–2.

46. This is Alexandra Salome, Hasmonean queen of Judea (76–67 BCE). She was the wife of Alexander Janneus (103–76 BCE). She appointed her elder son, Hyrcanus II as high priest. Cf. Josephus, *Ant* 20.242; 15.179.

47. This is Aristobulus II, the younger son of Alexander Janneus and Salome Alexandra.

48. Pompey captured Jerusalem and occupied the temple in 63 BCE. Aristobulus and his family were taken as captives to Rome. He was later liberated by Caesar in 49 BCE but was poisoned before he could reach Judea.

49. Cf. Josephus *Ant* 14.4.5.

50. Cf. Josephus *Ant* 20.10.5.

51. Courtray SC 602, 370n1 cites J. N. Guinot, "Théodoret imitateur d'Eusèbe," 289 to show that Jerome's second explanation of Eusebius is explained very briefly, and that the two solutions of Eusebius that Jerome reports in his commentary are incomplete. Jerome lacks the precision of Eusebius's long development on the interval that separates the first sixty-nine weeks from the last week and the interpretation of the last week. See: Theodoret of Cyrus, *Commentary on Daniel*, trans. Robert C. Hill (Leiden: Brill 2006), 245.

52. Again relying on Guinot's study, Courtray SC 602, 371n2 indicates that Jerome has made a mistake here, since Eusebius twice declares that the starting point of his explanation is the second year of Darius's reign, not the sixth year as Jerome writes. Eusebius leaves the completion of the reconstruction of the temple not to the reign of Cyrus, but that of Darius. The terminal date of the sixty-nine years is fixed at the reign of Herod and Augustus, at the

NOTES 215

time when Hyrcanus is murdered and when the succession of the high priests of God ceases according to the Law. Then comes the last week, with the true Christ, which Eusebius divides into two half-weeks: one half during the public life of Christ, when the worship of God is confirmed by the preaching of Christ, and another after the passion, when the sacrifices are definitively abolished in the temple because of the killing of Christ by the Jews. In the rest of his explanation, Eusebius explains that this period ends with the abomination of desolation, namely, the introduction by Pilate of the images of the emperor in the temple.

53. This was in 30 BCE. Cf. Josephus, *Ant* 15.173, 181.

54. Jerome's translation of Eusebius's *Chronicle* was carried out in 379–380.

55. Courtray SC 602, 374n1 thinks that this particular remark is aimed at the end of the explanation. Jerome is surprised that he can adopt two different computations for the sixty-nine weeks of years and for the last week.

56. Nero was emperor 54–68 CE.

57. Vespasian was emperor 69–79 CE.

58. Titus was Roman emperor 79–81 CE.

59. Trajan was emperor 98–117 CE.

60. Jerome mentions Hippolytus in *Vir Ill* 61 as a bishop of an unknown see and author of many commentaries on Scripture, including Daniel. He reports that Ambrosius urged Origen to write commentaries in emulation of Hippolytus.

61. Hippolytus separates the weeks of the prophecy into three units: 7, 62, and 1. He first explains the first seven weeks until the "christ-prince" of Dan 9:25. For him, this anointed one can only be Jeshua, son of Jozadac (Ezra 3:8; 5:2), who brought the people back, rebuilt the temple, and restored the sacrifice. He states that Daniel had this vision in the twenty-first year of his sojourn in Babylon—which, in addition to the seven weeks (forty-nine years) of the prophecy, gives a total of seventy years, according to the prophecy of Jeremiah (Jer 25:11–12), that the submission to Babylon was to last for seventy years. Hippolytus then reckons sixty-two weeks between the return of the Jews from Babylon—which had been authorized by an edict of Cyrus in the first year of his reign—and the birth of Christ, that is, 434 years.

62. Jerome bases this calculation on a number of testimonies, starting with Hippolytus himself (in Dan 4:24), who asserts that the Persians reigned 230 years and the Greeks 300 years; it is also the calculation proposed by Julius Africanus.

63. For Hippolytus there is a gap, since the seventieth week is reserved for the end of the world. In the first half of it, Elijah and Enoch will appear (cf. Mal 3:23; 1 Enoch 90.31; Rev 11:3). Then the antichrist will come and announce the desolation of the world. He will kill the two witnesses and take away victim and sacrifice. Cf. Hippolytus, *De Christo et Antichristo* 43, 46–47.

64. Courtray SC 602, 379n2 comments that this is the first time in the explanation of these seventy weeks that Jerome has shown such suspicion. Prior to this he sets forth the different hypotheses that were based on clearly identifiable past events. Apollinaris, however, declares that the second advent

of Christ will occur in the year 490 CE, that is, eighty-three years after the writing of the commentary of Jerome (in 407 CE).

65. Archer, *Jerome's Commentary on Daniel*, 104 inserts "i.e., 48 A.D."

66. Caligula succeeded Tiberius as emperor and ruled 37–41 CE.

67. Claudius ruled Rome 41–54 CE.

68. Archer, *Jerome's Commentary on Daniel*, 104 inserts "i.e. in 482 A.D."

69. See the note above on him.

70. Cf. Clement of Alexandria, *Strom* 1.21.126.1ff; 1.21.140.5–7. Jerome reports in *Vir Ill* 38 that Clement was a pupil of Pantaenus and led the theological school at Alexandria after the death of his master. He taught catechesis and was the author of notable volumes, full of eloquence and learning, both in Sacred Scripture and in secular literature; among these are the eight books of his *Stromata*. Courcelle, *Late Latin Writers and their Greek Sources*, trans. H. E. Wedeck (Cambridge, MA: Harvard University Press, 1969), 99 indicates that Jerome's notice on Clement in *Vir Ill* 38 is plagiarized entirely from Eusebius's *HE*. It is not clear whether Jerome was familiar with *Pedagogus* and *Protrepticus*, but he does make use of Clement's *Stromata*, as this passage shows.

71. According to Clement, the seven weeks are to be understood from the construction of the Temple in Jerusalem (started, after Cyrus, under Darius, from 520); the sixty-two weeks relate to the period when Judea was at rest, without war; as for the one week, one half corresponds to the reign of Nero (the repression of a revolt of the Jews in 67–68 is the abomination of Jerusalem); the other is after Nero, Otho, Galba, and Vitellius, to the reign of Vespasian, who destroyed Jerusalem and made the temple deserted. The latter operations were conducted by Titus in 70.

72. Courtray SC 602, 384n1 helpfully clarifies these matters. According to the *Chronicle of Eusebius*, which was translated and completed by Jerome, there are 629 years between the first year of Cyrus (first year of the 55th Olympiad) and the events of CE 70 under Vespasian (fourth year of the 211th Olympiad). Clement contradicts himself later in his *Stromata*, when he asserts that the Persians reigned 235 years, the Macedonians 312 years and 18 days until the death of Antony, before the establishment of the Roman Empire (27 BCE); we thus obtain, up to the events of 70, a total of 644 years.

73. Origen, *Strom* 10. In *Princ* 4.1.5, Origen reckons that the seventy weeks elapsed until Christ. Likewise, in his *Commentary on Matthew* 11, he relates Dan 9:24–25 to the incarnation of the Messiah-Prince.

74. Tertullian's *Adversus Judaeos* dates to 197–200 CE. In English, see Tertullian, *An Answer to the Jews* 8 (ANF 3.159–160).

75. Courtray, SC 602, 385n5 confirms that the text quoted by Jerome is, with a few variations, in conformity with that of Tertullian.

76. Lattey, *The Book of Daniel*, 121 gives the following commencement dates for the rulers of the Persian Empire: Cyrus 538 BCE; Cambyses 529; Darius I (Hystaspis) 522; Xerxes I (= Ahasuerus) 485; Artaxerxes I (Longimanus) 464; Xerxes II 424; Darius II (Nothus) 423; Artaxerxes II (Mnemon) 404; Artaxerxes III (Ochus) 359; Darius III (Codomannus) 338–1. Courtray SC 602, 386n1 notices that Tertullian appears to confuse Darius the Mede (Dan 9:1) with Darius II Nothos (424–405), whose reign lasted nineteen years.

NOTES 217

77. Lattey, *The Book of Daniel*, 121–22 gives the following commencement dates for the rulers of the Macedonian Empire: Philip II 359 BCE; Alexander the Great 336–323. Seleucids: Seleucus I (Nicator) 312; Antiochus I (Soter) 280; Antiochus II (Theos) 261; Seleucus II (Kallinikos) 246; Seleucus III (Keraunos) 226; Antiochus III (the Great) 223; Seleucus IV (Philopator) 187; Antiochus IV (Epiphanes) 175–164. Ptolemies: Ptolemy I Soter (ruler of Egypt) 323; Ptolemy II Philadelphus 283; Ptolemy III Euergetes I 246; Ptolemy IV Philopator 221; Ptolemy V Epiphanes 204; Ptolemy VI Philometor 181–145; Ptolemy VII Euergetes II 170–116.
78. Archer, *Jerome's Commentary on Daniel*, 107 inserts: "actually only twenty-nine years after Cleopatra's death—the language here is confusing."
79. Courtray SC 602, 389n2 clarifies that the total number of years does not add up to 437 years and five months but to 420 years and five months. Tertullian's error seems to come from the thirteen common years of the reigns of Cleopatra and Augustus. This explanation was offered by the Renaissance editor of Tertullian, Pamelius (cf. Migne, PL 25, 550 note j). Tertullian must have also counted the thirteen years of the reign of Augustus during which Cleopatra reigned at the same time as he and the forty-one years of Augustus before the birth of Christ—while the thirteen years are part of those forty-one years. Pamelius speaks of a lapse of memory.
80. Archer, *Jerome's Commentary on Daniel*, 107 inserts: "Note that Claudius' reign of 13 years is here omitted."
81. Cf. Tertullian, *An Answer to the Jews* 9 (ANF 3.160). Scholars (Archer, Courtray, et al.) have noticed weaknesses in Tertullian's chronology. He uses the two half-weeks separately by calculating 62.5 + 7.5 = 70. In addition, his chronology is incomplete: he leaves out the reigns of the Ptolemies and omits the reign of Emperor Claudius. Finally, the year totals do not tally—at least from the manuscripts we have. Courtray expresses surprise that Jerome quotes Tertullian's testimony without discussing it.
82. Lit.: to speak παραφραστικῶς.
83. Courtray SC 602, 395n3 (mistakenly written as 2) reports that the editions of the Vulgate did not retain the text *populus qui eum negaturus est* ("the people who will deny him"), which is found in the manuscripts, assuming that this was a comment that had been introduced very early. Courtray thinks that the expression was not part of the quotation but completed it: such is the explanation of the formula and *et non erit eius* according to Jerome, immediately followed by that of the Jews.
84. Jewish tradition sees the Roman general Tinius Rufus as the winner of the revolt led by Bar Kokhba that took place in Judea under Hadrian in 132–135. The emperor Hadrian then prohibited circumcision and founded on the ruins of Jerusalem the pagan city of Aelia Capitolina. In his *Commentary on Zechariah* 8:18–19, Jerome speaks of the temple being plowed over by Tyrannius Rufus to the shame of the oppressed nation.
85. Courtray SC 602, 397n5 comments: "This usage has indeed been kept in Latin for certain numbers (for example those between 11 and 17). For Hebrew, the rule given by Jerome is correct for numbers between 11 and 19, but not systematically."

86. Courtray SC 602, 398n1 comments that Jerome's example is inappropriate, because Gen 25:7 says, according to a literal translation from Hebrew, one hundred years and seventy and five years, in descending order. "Perhaps Jerome is remembering the paraphrase of Josephus on this passage (*Ant Jud* 1.17.256), which gives the numbers in the increasing sense, unless he has in mind Gen 12:4 ('Abram was aged five and seventy')."

87. Cf. Josephus, *Bell Iud?*

88. The Roman emperor Hadrian reigned 117–138 CE. He suppressed Bar Kokhba in 136.

89. This rebellion took place 132–36 CE. See: M. Mor, *The Second Jewish Revolt: The Bar Kokhba War, 132–136 CE* (Leiden: Brill, 2016).

90. Jerome calls this the final vision at 6:28 and at 10:21. It covers Dan 10—12.

91. Cyrus II was king of Persia 558–530 BCE.

92. Courtray SC 602, 401n2 clarifies this passage by saying that Jerome here justifies the apparent contradiction of the biblical text: Dan 1:21 adopts a chronology in accordance with the successive occupants of Babylon; Daniel thus passed first under the reign of Persian Cyrus, until his first year, before Darius the Mede in turn seized the kingdom of the Chaldeans. Dan 10:1 speaks of the third year of Cyrus, for, Darius being dead, the chronology of the story continues according to the reign of the Persian king.

93. This is Courtray's correction for the name "Aquila" which is found in the manuscripts.

94. Jerome's *Ep* 64 to Fabiola discusses the vestments of the high priest. See my new translation in the first volume of: St. Jerome, *Exegetical Epistles*, trans. Thomas P. Scheck, 2 vols., FOTC 147 and 148 (Washington, DC: Catholic University of America Press, 2023–24).

95. Cf. Jerome, *Commentary on Isaiah* Bk 1 on 2:16; Bk 18 on 66:18.

96. Glorie (CCSL) thinks this is a slip of memory on Jerome's part since Josephus speaks of it being Tarsus of Cilicia; *Ant* 9.10.1–2.

97. In *Commentary on Jonah* 1:3a Jerome cites 2 Chron 20:36–37 as a reference to a Tarsus in India.

98. See note at Dan 7:2 where Jerome's reading agreed with the Hebrew ("sons of Israel" instead of "God's angels"). Here he cites according to the Septuagint. The theory of the angels of the nations is testified in Origen: one finds it many times in his works, associated with the texts of Deut 32:8 and Dan 10:13. From Origen it was picked up by Rufinus and Jerome. See Origen, *Hom in Num* 11.5.2; *Hom on Luke* 35.6; *Princ* 3.3.3; *Cels* 5.30; Rufinus, *Exp Symb* 13; Jerome, *In Mic* Bk 2 on Micah 6:1–2.

99. Alexander the Great fought the Persians from the spring of 334 BCE, when he won a first victory over a Persian army on the banks of the Granicus, until July 330, when Darius was assassinated by conspirators.

100. This refers to the Old Latin translation of the LXX; cf. Prol and under Dan 1:3–4a.

101. Courtray SC 602, 417n3 clarifies that in Hebrew, Dan 11:1 begins in the first year of Darius the Mede, while, according to the Septuagint and Theodotion, this chapter commences in the first year of King Cyrus (as did chap. 10 in both the Hebrew and the LXX).

102. Cf. under Dan 6:1–2a; 7:1a.
103. Vision 9 opened in the first year of Darius (cf. Dan 9:1); vision 10 in the third year of Cyrus (cf. Dan 10:1), and vision 11 again in the first year of Darius (Dan 11:1). Jerome's explanation in Dan 10:1a seems to be that Darius must have succeeded Cyrus after the first year of his reign, in which case, the first year of Darius is effectively prior to the third year of Cyrus and contemporary with vision 9 (cf. Dan 9: 1).
104. Jerome has followed the Hebrew reading, which is also attested by Aquila and Symmachus. The LXX and Theodotion translated: "Cyrus." Baldwin, *Daniel* 31 finds in this evidence that the Greek translator knew that Darius the Mede and Cyrus were one and the same person.
105. Jerome explains Dan 11:1–20 from a purely historical point of view and mainly relates the vision to the Hellenistic period. Through the study of Greek and Latin historians, Jerome seeks to recognize the historical characters involved in each event predicted by the prophet. As Courtray SC 602, 420n1 indicates, in this case the prophetic interpretation is identified in the literal sense, and prophecy and history therefore correspond.
106. Smerdis was a brother of Cambyses, king of Persia, by whom he was put to death.
107. Cf. Herodotus, *Hist* 7–8; Thucydides 1.118.2.
108. Callias was archon of Athens in 480–479 BCE.
109. Sophocles (495–406) and Euripides (ca. 480–406) the two Greek tragic poets were active after Xerxes's death.
110. Themistocles (528–462 BCE) was an Athenian statesman and naval commander who persuaded the Athenians to evacuate the city after their defeat at Thermopylae and then defeated the Persians in the naval battle of Salamis.
111. Archer thought this referred to Tertullian, but Courtray traces it to Hippolytus, *In Dan* 4, 41.4–6.
112. Courtray SC 602, 423n6 provides the list that the *Chronicle* of Eusebius/Jerome has given for the Persian Empire: Cyrus II (559–530); Cambyses (530–522); the Magi (522); Darius I (522–486); Xerxes I (486–465); Artabanus (465); Artaxerxes I Long-Hand (465–424); Xerxes II (end of 424); Sogdianus (beginning of 423); Darius II (423–405); Artaxerxes II Mnemon (405–359); Artaxerxes III Ochus (359–338); Arses (338–336); Darius III Codomannus (336–330).
113. Alexander the Great (356–323 BCE) was the son of Philip II and Olympias and educated by Aristotle. He succeeded his father in 336. After consolidating power over Greece, he defeated Darius III at Issus (333) and again at Gaugamela in 331. Darius was assassinated by his own troops in 330. Alexander reached India in 326–25. His death in Babylon occurred in obscure circumstances.
114. Philip Arrhidaeus (357–317 BCE) was son of Philip II and Philinna of Larissa. He came unexpectedly to prominence in June 323 when the Macedonian phalanx troops found him at Babylon and proclaimed him Alexander's successor. He came to grief in 317 when his wife usurped his authority against the regent Polyperchon and was defeated and captured. Philip II's wife Olympias had him murdered in October of that year.

115. Seleucus I Nicator (the Conqueror) (358–281 BCE) fought as a general under Alexander the Great from Asia Minor to India. After Alexander's death, he gained the satrapy of Babylonia, which was to form the core of his later kingdom.

116. Antigonus I (382–301 BCE) was prominent under Philip II and governed Greater Phrygia for Alexander the Great (334–323).

117. This is the name of a Macedonian general under Alexander the Great; cf. Curt. 3, 9, 7; 4, 3, 1; 7, 6, 19; Cic. *Tuscul.* 5, 12, 34.

118. A general of Alexander the Great, cf. Curt. 4, 3, 1.

119. He was one of the generals of Alexander the Great, afterward king of Thrace, and founder of Lysimachia. Cf. Cicero, *Tuscul.* 1, 43, 102; 5, 40, 117.

120. A district of S.W. Asia Minor.

121. Ptolemy Philadelphus reigned 283–246 BCE.

122. Cf. Josephus, *Ant* 12.2.1–15.

123. An *artaba* is an Egyptian dry measure coming to 3 1/3 Roman pecks (*modii*).

124. Courtray, SC 602, 431n2 comments that the information Jerome mentions here may have come from Porphyry and his sources, since it is not found in extant sources, but it is possible to obtain a good idea of the power and the wealth of Ptolemy Philadelphus by reading the *Idyll* 17 of Theocritus, which was dedicated to him. Verses 86–92 relate to the first Syrian war (274–271 BCE) and enumerate the conquests of Ptolemy II. In the translation of Robert Wells, *Theocritus: The Idylls* (Harmondsworth: Penguin, 1988), 112, the passage reads:

> All these acknowledge Ptolemy's command.
> Syria, Phoenicia, Libya yield their land.
> Arab and black-skinned Ethiop feel his sword.
> Lycia, Pamphylia, Caria call him lord,
> Lord fierce Cilicia, sea-washed Cyclades.
> His ships proclaim him sovereign of the seas.
> Through both empires, the watery and the dry,
> All power begins and ends in Ptolemy.

125. See above under 11:4b.

126. Seleucus Nicator ruled 312–281 BCE.

127. Antiochus I Soter ruled 280–261 BCE.

128. Antiochus II Theos ruled 261–246 BCE.

129. In 261 BCE, Antiochos II waged a second Syrian war against Ptolemy II. In 252, the two kings signed a peace treaty with the result that Ptolemy lost his possessions in Asia Minor (in Ionia, Cilicia, and Pamphylia, with the exception of Caria), but retained Phoenicia and southern Syria.

130. Antiochus died by poison in Ephesus in 246 BCE.

131. Ptolemy III Euergetes ruled Egypt 246–221 BCE.

132. Courtray SC 602, 436n1 notes that Jerome is seemingly alone in reporting this. The historians who are extant recount that Cambyses II, during the campaign of Egypt (525–522), in the grip of a violent madness, profaned burial places and sanctuaries (Herodotus, *Hist* 3.37) and had temples demolished (Justin, *Epit* 1.9.2; Strabo, *Geogr* 17.1.27.46; Diodore, *Bibl* 1.46, 49).

133. Courtray SC 602, 437 placed v. 12b in square brackets even though it is found in all the manuscripts. It is cited below, but it is an uncertain addition because the passage is subsequently referred to Ptolemy and not to Antiochus.
134. Antiochus III the Great ruled 223–187.
135. Ptolemy IV Philopator ruled 221–204.
136. Cf. Polybius, *Hist* 5.80.3–82.1; 5.85.13–86.8.
137. Cf. Polybius, *Hist* 5.86.8; 5.87.
138. Cf. Polybius, *Hist* 14.11.5.
139. Cf. Livy, *Hist Rom* 31.14.5; Justin, *Epit* 30.2.8; Polybius, *Hist* 3.2.8; 15.20.
140. Cf. Polybius, *Hist* 15.20.2; Justin, *Epit* 31.1.1.
141. Cf. Josephus, *Ant* 13.3.1–3; 20:10.3; *Bell Jud* 1.1.1. Onias IV son of Onias III is reported to be the priest who fled to Egypt and received funds from the rulers of Egypt to build a Jewish temple at Leontopolis, to run a military colony, and to serve as a Ptolemaic general. Josephus offers conflicting accounts in *Antiquities* and *Jewish War*.
142. Cf. Jerome, *Commentary on Isaiah* Bk 5 on Isa 19:18.
143. Cf. Polybius, *Hist* 16.39.1–4; Josephus, *Ant* 12.3.3.
144. Jerome mentions Paneas in his *Commentary on Matthew* Bk 3 on Matt 16:13. The city is now called Banias. The original name derived from the fact that the village was dedicated to the god Pan. Jerome makes contradictory statements about this town, sometimes distinguishing it from Dan (*Onomasticon* 77), and sometimes identifying the two places (*Comm. in Ezek* 27.19), *Comm. in Amos*. According to J. F. Wilson, *Caesarea Philippi: Banias, the Lost City of Pan* (London: I. B. Tauris, 2004), Jerome received his information about the town not firsthand but from Eusebius, Jewish rabbis, and Josephus, *Ant* 18.2.1; cf. also *BJ* 2.167–68.
145. According to Courtray, SC 602, 447n1, Jerome's report here is our only source of knowledge about these events.
146. Cf. Polybius, *Hist* 16.18–20. This is the decisive battle of Panias (200 BCE) near the sources of the Jordan, where Antiochos III defeated Scopas, who took refuge in Sidon.
147. Cf. Livy, *Hist Rom* 33.20.4; 33.41.5; Polybius *Hist* 18.40a.
148. Cf. Polybius, *Hist* 28.17.9; Josephus, *Ant* 12.4.1; Euseb.-Hieron., *Chron* 136.24–137.2.
149. Jerome uses the Greek form. According to Jerome's teacher Donatus, *Ars Gramm.*, 3.3, a pleonasm is "the addition of an unnecessary word to give a fuller meaning," and he gives these same two examples. Thus in Dan 11:17 *of women* is redundant and unnecessary since all daughters are *of women*. In the Virgil quotes, "with the mouth" is unnecessary after "spoke"; and "with these ears" unnecessary after "drink in her voice."
150. Virgil, *Aen* 1:614; 4.276.
151. Virgil *Aen* 4.359.
152. Cleopatra was in conflict with her father because of her dowry. The friendship between Rome and Egypt dates from 273; it was renewed in 210 and 201.
153. These events date to 197–196 BCE, when Antiochus III aimed to reconstitute the empire of Seleucos I.

154. Scipio Africanus (236–184 BCE) was the hero of the Second Punic War against Hannibal, whom he defeated at the battle of Zama in 202 BCE. In Jerome's present context, Scipio had just exercised the consulate in 194 BCE, which prohibited him from receiving another immediately. His brother, Lucius Cornelius Scipio, was therefore elected in his place, and Scipio Africanus became his legate. The Romans viewed it as a favorable omen to entrust this war to the two Scipios.

155. Taurus is a high mountain range in the southeastern part of Asia Minor.

156. Courtray SC 602, 452n1 provides some of the historical background here: After his defeat at Thermopylae in April 191 BCE, Antiochus was forced to abandon Greece. In 190, the Roman army commanded by Lucius Scipio crossed into Asia, and Rome demanded that Antiochus leave all his possessions of Asia Minor and withdraw from Taurus, which he did after the victory of the Romans in Magnesia in January 189. The peace treaty was ratified in Apamee in 188. Antiochus had to abandon Asia up to the Taurus mountains. He was forced to pay fifteen thousand talents over ten years, to deliver Hannibal and the other Carthaginian refugees, to hand over almost all his fleet and his elephants to the Romans, and to forbid his warships to sail beyond Sarpedon. To pay the war indemnity, Antiochus attacked a rich temple of Elymais, but he was killed by the people of this city (July 187).

157. Courtray SC 602, 452n3 thinks this refers to the place of Antiochus's burial or the place where he fell.

158. Courtray SC 602, 453n5 notes that the interpretations given on this verse are divergent. Jerome thinks that the man described by the angel is Seleucus Philopator; according to Porphyry, it is Ptolemy Epiphanes; the Hebrews see it rather as an allusion to Trypho. Jerome thinks that Porphyry's interpretation does not hold up, since the person in question must not have had a great stature and did not carry out great warlike actions, which is certainly not the case with Ptolemy Epiphanes. Jerome cites as proof the translation of this same verse by the Septuagint, which insists even more on the incapacity of this character.

159. Cf. Justin, *Epit* 30.1.

160. Braverman, *Jerome's Commentary on Daniel*, 113 reports that there is no extant reference in rabbinical literature that identifies the figure in Dan 11:20 with Trypho.

161. The previous critical editor, F. Glorie, conjectured that this section Dan 11:21—12:13 was a treatise on the antichrist that Jerome had written in 399 and then completed when he was writing his *Commentary on Daniel*. Courtray SC 602, 456n1 dissents from this view and thinks it was actually written in 407, along with the rest of the commentary.

162. Antiochus IV Epiphanes reigned over the Seleucid empire 175–164 BCE. He conquered Jerusalem, desecrated the temple, and persecuted the Jews severely, as is recorded in the Books of Maccabees. A revolt against his measures to Hellenize the Jews of Palestine was led by the priest Mattathias and his five sons, among whom Judas Maccabeus was the military leader. In 164 BCE Judas Maccabeus retook Jerusalem and cleansed and rededicated the temple, thereby inaugurating the festival of Hanukkah. Cf. 1 Macc 1:10–15;

2 Macc 4:7–20. For Christian interpreters beginning with Jesus and Paul, Antiochus IV Epiphanes became a type of the antichrist, who will persecute the church prior to the second coming.

163. See under 11:2b.

164. M. Reaburn, "St Jerome and Porphyry Interpret the Book of Daniel," *Australian Biblical Review* 52 (2004): 9 is somewhat impressed by Jerome's balance and moderation in this section. She paraphrases his meaning: "Just as Solomon does not fulfil all the words of this Psalm in a literal sense, so the Maccabean interpretation does not fulfil all the elements of Dan 11:21ff in a literal sense. In Jerome's mind the eschatological interpretation which sees the little horn as the Antichrist is a much more complete interpretation. The surprise is not that Jerome upholds the traditional eschatological interpretation but that he goes to such lengths to legitimate a degree of agreement with Porphyry."

165. Archer, *Jerome's Commentary on Daniel*, inserts: "i.e. *manus*, 'hand,' may also signify a 'band of armed men.'"

166. I follow Courtray SC 602, 462 in understanding the remainder of this passage as Jerome's summary of Porphyry's explanation.

167. Cf. Polybius, *Hist* 27.19; Diodore, *Bibl* 30, fr. 2.

168. Cf. Josephus, *Ant* 12.5.2; Polybius, *Hist* 28.18; Diodore, *Bibl* 30 fr. 22a–b.

169. Callinicus Sutorius is mentioned in Jerome's prologue.

170. Jerome views the rise of the antichrist as "the rise of a political leader to world domination by means of military power." J. O'Connell, *The Eschatology of St. Jerome*, Dissertationes ad Lauream 16 (Mundelein, IL: Pontifical Theological Faculty of the Seminary of St. Mary of the Lake, 1948), 26.

171. In addition to Methodius, Eusebius, and Apollinaris, whose Christian responses to Porphyry's interpretations do not survive, Courtray cites Irenaeus, *Haer* 5.30.2; Hippolytus, *De Christo et Antichristo*; Cyril of Jerusalem, *Myst* 15.11.

172. Cf. Josephus, *Ant* 12.5.2.

173. See under 7:7c–8.

174. Courtray SC 602, 469n1 comments on this passage that the account of the events is not entirely accurate. Antiochus had let his nephew Ptolemy VI come home; he thus hoped that a feud would break out between the two Egyptian kings, Ptolemy VI and Ptolemy VII, and Euergetes II, his brother, whom he himself had placed on the throne. But this attempt was a failure: instead of fighting, the two Lagid kings came to an agreement to govern Egypt jointly. The event seems, in any case, unrelated to the reasons that pushed Antiochus to return to Syria at the end of his first campaign.

175. E. J. Young, *The Prophecy of Daniel: A Commentary* (Grand Rapids: Eerdmans, 1949), 244 notes that "and the Romans will come" is the LXX reading. He thinks that Jerome has discovered the correct meaning by his translation "triremes," and the reference to the Roman ships of Popilius Laenas.

176. Cf. Polybius *Hist* 19.11; Livy *Ab Urbe cond* 45.12; Josephus *Ant* 12.5.2; *De bello Iud* 1.1.

177. Cf. Jerome, *Ep* 121.11; Euseb.-Hieron., *Chron*, 114.16–19.

178. There are manuscript variants here. Some read "Domitian or Nero," "Domitian Nero." I am following Courtray's correction of the text, SC 602, 472, already made by Archer, *St. Jerome's Commentary on Daniel*, 133 with the insertion: "[A]ctually Domitius was the name of Nero's father, Ahenobarbus."

179. Nero was emperor 54–68 CE. He savagely persecuted the Christians after making them the scapegoat for the fire that destroyed Rome in 64. Peter and Paul were put to death under him. The idea of him being the antichrist is linked to Rev 13:3: "One of its heads seemed to have a mortal wound, but its mortal wound was healed, and the whole earth followed the beast with wonder." This mention of the death and healing of one of the seven heads of the first beast suggests an assassination or a violent death. Very quickly in Christian literature, an allusion to an emperor is made.

180. Cf. Josephus *Ant* 12.5.2–3.

181. The lemma had "abomination in the desolation." Cf. Josephus, *Ant* 12.5.4. J. Collins, *Daniel*, 358 comments: "Jerome, in his *Commentary* on Dan 11:31, says that Antiochus set up 'an image of Jupiter Olympius in the temple at Jerusalem.' Several modern commentators have inferred that the abomination was a statue. Yet this view is not attested before Jerome, and it does not fit well with the location of the abomination on the altar according to 1 Maccabees." Collins thinks that the abomination was a pagan altar.

182. Braverman, *Jerome's Commentary on Daniel*, 115–18 analyzes this section and says (p. 117) that the Jews, Jerome, and Porphyry all agree that the *chethim* in Dan 11:30 are identified as the Romans. "The uniqueness of the 'Jewish tradition' cited by Jerome is that the events in Dan 11:31 refer to the Romans as well, and particularly, to Vespasian and Titus who destroyed the Second Temple."

183. Courtray SC 602, 479n1 thinks that the use of the first person here may suggest that Jerome is giving his personal opinion rather than that of earlier Christian writers, unless he is simply varying his expressions.

184. Jerome referred to this Jewish tradition under 11:31.

185. Cf. Josephus *Ant* 12.6.1–4.

186. Courtray SC 602, 481n1 thinks this sentence has been inserted by Jerome into his paraphrase of Porphyry.

187. According to Braverman, *Jerome's Commentary on Daniel*, 120 this refers not to Septimius Severus (reigned 193–211), who was not favorable toward the Jews, but to Alexander Severus (reigned 222–235), who *was* favorable toward the Jews. Courtray SC 602, 482n1 dissents from Braverman's view and supports M. Simon, *Verus Israel* (Paris, 1964), 229, who thinks the reference is indeed to Septimus Severus (193–211).

188. It is very difficult to identify this Antoninus since many Roman emperors bore this name.

189. This is Julian the Apostate, who reigned 361–363. He favored the Jews in the sense that in his endeavor to restore the preeminence of paganism, specifically the Mithraic syncretistic creed, he enlisted Jewish support in his battle against the Christian Church. Julian abolished the special Jewish fiscal tax and spoke with admiration of Jewish customs and ceremonies. He also promised to rebuild Jerusalem and the Jewish temple. See M. Adler,

"The Emperor Julian and the Jews," *JQR* 5 o.s. (1893): 591–651; W. Bacher, "Emperor Julian and the Rebuilding of the Temple at Jerusalem," *JQR* 10 o.s. (1897): 168–72.

190. The reference is to a revolt of the Jews of Dio-Caesarea under Constantius Gallus (351–54), which Gallus repressed very brutally.

191. For a long list of parallel passages in Jerome's commentaries, see Courtray SC 602, 482.

192. Braverman, *Jerome's Commentary on Daniel* 124–25 reports that there are no extant rabbinic sources that identify the figure in Dan 11:36 with the antichrist of Jerome's Jewish tradition. However, the background text of 2 Thess 2:1–12 that Jerome integrates does have such links.

The entire passage in Thessalonians is probably based on a Jewish conception of the antichrist. The appellations "man of lawlessness" (2 Thess 2:3) and "the lawless one" (2 Thess 2:8) correspond to the name Belial found elsewhere as an opponent of the Messiah. The name Belial is explained by rabbinic texts as a contraction of two Hebrew words that mean "without a yoke," signifying the refusal to bear the yoke of the law. The death of the antichrist "with the breath of his [Jesus's] mouth" (2 Thess 2:8) is similar to Targum Jonathan in Isa 11:4: "with the speech of his lips he will kill the evil Armillus." Armillus is the name of the antichrist and appears often in later Midrashim. According to later Midrashim, the antichrist Armillus is portrayed as a false messiah. He arises after the coming of the Messiah ben Joseph and kills this Messiah in battle. He himself is then killed by the breath of the Messiah ben David.

193. Courtray SC 602, 485n3 explains this to mean that the statue of Olympian Zeus had the features of Antiochos Epiphanes, and that the king forced the Jews to celebrate his birthday every month in the temple of Jerusalem.

194. Diodorus Siculus of Agyrium, Sicily is the author of the Library, a universal history from mythological times to 60 BCE. It survives only in fragments.

195. Scholars generally believe that Jerome's testimony is second-hand.

196. Cf. Polybius, *Hist* 31.4, 9, 11; Josephus, *Ant* 12.9.1. To enrich himself personally and to pay the Romans the contributions that had been imposed on his father Antiochos III and that had not yet been paid, Antiochos IV launched this campaign toward the East in the spring of 165 BCE.

197. Jerome follows Josephus, *Ant* 12.9.1, who faults Polybius of Megalopolis for saying that Antiochus died because he purposed to plunder the temple of Diana in Persia: "For the purposing to do a thing, but not actually doing it, is not worthy of punishment." He says it is much more probable that he was punished for plundering the temple of Jerusalem.

198. Courtray SC 602, 489n2 helps to clarify this: "The ambiguity comes from the fact that we do not know if the verb *intellegere* ('understand') relates only to the phrase *super omnem deum* ('over every god') or also to *super concupiscentiam feminarum* ('over the lusts of women'), as Jerome will develop it later."

199. Archer, *Jerome's Commentary on Daniel*, 138 defines this Greek phrase (used frequently by Jerome) as: "the use of a common word in two different

clauses." The figure consists in putting an expression in one proposition and not repeating it in the following one.
   200. Cf. Polybius, *Hist* 26.1.1; 30.26; Livy, *Hist Rom* 41.20.
   201. Jerome, *Commentary on Isaiah* Bk 9 on Isa 30:1–5 writes of v. 2: "For *strength of pharaoh*, which is recorded twice in this passage, the Hebrew has written *maoz*. We have taken note of this, that what we read in Daniel's last vision as '*god maozim*' [Dan 11:38], not as Porphyry dreams up, 'god of the hamlet of Modein,' but we should understand this as 'strong and powerful god.'"
   202. The lemma had added "over many" here.
   203. With the exception of Porphyry, ancient historians are silent on the subject of a second Egyptian campaign of Antiochus IV Epiphanes. Some have posited such a campaign in 168 BCE, but to most scholars it seems highly unlikely that after the intervention of the Roman legate Popilius in the affairs of Egypt, Antiochus would have returned to the kingdom of the Ptolemies. Courtray SC 602, 494n1 thinks that the testimony of Porphyry, quoted by Saint Jerome, does not need to be retained as historically reliable. For Porphyry was concerned to show against the Christians that all the events of Daniel 11 had already been carried out and were related to Antiochus IV Epiphanes. One can conjecture that Porphyry could have contrived a new campaign of Antiochus in Egypt based precisely on these lines from Daniel. One can assume that these lines were inspired in Porphyry by 1 Macc 1:16–20.
   204. Aradus was an island off the coast of Phoenicia.
   205. Archer, *Jerome's Commentary on Daniel*, 141 inserts a comment about Theodotion's rendering: "The Massoretic text has the common noun, *sebiy*, which means 'beauty' or 'honor,' and gives no room for any proper noun, *Saba*." The proper noun might have referred to southern Arabia whence came incense products (cf. Jer 6:20; Isa 60:6; Herodotus 3.97) and whence came the Queen of Sheba (1 Kgs 10:1–13).
   206. Cf. Polybius, *Hist* 31.4, 9, 11; Josephus, *Ant* 12.9.1.
   207. S. R. Driver, *The Book of Daniel with Introduction and Notes*, Cambridge Bible for Schools and Colleges (Cambridge: Cambridge University Press, 1900), 197 discusses Porphyry's historical interpretation in detail and tentatively surmises that elements of it (a fourth Egyptian expedition of Antiochus) may have been derived from Daniel's verses and not from reliable history. As mentioned above, Courtray concurs with this.
   208. Driver, *The Book of Daniel with Introduction and Notes*, ciii, n. 1 calls Jerome's comment "notable and far-sighted words."
   209. Young, *The Prophecy of Daniel*, 316n3 comments: "The Latin word is *mentitum*. All honor to Porphyry for thus candidly and accurately stating the case. (There seems no sufficient reason for denying this language to Porphyry). For if an unknown author, living at the time of the Maccabees, wrote under the name of Daniel, he did just what Porphyry declares he did—he lied."
   210. Cf. Jerome, *Commentary on Isaiah* Bk 8.12 on Isa 25:6–8.
   211. Archer, *Jerome's Commentary on Daniel*, 143 inserts the comment: "An interesting observation, but rather puzzling. Ordinarily the Hebrew pe is spirantized only after a vowel sound, and is hard the rest of the time. It is hard and doubled in this particular word, '*appadnow*, according to the Massoretic pointing."

NOTES   227

212. Glorie, CCSL refers in the apparatus to Aquila and Symmachus as the versions Jerome is rendering here.

213. Lattey, *The Book of Daniel*, 111 notes that Dan 12:1 is quoted in Matt 24:21 and Mark 13:19 and applied by Jesus to the end of Jerusalem and possibly to the end of the world and the time of the second coming of Christ. He writes: "Already the lesser deliverance is embraced within the greater, much as the prophet Isaiah passes from the deliverance from exile (e.g., 48:20–21; 52:7–12) to the full messianic deliverance (e.g., ch. 62)." Lattey uses the term *compenetration* to describe this embracing of the eschatological within the historical.

214. Lysias was a general in the Seleucid army of Antiochus IV Epiphanes. On Antiochus's orders, he marched against Jerusalem and in 165 BCE his commanders met defeat at Emmaus in a battle with Judas Maccabeus (1 Macc 4:1–24). Lysias's eventual departure from Israel allowed Judas to rededicate the temple (1 Macc 4:36–59).

215. Cf. Josephus *Ant* 12.9.1–2.

216. Greek: μεταφορικῶς.

217. I believe Jerome's paraphrase of Porphyry's interpretation ends here. J. Collins, *Daniel: A Commentary on the Book of Daniel*, Hermeneia (Minneapolis: Augsburg Fortress, 1993), 391–93 comments: "According to Jerome, Porphyry interpreted this passage as a metaphorical account of the Maccabean rebellion. Resurrection language is certainly used metaphorically in the Hebrew Bible (e.g., Ezekiel 37; Hos 6:2), but there is virtually unanimous agreement among modern scholars that Daniel is referring to the actual resurrection of individuals from the dead, because of the explicit language of everlasting life."

218. Courtray SC 602, 514n1 discusses the difficulty of the text here and the uncertainty of the reading. The expression "common edition" always designates the text of the Septuagint; but for Daniel, as Jerome reports in his prologue, it is the revision of Theodotion that was used by the churches and that constitutes the current edition.

219. A passage in *Ep* 53.3 to Paulinus of Nola (394 CE) resembles this one: "For holiness that is uneducated (*sancta rusticitas*) benefits only the person who possesses it, and however much he builds up the church of Christ due to the merit of his life, to the same extent he harms it, if he does not offer resistance to those who speak against it [cf. Titus 1:9]. The prophet Malachi [*sic*] or, rather, the Lord through Malachi, says: 'Ask now the priests concerning the law' [Hag 2:12]. That shows how much it is incumbent upon the priest to be able to answer, if they are asked about the law. And in Deuteronomy we read: 'Ask your father, and he will tell you; [ask] your elders, and they will tell you' [Deut 32:7]. And in Psalm 118: 'My songs were your statutes in the place of my pilgrimage' [Ps 119:54]. And in the description of the just man, whom David compares with the tree of life, which is in paradise, among his other virtues he added this one as well: 'His will was in the law of the Lord, and he will meditate on his law day and night' [Ps 1:2]. At the end of his most sacred vision, Daniel says that the just will shine like stars, and the intelligent, that is, the learned, like the firmament. Do you see the significant differences between just rusticity and learned justice? The former are compared to the stars, the latter

to the heavens. Although, according to the Hebrew truth, both can apply [to the learned], since we read the following in the Hebrew text: 'Those who are learned will shine like the brightness of the firmament, and those who instruct many in justice, like stars for all eternity.'" This is from my forthcoming translation: St. Jerome, *Exegetical Epistles*, 2 vols., trans. Thomas P. Scheck, FOTC (Washington, DC: Catholic University of America Press, 2023–24).

220. Cf. J. R. Webb, "Knowledge Will Be Manifold: Daniel 12.4 and the Idea of Intellectual Progress in the Middle Ages," *Speculum* 89 (2014) 307–57 (311–13).

221. Greek: ἰδίωμα.

222. This word, *efferatio* is found in Jerome *Ep* 107.2.

223. Josephus, *Ant* 11.10; 12.5, 4; 7.6.

224. Cf. Josephus, *Ant* 12.5, 4; 7.6.

225. Josephus, *Ant* 12.5.4; 7.6 (three years). In *Bell Iud* 1.1.1 Josephus records three and a half years.

226. This is Theodotion's translation.

227. See above at 8:9b–12.

228. Reaburn, "St. Jerome and Porphyry," 15, describes Jerome's repeated criticism of Porphyry on this exegetical point about the three versus the three and a half years of Dan 12:7 as his *pièce de résistance* in his historical/exegetical arguments against Porphyry. I would judge Jerome's exposé of Porphyry's faulty textual emendation of "god Maozim" (Dan 11:37–39) as perhaps an even stronger criticism (not mentioned or discussed by Reaburn).

229. Reaburn, "St Jerome and Porphyry," 16–17, comments on these words: "This makes clear what Jerome has hinted at: he is not bothered so much by the Maccabean interpretation but by the understanding by some that this is the only interpretation; the eschatological interpretation remains not only a possibility but for Jerome the interpretation which is true to the details of the text." I find it noteworthy that Josephus, *Ant* 10.11.7 acknowledged that much of Daniel's prophecy was fulfilled in the time of Antiochus Epiphanes but added that Daniel also wrote about the Roman Empire and the laying waste of Jerusalem.

230. As Courtray SC 602, 529n3 indicates, one senses a concluding tone to this last remark of Jerome, which is confirmed by the fact that the rest of Jerome's commentary is comprised of excerpts from Origen's *Stromata*. But here Jerome recalls the main themes he has developed over the course of the commentary: Porphyry does not know how to read the biblical text; Antiochus IV Epiphanes was only a type of the antichrist, of whom the biblical text speaks here. Notice how Jerome refers back to his prologue by naming Eusebius, Apollinaris, and Methodius, Porphyry's ecclesiastical adversaries. Such remarks bring natural closure to the commentary and make the remaining section a kind of appendix.

The Stories of Susanna and Bel

1. This heading was added by Courtray.

2. The CCSL editor F. Glorie comments that Jerome has clearly made several additions on his own, and Courtray concurs with this.

3. In addition to the *Stromata*, Origen refers to this Jewish tradition in *Letter to Africanus* 7–8 (ANF 4.388). See the appendix to this volume. Jerome refers to it again in his final work, *Commentary on Jeremiah* 29:21–23, in a passage that is highly dependent on Origen. In rabbinic literature, there are many versions and variants of the tradition concerning the evil deeds of Achias (Ahab) and Zedekiah but without any link to the Susanna story. J. Braverman, *Jerome's Commentary on Daniel: A Study of Comparative Jewish and Christian Interpretation of the Hebrew Bible* (Washington, DC: Catholic Biblical Association, 1978), 130–31 summarizes this material as follows:

> The similarities of all the above rabbinic versions of the Ahab and Zedekiah tradition with the Hebrew tradition of Origen and Jerome are indeed self-evident. It is the differences that are more subtle. In the patristic version, Ahab and Zedekiah consort with *Jewish* women in Babylonia, promising to cause them to give birth to the *Messiah*. In extant rabbinic tradition, they consort with *Babylonian* women, even Nebuchadnezzar's *daughter and wife*, promising to cause them to give birth to *prophets*. It seems quite plausible that the earlier version of the tradition was preserved by Origen. The seduction of *Jewish* wives in Babylonia by Ahab and Zedekiah sets the scene for the Susanna story, which takes place, according to its opening verses, in Babylonia. Thus it is plausible that in Origen's time a Jewish tradition linking Susanna with Ahab and Zedekiah was current. Perhaps the same motivation and circumstances which caused the Susanna story to be absent from rabbinic records until the eleventh century caused the tradition concerning the seduction of "Jewish wives" to be changed to read "Babylonian women." In any event, once again we are indebted to Origen and Jerome for the only written record of a Jewish tradition. Our debt to these Fathers of the Church is the greater because none of the other early patristic commentators on Susanna mention this tradition.

Italics in original.

4. According to Courtray, SC 602, 534n1, this is Jerome's insertion into what otherwise comes from Origen. Cf. Cicero, *Tuscul.* 4.10; A. Canellis, "Saint Jérôme et les passions: sur les quattuor perturbationes des Tusculanes," *Vigiliae Christianae* 54 (2000): 178–203.

5. G. Archer, *Jerome's Commentary on Daniel* (Grand Rapids: Baker, 1958), 153 inserts: "This is Verse 13 according to the Septuagint, not according to Theodotion, who does not include the verse at all."

6. Again, Jerome intervenes to remark on the text followed by Origen. One can deduce from it that elsewhere, Origen resorts to the translation of Theodotion. This is a defense of Jerome's textual method, which looks beyond the LXX.

7. Courtray SC 602, 537n1 describes this passage as a "Philonian theme dear to Origen." Cf. Origen, *Heracl* 25–26.

8. Courtray SC 602, 539n2 summarizes that Jerome will subsequently bring together all of Origen's remarks on the expression "great voice." According

to Origen, the phrase applies only to the saints: the great voice can come from chastity (v. 24a), from the feelings of the heart, from the pure confession of the soul, and from the uprightness of the conscience (vv. 42–43), from a holy spirit who speaks in humanity (v. 46). It remains to be seen why, in Dan 14:17, King Cyrus praises the god Bel with a loud voice.

9. Cf. under 13:24a; 13:42–43a; 14:17.

10. Notice how Jerome successfully replicates the Greek pun in Latin.

11. Cf. Origen, *Epistle to Julius Africanus* 2, 6, 11–12 (ANF 4.386–91). See appendix. I have discussed this passage in the notes to Jerome's Preface to the Vulgate Version of Daniel.

12. *Prio* in Greek means "to saw."

13. Jerome seems to be assuming the truth of Julius Africanus's objection to the authenticity of this story, namely, the claim that the Jews would not have been allowed to pass and carry out a death sentence while in captivity. Origen replied to this objection, that it was not uncommon for conquering kings to allow captives to use their own laws and courts of justice. ANF 4.392.

14. I believe he means, if Susanna had died while being innocent, she would have died holy. The worst thing would have been to die in a state of sin.

15. This is v. 17 in the Vulgate but v. 18 in Theodotion, the text followed by Origen.

16. See under Dan 13:46.

17. Courtray SC 602, 547n4 comments on the seemingly abrupt nature of the ending of Jerome's *Commentary on Daniel*. On the one hand, ancient works rarely contain a conclusion; moreover, if there is a conclusion to this commentary, it is rather located at Dan 12:13. The brief comments on Dan 13—14 are additional excerpts from Origen's *Stromata* added to Jerome's commentary.

Appendix

1. This summary is drawn from Nicholas de Lange's introduction to *La Lettre à Africanus sur l'histoire de Suzanne* in Marguerite Harl and Nicholas de Lange, *Philocalie 1–20 sur les Écritures*, introduction, texte, traduction, et notes par Marguerite Harl; *La Lettre à Africanus sur l'histoire de Suzanne*, introduction, texte, traduction, et notes par Nicholas de Lange, SC 302, 478–79.

2. The translation is that of Frederick Crombie, ANF 4.385–392: https://www.newadvent.org/fathers/0413.htm. I have made slight changes based on the suggestions and critical remarks of Nicholas de Lange, SC 302 and have followed de Lange's paragraph enumeration, with Crombie's in parentheses.

3. Crombie rendered this as a personal name, Agnomon. The word means "ignorant." In his reply (2), Origen names him Bassus—I have followed de Lange in rendering this as an adjective.

4. De Lange, SC 302, 516n1 asks why Julius insists that Daniel did not prophesy by inspiration. He thinks there could be an indirect allusion to a famous ancient dispute. In rabbinical thought, the gift of prophecy is linked to the Holy Spirit: when the last prophets died, the Holy Spirit no longer works in Israel. Although Flavius Josephus considered Daniel a prophet

(*Ant* 10.266f.) and the Greek Bible placed his book among the writings of the prophets, in the Hebrew Bible Daniel was placed in the Hagiographa, not in the Prophets.

    5. Philistion was an author of mimes celebrated in the time of Augustus. De Lange SC 302, 517n2 thinks that the allusion is probably aimed at a lost mime of Philistion, where a conviction was being made in a very artificial way.

    6. The Greek word means strike, clap, tap, and can refer to striking a musical instrument.

    7. Again, this is Crombie's translation (ANF 4, 386–92) with minor revisions, but adapted to de Lange's paragraph enumeration. I have taken it from: https://www.newadvent.org/fathers/0414.htm.

    8. Africanus 2.

    9. See G. B. Gray, "The Additions in the Ancient Greek Version of Job," *Expositor* 8, no. 19 (1920): 422–38; H. M. Orlinsky, "Studies in the LXX of the Book of Job," *HUCA* 28 (1957): 53–74.

    10. Cf. Matthew J. Thomas, "Origen on Paul's Authorship of Hebrews," *New Testament Studies* no. 65, no. 4 (October 2019): 598–609.

    11. Jerome includes some of Origen's reflections on Susanna in the final portion of his commentary.

BIBLIOGRAPHY

Texts and Translations

Archer, G., trans. *Jerome's Commentary on Daniel.* Grand Rapids: Baker, 1958.
Cain, A., trans. *St. Jerome: Commentary on Galatians.* FOTC 121. Washington, DC: Catholic University of America Press, 2010.
Canellis, Aline, ed. *Jérôme: Préfaces aux Livres de la Bible. Textes Latins des Éditions de R. Weber et R. Gryson et de L'Abbaya Saint-Jérôme (Rome), Revus et Corrigés.* SC 592. Paris: Cerf, 2017.
Courtray, Régis, ed. *Jérôme, Commentaire sur Daniel,* SC 602. Paris: Cerf, 2019.
Ewald, M. L., trans. *The Homilies of Saint Jerome.* 2 vols. FOTC 48, 57. Washington, DC: Catholic University of America Press, 1964, 1966.
Fremantle, W. H., trans. *The Principal Works of St. Jerome.* NPNF2 6. Grand Rapids: Eerdmans, 1893.
―――. *St. Jerome: Apology to Rufinus.* NPNF2 3. Grand Rapids: Eerdmans, 1892.
Glorie, Franciscus. *S. Hieronymi Presbyteri Commentariorum in Danielem Libri III <IV>.* CCSL 75A. Turnholt: Brepols, 1964.
Graves, M., trans. *Jerome: Commentary on Jeremiah.* Ancient Christian Texts. Downers Grove, IL: InterVarsity Press, 2011.
Halton, T., trans. *St. Jerome: On Illustrious Men.* FOTC 100. Washington, DC: Catholic University of America Press, 1999.
Harl, Marguerite, and Nicholas de Lange, *Philocalie 1–20 sur les Écritures.* Introduction, texte, traduction, et notes par Marguerite Harl. *La Lettre à Africanus sur l'histoire de Suzanne.* Introduction, texte, traduction, et notes par Nicholas de Lange. SC 302.
Hayward, C. T. R., trans. *Saint Jerome's Hebrew Questions on Genesis.* With introduction and commentary. Oxford: Clarendon, 1995.
Heine, R., trans. *The Commentaries of Origen and Jerome on St. Paul's Epistle to the Ephesians.* Oxford: Oxford University Press, 2002.
Richardson, E. C., trans. *St. Jerome: Lives of Illustrious Men.* NPNF2 3. Grand Rapids: Eerdmans, 1892.
Scheck, Thomas P., ed. *St. Jerome: Commentaries on the Twelve Prophets.* 2 vols. Ancient Christian Texts. Downers Grove, IL: InterVarsity Press, 2016, 2017.
―――, trans. *St. Jerome: Commentary on Ezekiel.* ACW 71. Mahwah, NJ: Newman Press, 2017.

234 ST. JEROME: COMMENTARY ON DANIEL

———, trans. *St. Jerome: Commentary on Isaiah. Origen: Homilies 1–9 on Isaiah.* ACW 68. Mahwah, NJ: Newman Press, 2015.

———, trans. *St. Jerome: Commentary on Matthew.* FOTC 117. Washington, DC: Catholic University of America Press, 2008.

———, trans. *St. Jerome's Commentaries on Galatians, Titus, and Philemon.* Notre Dame, IN: University of Notre Dame Press, 2010.

Secondary Works

Anastos, M. V. "Porphyry's Attack on the Bible." In *Studies in Honor of H. Caplan,* edited by L. Wallach, 421–50. Ithaca, NY: Cornell University Press, 1966.

Baldwin, Joyce G. *Daniel.* Tyndale Old Testament Commentaries 23. Downers Grove, IL: Intervarsity, 1978.

———. "Is There Pseudonymity in the Old Testament?" *Themelios* 4, no. 1 (1978): 6–12.

Bardy, G. "Jérôme et ses maîtres hébreux." *Revue Bénédictine* 46 (1934): 145–64.

Barr, James. "St. Jerome and the Sounds of Hebrew." *Journal of Semitic Studies* 12, no. 1 (1967): 1–36.

Bergsma, J., and B. Pitre. "Daniel." In *A Catholic Introduction to the Bible.* Vol. 1: *The Old Testament,* 875–906. San Francisco: Ignatius, 2018.

Braverman, J. *Jerome's Commentary on Daniel: A Study of Comparative Jewish and Christian Interpretation of the Hebrew Bible.* Washington, DC: Catholic Biblical Association, 1978.

Brown, D. *Vir Trilinguis: A Study in the Biblical Exegesis of Saint Jerome.* Kampen, The Netherlands: Kok Pharos Publishing House, 1992.

Cain, A., and J. Lössl, eds. *Jerome of Stridon: His Life, Writings and Legacy.* Aldershot, UK: Ashgate, 2009.

Calvin, John. *Commentary on Daniel.* Translated by Thomas Myers. 2 vols. Edinburgh: T. Constable, 1849.

Canellis, A. "Saint Jérôme et les passions: sur les quattuor perturbations des Tusculanes." *Vigiliae Christianae* 54 (2000): 178–203.

Casey, P. M. "Porphyry and the Origin of the Book of Daniel." *JTS* n.s. 27, no. 1 (1976): 15–33.

Cavallera. F. *Saint Jérôme: Sa vie et son oeuvre.* Spicilegium sacrum Lovaniense. 2 vols. Paris: E. Champion, 1922.

Charles, R. H., ed. *The Apocrypha and Pseudepigrapha of the Old Testament.* Vol. 1. Oxford: Oxford University Press, 1913.

Collins, John J. *Daniel: A Commentary on the Book of Daniel.* Hermeneia. Minneapolis: Augsburg Fortress, 1993.

———. *Daniel, First Maccabees, Second Maccabees, with an Excursus on the Apocalyptic Genre.* Wilmington, DE: Michael Glazier, 1981.

Courcelle, P. *Late Latin Writers and Their Greek Sources.* Translated by H. E. Wedeck. Cambridge, MA: Harvard University Press, 1969.

Courtray, Régis. "Daniel et Ashpenaz: sur quelques lectures contemporaines de Daniel 1, 7 et 9." *Anabases* 13 (2011): 55–78.

———. "Jérôme, traducteur de Livre de Daniel." *Pallas* 75 (2007): 105–24.

———. "La figure de l'Antichrist chez Jérôme." In *Les forces du bien et du mal dans les premiers siècles de l'Église*, edited by Y.-M Blanchard, B. Pouderon, and M. Scopello. Coll. *Théologie historique* 118 (Paris 2011): 335–61.

———. "Le roi Nabuchodonosor change en bête (Dn 4). Du récit biblique à quelques lectures chrétiennes anciennes." In *La metamorphose et ses metamorphoses*, edited by V. Adam and C. Noacco, 49–64. Albi: Presses du Centre universitaire Champollion, 2010.

———. "Les Maccabées chez Jérôme: de la liberation juive à la véritable victoire dans le Christ." In *Le mémoire des persecutions. Autour du livre des Maccabées*, edited by M.-F Baslez and O. Munnich, 385–97. *Collection de la Revue des Études juives* 56. Paris-Louvain, 2014.

———. "Nabuchodonosor, figure biblique de l'homme sauvage (Daniel 4)? Examen de la question à travers les âges." In *L'homme sauvage dans les lettres et les arts*, edited by C. Noacco and S. Duhem. Colloquium. "Interférences," 375–86. Rennes: 2019.

———. "Nabuchodonosor, figure du diable chez Jérôme." *Connaissance des Pères de l'Église* 120 (2010): 18–26.

———. *Prophète des temps derniers. Jerome commente Daniel*. Theologie historique 119. Beauchesne: Paris, 2009.

———. "Questions critiques autour du Commentaire sur Daniel de Jérôme." In *L'exégèse de saint Jérôme*, edited by É. Ayroulet and A. Canellis, 201–20. Saint-Étienne: Publications de l'Université de Saint-Étienne, 2018.

Crouzel, H. *Origen*. Edinburgh: T & T Clark, 1989.

Daley, B. *The Hope of the Early Church: A Handbook of Patristic Eschatology*. Cambridge: Cambridge University Press, 1991.

Di Berardino, A., ed. *Encyclopedia of the Early Church*. 2 vols. New York: Oxford University Press, 1992.

Driver, S. R. *The Book of Daniel with Introduction and Notes*. Cambridge Bible for Schools and Colleges. Cambridge: Cambridge University Press, 1900.

Dulaey, M. "Daniel dans la fosse aux lions. Lecture de Dn 6 dans l'Église ancienne." *RevSR* 72 (1998): 38–50.

———. "Jérôme, Victorin de Poetovio et le millénarisme." In *Jérôme entre l'Occident et l'Origent. XVIe centenaire du depart de saint Jérôme de Rome et de son installation à Bethléem*, edited by Y.-M. Duval. Actes du Colloque de Chantilly (September 1986), EAA 122, 1988.

Emerton, J. A. "The Purpose of the Second Column of the Hexapla." *JTS* 7 (1956): 79–87.

Freedman, David Noel, ed. *Eerdmans Dictionary of the Bible*. Grand Rapids: Eerdmans, 2000.

Gallagher, Edmon L. "The Old Testament 'Apocrypha' in Jerome's Canonical Theory." *Journal of Early Christian Studies* 20, no. 2 (2012): 213–33.

Graves, Michael. *Jerome's Hebrew Philology: A Study Based on His Commentary on Jeremiah*. Leiden: Brill, 2007.

Grützmacher, G. *Hieronymus: Eine biographische Studie zur alten Kirchengeschichte*. 3 vols. Leipzig, 1901–8, repr. Berlin: Scientia Verlag Aalen, 1969.

Hagendahl, H. *Latin Fathers and the Classics: A Study on the Apologists, Jerome and Other Christian Writers*. Gothenburg, Sweden: Almquist & Wiksell, 1958.

Hale Williams, Megan. *The Monk and the Book: Jerome and the Making of Christian Scholarship.* Chicago: University of Chicago Press, 2006.
Harrison, R. K. *Introduction to the Old Testament.* Grand Rapids: Eerdmans, 1969.
Hartman, Louis F. "Daniel." In *The Jerome Biblical Commentary,* edited by R. E. Brown, J. A. Fitzmyer, and R. E. Murphy, 446–60. Englewood Cliffs, NJ: Prentice-Hall 1968.
Hartman, Louis F., and Alexander A. Di Lella. *The Book of Daniel.* Anchor Bible 23. Garden City, NY: Doubleday, 1978.
Hartmann, L. N. "St. Jerome as an Exegete." In *A Monument to St. Jerome,* edited by F. X. Murphy, 37–81. New York: Sheed and Ward, 1952.
Hornblower, S., and A. Spawforth, eds. *The Oxford Classical Dictionary.* 3rd ed. Oxford: Oxford University Press, 1996.
Jeanjean, Benoît. *Saint Jérôme et l'Hérésie.* Paris: Institut d'Études Augustiniennes, 1999.
Jellicoe, S. *The Septuagint and Modern Study.* Oxford: Clarendon Press, 1968.
Kamesar, A. *Jerome, Greek Scholarship, and the Hebrew Bible: A Study of the Quaestiones Hebraicae in Genesim.* Oxford: Oxford University Press, 1993.
Kelly, J. N. D. *Jerome: His Life, Writings, and Controversies.* New York: Harper & Row, 1975.
Kritzinger, J. P. K. "St. Jerome's Commentary on Daniel 3." *Acta Patristica et Byzantina* 16 (2005): 54–69.
Lacocque, André. *The Book of Daniel.* Atlanta: John Knox Press, 1979.
Lampe, G. W. H. *A Patristic Greek Lexicon.* Oxford: Oxford University Press, 1961. Abbreviated PGL.
Lataix, Jean (= A. Loisy). "Le commentaire de s. Jérôme sur Daniel." *Revue d'histoire et de littérature religieuses* 2 (1897): 164–73; 268–77.
Lattey, C., SJ. *The Book of Daniel.* Dublin: Richview Press, 1948.
Liddell, Henry George, and Robert Scott. *An Intermediate Greek-English Lexicon.* Founded upon the seventh edition of Liddell and Scott's Greek English Lexicon. Oxford: Clarendon Press, 1997.
Lucas, Ernest. *Daniel.* Apollos Old Testament Commentary 20. Downers Grove, IL: InterVarsity, 2002.
Lust, J., E. Eynikel, and K. Hauspie with collaboration of G. Chamberlain. *A Greek-English Lexicon of the Septuagint.* 2 vols. Stuttgart: Deutsche Bibelgesellschaft, 1992.
Montgomery, James A. *A Critical and Exegetical Commentary on the Book of Daniel.* International Critical Commentary. Edinburgh: Clark, 1927.
Murphy, F. X., ed. *A Monument to Saint Jerome.* New York: Sheed & Ward, 1952.
———. *Rufinus of Aquileia (345–411): His Life and Works.* Washington, DC: Catholic University of America Press, 1945.
———. "Saint Jerome." In *New Catholic Encyclopedia,* 7:756–59. 2nd ed. Washington, DC: Catholic University of America Press.
O'Connell, John P. *The Eschatology of Saint Jerome.* Dissertationes ad Lauream 16. Mundelein, IL: Pontifical Theological Faculty of the Seminary of St. Mary of the Lake, 1948.
Quasten, J., et al. *Patrology.* 4 vols. Utrecht-Antwerp: Spectrum, 1975.
Radice, B. *Who's Who in the Ancient World: A Handbook to the Survivors of the Greek and Roman Classics.* Harmondsworth, UK: Penguin Books, 1973.

Reaburn, Mary. "St. Jerome and Porphyry Interpret the Book of Daniel." *Australian Biblical Review* 52 (2004): 1–18.
Saydon, P. P. "Daniel." In *A Catholic Commentary on Holy Scripture*, edited by B. Orchard et al., 621–43. New York: Thomas Nelson & Sons, 1953.
Steinmann, Jean. *Saint Jerome and His Times*. Translated by R. Matthews. Notre Dame, IN: Fides Publishers, 1959.
Sutcliffe, Edmund F. "Jerome." In *The Cambridge History of the Bible.* Vol. 2: *The West from the Fathers to the Reformation*, edited by G. Lampe, 80–101. Cambridge: Cambridge University Press, 1969.
———. "St. Jerome's Pronunciation of Hebrew." *Biblica* 29 (1948): 112–25.
Swete, H. *An Introduction to the Old Testament in Greek*. Revised by R. R. Ottley. Peabody, MA: Hendrickson, 1989; originally published by Cambridge University Press, 1914.
Webb, J. R. "Knowledge Will Be Manifold: Daniel 12.4 and the Idea of Intellectual Progress in the Middle Ages." *Speculum* 89 (2014): 307–57.
Young, Edward J. *The Prophecy of Daniel: A Commentary*. Grand Rapids: Eerdmans, 1949.

GENERAL INDEX

Citations according to the lemma of Jerome's Commentary on Daniel
Abbreviations: DnVgPf = Jerome's Preface to the Latin Vulgate version of
Daniel; DnPf = Jerome's Preface to Book 1 of his Commentary on Daniel

Abda, DnPf
Abiesdri, 1:3–4a
Adler, M., 11:34–35
Africanus, Julius, DnVgPf 3; 9:24a;
   Appendix 1
Africanus, Scipio, 11:17b–19
Agathoclea, 11:13–14a
Agathocles, 11:13–14a
Albright, W., 9:1
Alexander the Great, 2:31–35;
   2:47b; 7:5; 7:6; 7:7b;
   8:3c–4a; 8:5b–9a; 8:14; 9:1; 9:24a;
   10:20b; 10:21a; 11:2b; 11:3–4a;
   11:4b; 11:21
Alypius, DnPf
Ambrosiaster, 3:92b
Anagogy, 1:2b; 10:2–3
Andronicus, DnPf
Antigonus, 7:6; 8:5b–9a; 11:4b;
   11:5a
Antin, P., 2:3
Antiochus I Soter, DnPf; 11:6
Antiochus II Theos, 11:6
Antiochus III (the Great), 11:10;
   11:11–12; 11:13–14a; 11:14b;
   11:15–16; 11:17a; 11:17b–19;
   11:20; 11:21
Antiochus IV Epiphanes, DnPf;
   7:7b; 7:7c–8; 7:14b; 7:25c;
   8:5b–9a; 8:13b; 8:14; 9:24a;

11:21; 11:25–26; 11:27–28a;
11:28b–30a; 11:31; 11:33;
11:34–35; 11:36; 11:37–39;
11:40–41a; 11:41b; 11:42–43;
11:44–45; 12:1–3; 12:5–6; 12:7a;
12:7b; 12:11; 12:12; 12:13
Antiochus VI, 11:20
Antoninus, 11:34–35
Apaturius, 11:10
Apedno, 11:44–45
Apollinaris, DnVgPf 5; DnPf; 9:24a;
   11:44–45; 12:13
Aquila, DnPf; 1:3–4a; 3:21; 4:5a;
   6:4a; 6:4c; 8:2b; 8:13a; 10:5b;
   10:5c; 11:15–16; 11:30b;
   11:37–39; 11:40–41a; 11:44–45
Arabic, DnVgPf 1
Aradian, 11:44–45
Aramaic. See Chaldean
Archer, G., 1:3–4a; 1:7; 2:2a; 2:27b;
   3:4–6; 3:16b; 3:19a; 3:21; 3:23;
   3:29; 4:31d; 5:1; 5:6a; 5:7d;
   5:30–31; 6:4a; 7:4; 7:5; 7:6; 7:7a;
   7:10b; 7:25c; 8:2b; 8:5b–9a; 8:14;
   8:16; 9:2b–3; 9:24a; 11:2b; 11:21;
   11:28b–30a; 11:37–39; 11:44–45;
   13:8b–9
Aristotle, 7:4; 11:3–4a
Arses, 7:5; 11:2b
Artabanus, 7:5; 11:2b

Artaxerxes I Longimanus, 7:5; 9:24a
Artaxerxes II Mnemon, 7:5
Artaxerxes III Ochos, 7:5
Artaxerxes IV Arses, 7:5
Artaxias, 7:7c–8; 11:44–45
Asterisks, DnPf
Astyages, 5:1; 6:1–2a; 8:3b
Augustine, DnPf; 1:9; 4:5a
Augustus, Caesar, DnPf; 9:24a

Bacher, W., 11:34–35
Baldwin, J., 5:1; 5:30–31; 9:1; 11:1
Banereem, 1:7
Bar Kokhba, 9:24a
Basilides, 2:29c
Benacus, Lake, 6:19
Bernice, 11:6; 11:7–9
Berosus, 5:1
Boanerges, 1:7
Bonner, Alison, 1:9; 4:24; 9:2b–3
Braverman, J., DnVgPf 3; 1:3–4a; 2:1a; 2:12–13; 2:25b; 5:2; 6:1–2a; 6:4a; 7:5; 7:7a; 8:16; 9:2b–3; 11:20; 11:31; 11:34–35; 11:36; 13:3

Caesar, Julius, 9:24a
Caligula, 9:24a
Callias, 11:2b
Cambyses, 7:5; 9:24a; 11:2b; 11:7–9
Canellis, DnVgPf 2; 5:7c; 13:5b
Carmentalis, 8:2b
Centaurs, 4:1a
Chaldee/Chaldean, DnVgPf 1–3; 1:4a, c; 1:8a; 1:17; 1:20; 2:1a; 2:2a; 2:4a; 2:12–13; 2:15a; 2:48; 3:8; 3:16b; 3:21; 4:1a; 4:5c; 4:6a; 4:7–8; 4:10b; 5:1; 5:7a; 5:11a; 5:25–28; 5:30–31; 6:4c; 6:28; 7:4; 7:28b; 9:1; 9:24a; 10:1a; 11:1
Charles, R., 9:24a
Chiliasm, 7:17–18a
Chimaera, 4:1a
Cicero, DnVgPf 2; 5:7c

Claudius Caesar, emperor, 9:24a
Claudius Theon, DnPf
Clement of Alexandria, 3:39; 5:1; 9:24a
Cleopatra, 9:24a; 11:17a; 11:17b–19; 11:21; 11:28b–30a
Collins, J., 7:14b; 11:31; 12:1–3
Consolation, 2:1b; 2:48
Courcelle, P., DnPf; 1:4a, c; 5:1; 9:24a
Courtray, R., DnPf; 1:3–4a; 1:20; 2:28c; 2:29a; 2:29c; 2:31–35; 3:18a; 3:19a; 3:37–39; 3:39; 3:87; 3:96; 3:97; 4:1a; 4:5a; 4:14a; 4:31b; 5:7c; 5:30–31; 7:4; 8:3b; 8:5b–9a; 8:14; 9:1; 9:18a; 9:24a; 10:1a; 10:21b; 11:2; 11:2b; 11:5b; 11:7–9; 11:17b–19; 11:20; 11:21; 11:27–28a; 11:28b–30a; 11:32; 11:34–35; 11:36; 11:37–39; 11:40–41a; 11:44–45; 12:1–3; 12:13; 13:5b; 13:22; 13:24; 14:17
Craterus, 11:4c
Cyaxares, 8:3b
Cyrus the Great, 5:1; 5:25–28; 5:30–31; 6:28; 7:5; 9:24a; 10:1a; 11:2b

Dabar, 1:20
Damoxenus, 11:15–16
Darius I, 5:25–28; 7:5; 9:24a; 10:1a; 11:2b
Darius II Ochus, 7:5; 9:24a
Darius III Codomannus (son of Arsamus), 7:5; 8:3c–4a; 8:5b–9a; 9:1; 10:20b; 11:2b; 11:3–4a
Darius the Mede, 1:21; 5:1; 5:29; 5:30–31; 6:1–2; 6:8a; 6:12d; 6:25a; 6:28; 7:1a; 7:5; 8:3b; 9:1; 10:1a; 10:21b; 11:1; 11:2b
Demetrius of Phalerum, 11:5a, b
Diana, 8:44; 11:44–45

GENERAL INDEX 241

Diodorus (Siculus), DnPf; 8:3c–4a; 11:7–9; 11:36
Diogenes Laertius, 1:20
Domitius, 11:28b–30a
Donatus, 11:17a
Driver, S., DnVgPf 1; 11:44–45
Dulaey, 3:1a; 7:17–18a
Duval, 3:18a

Ebion/Ebionite, DnPf
Elymais/Elam, 8:2a; 8:14; 11:17b–19; 11:36; 11:44–45
Ephraim of Syria, 2:31–35
Epiphanius, DnVgPf 5; 3:96
Eropus, 11:15–16
Eucles of Rhodes, 11:17a
Eunuch, 1:3–4a; 1:7; 1:9; 1:18; 6:4a; 11:21
Euripides, 6:4c; 11:2b
Eusebius of Caesarea, DnVgPf 5; DnPf; 9:24a; 12:13
Eustochium, DnVgPf 5; DnPf

Foreknowledge, 2:9b, 11; 4:24; 4:24b

Gabriel, 8:5b–9a; 8:16; 8:26b; 9:21a; 9:24a
Galba, 9:24a
Gallus Caesar (Constantius), 11:34–35
Genneus, 11:6
Glorie, F., 2:31–35; 3:87; 4:31d; 5:7c; 9:24a; 10:6a; 11:21; 11:44–45; 13:3
Granicus River, 8:5b–9a; 10:21a
Graves, M., 7:1a
Guinot, N., 9:24a

Habakkuk, prophecy of, DnVgPf 3; DnPf
Hadrian, Aelius, 9:24a
Hagendahl, DnPf; 1:2b; 5:7c
Hagiographa, DnVgPf 4
Hannibal, 11:17b–19

Harrison, R. K., 4:1a; 5:1
Hegemonikon, 2:28c
Heliopolis, 11:14b
Herodotus, 3:21; 9:1; 11:2b; 11:7–9; 11:44–45
Hexapla, 1:3–4a
Hieronymus (historian), DnPf
Hippolytus, 1:1; 1:12; 2:1b; 2:9b; 2:11; 2:31–35; 2:48; 2:49a; 3:23; 3:92b; 7:4; 7:7a; 9:24a; 11:2b
Horace, 4:1a
Hydra, 4:1a

Icadio, 11:6
Irenaeus, 2:31–35; 3:92b; 11:21
Italians, 11:31

Jeanjean, B., 2:29c
Jelicoe, DnVgPf 1
Josephus, Flavius, DnPf; 1:1; 2:1a; 2:47b; 3:23; 5:1; 5:10a; 5:30–31; 6:1–2a; 8:2a; 8:3b; 8:14; 9:24a; 10:6a; 11:5b; v11:14b; 11:21; 11:25–26; 11:30b; 11:34–35; 12:1–3; 12:7a; 12:11; 12:13
Jovinian, DnPf; 1:3–4a; 7:5
Judas Maccabeus, DnPf
Julian (the Apostate), 11:34–35; 11:36
Julius. *See* Africanus
Jupiter, 8:5b–9a; 8:13b; 8:14; 11:31; 11:37–39; 12:7a
Justin (the historian), DnPf; 5:1; 8:3c–4a; 11:7–9; 11:13–14a; 11:20
Justin Martyr, 2:31 35

Kamesar, A., DnVgPf 1; 1:3–4a; 4:5a
Kelly, J. N. D., 6:25a
Kokhba. *See* Bar Kokhba
Kritzinger, 3:1a; 3:29; 3:92b

Labor-sordech, 5:1
Laenas, Marcus Popilius, 11:28b–30a; 11:40–41a
Lampe, DnPf; 1:2b; 2:2a; 2:27b; 3:1b
Laodice, 11:6; 11:7–9
Laricus, Lake, 6:19
Lattey, 1:1; 1:21; 7:5; 9:24a; 12:1–3
Lentil, DnVgPf 3
Liburnians, 11:5b
Livy, Titus, DnPf; 5:7c; 11:13–14a; 11:15–16; 11:28b–30a; 11:37–39
Lucas, E., 8:5b–9a
Lucretius, 4:1a
LXX (Seventy), DnVgPf 1; 1:3–4a
Lysias, 12:1–3
Lysimachus, 11:4c

Macarius, 1:8a
Man of desires, 9:23c; 10:11a
Maozim, 11:37–39
Marcella, DnPf
Marcion, 2:29c
Mattathias, DnPf
Menocles, 11:15–16
Methodius, DnVgPf 5; DnPf; 12:13
Michael, 8:16; 10:13b, c; 10:21a; 10:21a, b; 12:1–3
Millennialism. *See* Chiliasm
Minucius Felix, 3:1a; 6:20c
Montanists, DnVgPf 5
Montgomery, James A., DnPf

Nabonidus, 1:1; 4:1a; 5:1
Neglisar, 5:1
Nero, 7:7c–8; 9:24a; 11:28b–30a
Nicanor (Nicator). *See* Seleucus Nicanor

Obelus, DnVgPf 3; DnPf
O'Connell, J. P., 3:92b; 7:7c–8; 7:17–18a; 7:25b; 11:21
Onias I, 9:24a
Onias II, 9:24a

Onias III, 9:24a; 11:14b
Onias IV, 11:14b
Origen, DnVgPf 1, 3; DnPf; 1:3–4a; 1:4a, c; 1:7; 1:8a; 1:20; 2:2a; 2:29c; 2:31–35; 3:1a; 3:4–6; 3:26–28a; 3:29; 3:37–39; 3:39; 3:96; 4:1a; 4:5a; 4:7–8; 4:23b; 4:33b; 5:10a; 5:22; 6:10a; 6:25a; 8:16; 9:24a; 10:13a; 12:13; 13–14 passim
Otho, 9:24a
Ovid, 4:1a

Pammachius, DnPf
Pamphilus, DnVgPf 5
Paneas, 11:15–16
Panthaptes, 11:2b
Parthians, 1:3–4a
Paula, DnVgPf 5; DnPf
Paulinus of Nola, 12:1–3
Perdicas, 11:4c
Persona, 3:29; 7:13b; 9:5a; 11:1
Philip Arrhidaeus, 7:6; 8:5b–9a; 11:4b
Philip of Macedon, 11:13–14a
Philip II of Macedon (father of Alexander the Great), 8:3c–4a; 11:3–4a
Philo, 1:4a, c; 2:29a; 13:22
Plato, 1:2b; 1:20; 2:28c
Plautus, DnVgPf 2; 3:98
Pleonasm, 11:17a
Pliny the Elder, DnVgPf 2; 7:4
Plutarch, 3:97; 8:3c–4a
Polybius, DnPf; 11:11–12; 11:13–14a; 11:15–16; 11:21; 11:28b–30a; 11:36; 11:37–39; 11:44–45
Pompeius Trogus, DnPf; 5:1
Popilius. *See* Laenas, Marcus Popilius
Porphyry, DnVgPf 5; DnPf; 1:1; 2:31–35; 2:46; 2:47b; 2:48; 3:98; 5:10a; 7:7b; 7:7c–8;

GENERAL INDEX

7:14b; 9:1; 11:20; 11:21;
11:25–26; 11:34–35; 11:36;
11:37–39; 11:40–41a; 11:41b;
11:44–45; 12:1–3; 12:5–6;
12:7a; 12:7b; 12:11; 12:12;
12:13
Posidonius, DnPf
Ptolemy I Soter (son of Lagos),
DnPf; 7:6; 8:5b–9a; 9:24a;
11:3–4a; 11:4b; 11:5a, b
Ptolemy V Epiphanes, 11:13–14a;
11:17b–19; 11:20; 11:21
Ptolemy VI Philometor, 7:7c–8;
8:5b–9a; 11:21; 11:40–41a
Ptolemy VII Euergetes II, 7:7c–8;
9:24a; 11:7–9
Ptolemy Philadelphus, 5:1; 9:24a;
11:5b; 11:6; 11:7–9
Ptolemy Philopator, 11:10;
11:11–12; 11:13–14a
Pyrrhus, King of Epirus, 11:5a

Quintilian, DnVgPf 2; 3:39
Quintus Curtius, 8:3c–4a

Raphael, 8:16
Raphia, 11:11–12
Reaburn, DnPf; 3:98; 11:21; 12:12;
12:13
Romans, 2:31–35; 7:7a, b; 8:2b;
9:5a; 9:24a; 11:14b; 11:28b–30a;
11:30b; 11:31; 12:7a
Rufinus, DnVgPf 3; DnPf; 1:8a; 3:23;
3:98; 4:5a; 5:7c; 10:13a

Salamis, DnPf; 11:2b
Sallust, 3:39
Scipio Africanus, 11:17b–19
Scipio Nasica, 11:17b 19
Scopas, son of Aetholus, 11:14b;
11:15–16
Scylla, 4:1a
Seleucus I Nicanor (Nicator), DnPf;
7:6; 8:5b–9a; 9:24a; 11:4b; 11:6;
11:10; 12:7a

Seleucus Callincius, 11:6; 11:7–9;
11:10
Seleucus Philopator, 8:5b–9a; 9:24a;
11:20
Severus, 11:34–35
Sirach, 9:24a
Skaia, 8:2b
Smerdis the Magus, 7:5; 11:2b
Socrates (church historian), 9:24a
Socrates (philosopher), 1:2b; 1:20;
5:1
Sogdianus, 7:5; 11:2b
Sophists, 1:20
Sophocles, 11:2b
Spartans, 7:5
Stoics, 1:2b; 2:28c
Strabo, 3:39; 3:97; 11:7–9
Sutorius Callinicus, DnPf; 11:21
Sycophant, 3:98
Symmachus, DnPf; 1:3–4a; 1:17;
2:27b; 2:31–35; 3:1b; 3:18b; 3:21;
3:92b; 4:5a; 5:11a; 6:4a; 7:25a;
8:2a; 8:2b; 8:13a; 10:5b; 10:6a;
10:11a; 11:15–16; 11:37–39;
11:40–41a; 11:44–45
Syriac, DnVgPf 1, 3; 2:4a; 7:28b

Tabes, 11:44–45
Tacitus, 3:39
Tanakh, DnVgPf 4
Terence, DnVgPf 2; 3:98
Tertullian, 1:12; 2:21a; 2:28c;
2:31–35; 3:39; 3:92b; 6:10a;
6:20c; 6:25a; 9:24a; 11:2b
Themistocles, 11:2b
Theocritus, 11:5b
Theodotion, DnVgPf 1; DnPf;
1:3–4a; 3:1b; 3:21; 3:91a; 4:1b;
4:5a, c; 4:7–10; 4:10b; 6:4a, c;
8:2b; 8:13a; 10:5b; 10:6a; 10:16b;
11:6; 11:10; 11:11–12; 11:15–16;
11:37–39; 11:40–41a; 11:44–45;
12:1–3; 12:13
Theodotius, 11:10; 11:11–12

Thucydides, 11:2b
Tiberius, 9:24a
Tinius Rufus, 9:24a
Titus (Roman general and emperor), 9:24a; 11:31; 11:33
Torques, 5:7c
Trajan, 9:24a
Triremes, 11:28b–30a; 11:31
Troy, 8:2b
Trypho, 11:20

Valentinus, 2:29c
Varro, 5:7c
Vespasian, 9:24a; 11:14b; 11:31; 11:33

Virgil, DnVgPf 3; 3:21; 4:1a; 5:7c; 11:17a
Vitellius, 9:24a

Webb, J. R., 12:4

Xanthippus, 11:7–9
Xenophon, 3:21; 5:1; 7:5; 8:3b
Xerxes I, 7:5; 11:2b

Young, E. J., 2:31–35; 4:24b; 7:7c–8; 11:28b–30a; 11:44–45

Zeno, 1:2b

INDEX OF HOLY SCRIPTURE (RSVCE)

Citations are according to the lemma of Jerome's *Commentary on Daniel*
Abbreviations: DnVgPf = Jerome's Preface to the Latin Vulgate version of Daniel; DnPf = Jerome's Preface to Book 1 of his Commentary on Daniel

OLD TESTAMENT

Genesis
2:7, 2:29c
3:15, 12:1–3
6:1–4, 3:92b
6:3, 9:2b–3
11:1–8, 1:2b
11:9, 1:2b
11:27–28, 1:4a, c
11:31, 1:4a, c
15:7, 1:4a, c
17:5, 1:7
17:15, 1:7
18:1–3, 8:15b
18:27, 8:27a
25:7, 9:24a
26:18, 2:22
41:1–13, 2:1b
41:37–46, 2:48
41:45, 1:7

Exodus
2:9–10, 1:8a
20:21, 2:22
29, 2:25b
29:38, 8:5b–9a
30:8, 8:5b–9a
32:4, 3:14b
32:7, 9:24a
32:34, 9:14a
33:11, 2:22

Leviticus
18:25, 9:14a
19:2, 9:24a
26:16, 9:14a
26:28, 9:11a

Numbers
1, 2:25b
14:18, 9:14a

Deuteronomy
4:24, 7:9d
12:5, 6:10a
12:5–6, 11:14b
12:11, 6:10a
19:16–19, 13:61b–62a
27:15—28:68, 9:11b
32:8, 10:13a
32:8–9, 7:2–3
32:15, 5:4

1 Samuel
16:1, 9:2b–3

2 Samuel
12:25, 9:23c

1 Kings
8:29–30, 6:10a
12:28, 3:14b
12:32–33, 3:14b

2 Kings
22:14, 1:1
23:34, 1:1
23:36, 1:1
24:6, 1:1
24:6–17, 1:1
24:8, 1:1
24:17, 1:1
25:2–10, 1:1

2 Chronicles
7:15–16, 6:10a
36:5, 1:1
36:8, 1:1
36:17–20, 1:1
36:22, 9:24a
36:22–23, 9:24a

Ezra
1, 10:2–3
1—5, 9:24a
1:1–4, 9:24a
3—4, 9:24a
3:2ff., 9:24a
4:24, 9:1
6:14–15, 9:24a
7:6, 9:24a
8:2, 2:25b

Nehemiah
1:11, 9:24a
2:1, 9:24a
2:5–9, 9:24a
3—4, 9:24a
8:4, 2:25b
10:3, 2:25b
10:7, 2:25b
10:24, 2:25b
12:10–11, 9:24a

Tobit
5:4, 8:16

Esther
3:13, 7:5
8:1–2, 2:48

1 Maccabees
1:1–42, 8:5b–9a
1:7, 11:3–4a
1:8–11, 9:24a
1:10, 11:21
1:11—4:58, 8:14
1:16–20, 11:40–41a
1:18–19, 11:25–26; 11:40–41a
1:19–20, 8:5b–9a
1:20–24, 11:28b–30a
1:20–28, 11:30b
1:21–28, 8:5b–9a
1:29–30, 11:31
1:30–42, 8:5b–9a
1:35–49, 11:37–39
1:41–42, 11:37–39
1:43, 11:36
1:43–57, 8:5b–9a
1:43–67, 9:24a
1:52, 11:32
1:57, 12:11; 12:12
1:58–67, 8:5b–9a
1:59, 12:7a
1:62, 11:32
2:1, 8:14; 11:37–39
2:1–70, 11:34–35
2:15–28, 11:37–39
2:18, 11:37–39
2:28–30, 12:1–3
3:1–4, 7:14b
3:35, 7:14b
4:3–25, 8:14
4:30–58, 12:12
4:36–58, 9:24a
4:52, 12:7a; 12:11; 12:12
5:1–7, 7:14b

INDEX OF HOLY SCRIPTURE

5:47, 7:14b
6:1–3, 8:14
6:1–4, 11:36
6:8–16, 11:36
6:9–16, 8:14
6:12–13, 11:36
6:16, 9:24a
9:17–18, 11:34–35
12:39–40, 11:20; 11:34–35
13:31–32, 11:20
14:48, 9:24a
16:14–16, 9:24a

2 Maccabees
1:10, 9:24a
1:13–14, 11:36
1:13–16, 11:36
1:24, 9:9a
4:7, 11:21
4:7—10:8, 8:14
4:10–11, 11:37–39
5:1—6:7, 8:5b–9a
5:11–21, 11:28b–30a
5:11–26, 8:5b–9a
5:24–27, 8:5b–9a
6:1–2, 11:31; 11:37–39
6:1–7, 8:5b–9a
6:1–11, 9:24a
6:2, 11:36
6:8—7:42, 8:5b–9a
6:18–31, 11:33
7:1–42, 11:33
8—15, 7:14b
8:1–36, 8:14
9:1–2, 8:14
9:5–10, 8:14
9:5–27, 11:36
9:12–13, 11:36
9:28, 8:14
9:28—10:5, 9:24a
10:5, 12:7a
10:38, 9:20a

Job
1:6, 3:92b
2:1, 3:92b
38:7, 3:92b
41:25, 7:2–3

Psalms
11:2, 3:49–50; 5:4
18:11, 2:22
24:8, 8:16
29:1, 3:92b
32:7, 11:1
32:8, 11:1
34:20, 9:14a
37:35, 4:7–8
42:5, 9:20a
45:1, 3:19a; 5:6a
45:7, 9:24a
45:13, 10:16b
48:7, 10:6a
57:10, 2:22
60:1, 5:6a
68:17, 7:10b
69:1, 3:19a; 5:6a
69:28, 7:10c
72:5, 11:21
72:8, 11:21
72:11, 11:21
72:17, 11:21
73:20, 9:14a
74:14, 7:2–3
78:65, 9:14a
80:1, 3:19a; 5:6a
80:13, 7:7a
81:10, DnPf
89:6, 3:92b
89:32, 9:14a
95:2, 9:20a
97:3, 7:9d
97:8, 3:26–28
103:1, 10:16b
104:4, 7:10b
104:15, 10:2–3

108:4, 2:22
112:4, 9:9a
116:5, 9:9a
121:4, 4:10b; 9:14a
137:4, 1:7

Proverbs
1:3–6, 12:4
1:5, 2:21b
1:6, 2:22
5:15, 2:22
21:1, 5:19b

Ecclesiastes
2:14, 2:28c
3:20, 7:17–18a

Wisdom
1:4, 2:21b; 12:8–10
13:5, 3:57a

Sirach
39:19–20, 3:57a
48:10, 9:24a

Isaiah
10:14, 4:7–8
13:17–18, 5:30–31
14:12, 4:1a
14:13–14, 4:7–8; 7:4
19:19, 11:14b
21:4–5, 5:30–31
21:7, 5:1
21:9, 5:1
25:7, 11:44–45
29:11–12, 12:4
38:1, 4:24
38:5, 4:24
39:7 LXX, 1:3–4a
44:17, 3:14b
56:11, 3:1a
58:9, 9:21a

Jeremiah
1:2–3, 1:1

6:13, 3:1a
7:16, 9:2b–3
8:10, 3:1a
10:11, DnVgPf 1; 2:19a
17:13, 7:10c
18:7–9, 4:24
21:1–2, 7:1a
25:11–12, 5:2; 9:1
25:12, 9:2b–3
29:7, 4:24b
29:10, 5:2
29:10–11, 9:1
29:12, 9:2b–3
29:22–23, 13:3; 13:61b–62a
31:28, 9:14a
44:27, 9:14a
51:28, 5:30–31
51:33, 5:30–31
52:31, 5:1

Ezekiel
1:1, 10:4b
1:2, 1:1
1:14–15, 7:9d
1:26–27, 7:9d
2:1–47, 8:17b
6, 8:17b
8:3, DnVgPf 3
13:16, 6:10a
29:17–21, 7:1a
31:10–14, 4:7–8
42:7, 9:24a

Daniel
1:2, 1:1
1:4, 1:8a; 4:6a
1:5, 1:18; 2:1a
1:6, DnPf
1:8, 1:9
1:18, 2:1a
1:20, 4:1b
1:21, 6:28; 10:1a
2:6, 2:5b; 2:12–13
2:10–11, 2:26b

INDEX OF HOLY SCRIPTURE

2:12, 2:30a
2:17–18, 2:16
2:24, 2:25b
2:25, DnPf
2:32, 7:4; 7:5; 7:6; 8:5a
2:33, 7:7a
2:34, 8:14
2:34–35, 2:28b; 7:13b; 11:44–45
2:35, 2:31–35
2:38, 2:31–35
2:39, 2:31–35; 8:5a
2:40, 2:28b; 2:31–35
2:41, 2:31–35
2:44–45, 2:28b
2:45, 2:31–35
2:46, 3:1a; 3:15c
2:46–47, 3:95a
2:47, 3:15c; 6:16b
2:48, 4:16a
2:49, 3:97
2:49b, 2:49a
3:1, 1:2b
3:17, 3:18a
3:24–90, DnVgPf 3
3:25, 6:16b
3:51–90, DnVgPf 3
3:58–59, 3:57a
3:60–61, 3:57a
3:62, 3:57a
3:64, 3:57a
3:66–67, 3:57a
3:67, 3:57a
3:77–78, 3:57a
3:79–81, 3:57a
3:82, 3:57a
3:83, 3:57a
3:84–85, 3:57a
3:86, 3:57a
3:87, 3:57a
3:88, 3:57a
3:92, 3:95a
3:93b, 3:93a
3:95–100, 6:25a
4:5, 4:6a

4:12, 4:20b
4:19, 4:7–8
4:22, 4:1a
4:23, 4:34b
4:27, 4:24
4:28, 5:5
4:28–37, 7:4
4:29–30, 4:1a
4:34, 4:1a; 4:31d
5:1, 5:2
5:9, 5:6a
5:20, 5:22
5:20–21, 4:1a
5:28, 5:30–31
5:30, 7:1a
5:30–31, 7:4; 9:24a
5:31, 6:1–2a
6:1, 5:30–31
6:1–2, 6:12d; 7:5
6:12, 6:14a
6:16, 6:20d
6:17, 11:1
6:18, 6:14a; 11:1
6:28, 6:12d
7:1, 6:1–2a; 8:1a
7:4–6, 7:7a
7:5, 8:5a
7:8, 7:7b; 7:26; 11:25–26; 11:40–41a; 11:44–45
7:13–14, 11:44–45
7:16–27, 8:17b
7:17, 7:2–3
7:24–26, 12:7a
7:27, 12:7a
8:1, 6:1–2a; 7:1a
8:1–2, 2:4a
8:10, 8:5b–9a
8:11, 8:5b–9a
8:12, 8:5b–9a
8:14, 9:24a
8:15–16, 9:21a
8:15–26, 8:17b
8:16, 12:5–6
8:20, 8:5b–9a

8:21, 8:5b–9a
8:22, 8:5b–9a
8:22–23, 8:5b–9a
8:25, 8:14
9:1, 1:21; 9:24a; 10:1a
9:2, 5:2; 9:17b
9:7, 9:9a
9:15, 9:24a
9:17–18, 9:2b–3
9:19, 9:24a
9:21, 12:5–6
9:21–27, 8:17b
9:23, 9:24a
9:24, 10:1a
9:25, 9:24a
9:26, 9:24a
9:27, 9:24a
10:1, 1:21; 6:1–2a; 6:28; 10:21b
10:2, 10:12
10:4, 10:12; 12:5–6
10:4–20, 12:5–6
10:5—12:13, 8:17b
10:13, 10:20b
10:14, 10:20a; 10:20b
11, 12:8–10
11:1, 10:21b
11:1–20, 11:44–45
11:22, 11:21
11:23, 11:21
11:24, 11:21
11:25, 11:21
11:30, 11:31
11:34, 11:36
11:45, 12:11
12:1, 7:10c
12:11, 12:7a
13, DnVgPf 3
13:54–59, DnVgPf 3; DnPf
13:60, 13:61b–62a
13:65, DnPf
14, DnVgPf 3
14:1, DnPf
14:1–21, DnVgPf 3
14:26–27, DnVgPf 3

14:27, 2:25b
14:32–38, DnVgPf 3

Amos
9:3, 7:2–3

Obadiah
4, 7:4

Jonah
1:3, 10:6a
3:4, 4:24
3:6, 3:96
3:10, 3:96; 4:24

Haggai
1:1, 9:24a

Zechariah
1:1, 9:24a
1:8, 7:5
1:9–14, 8:17b
1:12–17, 5:2
2:2, 8:17b
2:7, 8:17b
4:4–5, 8:17b
6:3, 7:5
6:4–5, 8:17b
6:6, 7:5

Malachi
4:5, 9:24a

New Testament

Matthew
1:11–12, 1:1
2:1–11, 2:2a
3:13–16, 10:4b
4:9, 3:4–6; 4:1b
5:3, 3:87
5:8, 2:28c
5:45, 2:29c
9:4, 2:28c
9:14–15, 10:2–3
10:2, 1:7

INDEX OF HOLY SCRIPTURE

10:8, 5:17
10:19, DnPf
11:13, 9:24a
11:29, 3:87; 4:7–8
13:12, 2:21b
13:13–14, 8:15a
13:19, 8:15a
13:47–50, 7:2–3
16:17–18, 1:7
17:2, 7:9b
19:28, 7:9a
22:21, 8:27a
24:12, 11:32
24:15, DnPf; 11:31
24:22, 7:25c
24:29–31, 12:1–3
25:29, 2:21b
26:64, 7:13b
27:25, 9:24a

Mark
1:9–10, 10:4b
2:8, 2:28c
2:18–20, 10:2–3
3:16, 1:7
3:17, 1:7
4:12, 8:15a
4:25, 2:21b
5:9, 3:14b
9:2–3, 7:9b
12:17, 8:27a
13:11, DnPf
14:15–17, 6:10a
15:13, 13:61b–62a

Luke
1:11–19, 8:16
1:17, 9:24a
1:26–27, 8:16
3:1, 9:24a
3:21, 10:4b
3:23, 9:24a
5:22, 2:28c
5:34–35, 10:2–3

6:14, 1:7
8:10, 8:15a
8:18, 2:21b
9:29, 7:9b
10:18, 4:1a
12:11, DnPf
16:16, 9:24a
18:8, 11:32
20:25, 8:27a
20:35, 12:1–3
21:12–14, DnPf
22:12–14, 6:10a
22:30, 7:9a
23:21, 13:61b–62a
23:34, 2:24b
24:51, 11:44–45

John
1:42, 1:7
2:13, 9:24a
2:20, 9:24a
6:4, 9:24a
6:58–59, 10:2–3
8:6, 7:10c
8:56, 8:15b
10:28–29, 5:19b
11:55, 9:24a
12:40, 8:15a
14:2, 12:1–3
15:6, 7:9d
19:6, 13:61b–62a
19:15, 9:24a; 13:61b–62a

Acts of the Apostles
1:6–12, 11:44–45
1:11, 7:13b
1:13–15, 6:10a
2:1–5, 6:10a
2:4, 6:10a
2:15, 6:10a
3:1, 6:10a
7:4, 1:4a, c
7:22, 1:8a
9:7, 10:7

10:9–10, 6:10a
14:10–12, 2:46
22:6–9, 10:7
26:4–5, DnVgPf 3
28:26, 8:15a

Romans
1:20–23, 3:19a
5:8, 9:5a
6:12, 5:19b
7:6, 12:4
7:14–25, 9:5a
11:26, 9:24a
11:33, 2:22
13:7, 8:27a

1 Corinthians
1:21, 2:19a
2:6, 10:13a
2:8, 10:13a
2:10, 2:22
3:12–15, 7:9d
3:15, 7:9c
9:22, 8:27a
11:19, 11:34–35
13:12, 12:4
15:47–48, 2:29c

2 Corinthians
3:6, 12:4
12:2, DnVgPf 3

Ephesians
3:5, 2:19a
6:16, 3:49–50

Philippians
2:6–8, 7:13c
3:13, 2:22; 9:24a
4:3, 7:10c

Colossians
1:16, 7:9a
1:26, 2:19a

2 Thessalonians
2:3, 7:7c–8
2:3–4, 11:31
2:4, 7:7c–8; 7:25b; 9:24a; 11:36
2:8, 9:24a; 12:1–3
2:9–10, 11:21
2:10–11, 7:25c
2:11, 9:24a

1 Timothy
1:6–7, 6:4a
6:20, 6:4a

2 Timothy
4:3–4, 6:4a

Titus
1:14, 6:4a
3:9, 6:4a

James
4:6, 5:22

1 Peter
3:19, 3:92b
5:5, 5:22
5:8, 6:22

2 Peter
1:13, DnVgPf 5
1:16, 6:4a

1 John
5:19, 4:1b

2 John
7, 11:21
9, 1 Cor 13:5

Jude
4, 2 Tim 3:6

Revelation
1:13–14, 7:9a
3:5, 7:10c
4:1–6, 7:9a

INDEX OF HOLY SCRIPTURE

5:1–3, 12:4
5:4–5, 12:4
5:5, 7:9a
12:3–4, 4:1a
12:10, 7:10c
13:8, 7:10c
13:10, 11:34–35
14:12, 11:34–35
17:8, 7:10c

17:14, 8:14
19:16, 8:14
20:1–6, 7:17–18a
20:8, 11:21
20:12, 7:10c
20:15, 7:10c
21:27, 7:10c